GRAMMARS OF IDENTITY/ALTERITY

LEARNING FIELDS
Volume 1
Educational Histories of European Social Anthropology
Edited by Dorle Dracklé, Iain R. Edgar and Thomas K. Schippers

LEARNING FIELDS
Volume 2
Current Policies and Practices in European Social Anthropology Education
Edited by Dorle Dracklé and Iain R. Edgar

GRAMMARS OF IDENTITY/ALTERITY
Edited by Gerd Baumann and Andre Gingrich

Grammars of Identity/Alterity

A Structural Approach

Edited by
Gerd Baumann and Andre Gingrich

Berghahn Books
New York • Oxford

First published in 2004 by

Berghahn Books

www.berghahnbooks.com

©2004 Gerd Baumann and Andre Gingrich

All rights reserved. Except for the quotation of short passages for the purposes of criticism and review, no part of this book may be reproduced in any form or by any means, electronic or mechanical, including photocopying, recording, or any information storage and retrieval system now known or to be invented, without written permission of the publisher.

Library of Congress Cataloging-in-Publication Data

Grammars of identity/alterity : a structural approach / edited by Gerd Baumann and Andre Gingrich.
    p. cm.
    Includes bibliographical references.
    ISBN 1–57181–698–4 (alk. paper)
    1. Group identity. 2. Other (Philosophy). 3. Violence. I. Baumann, Gerd. II. Gingrich, Andre.

HM753.G73 2004
302.4--dc22   2004046272

British Library Cataloguing in Publication Data

A catalogue record for this book is available from the British Library.
Printed in Canada on acid-free paper

ISBN 1–57181–698–4 hardback

Contents

List of Figures	vii
Foreword *Gerd Baumann and Andre Gingrich*	ix
Acknowledgments	xv

Step I:	*From an Essentialised Use of 'Othering' to a Differentiation of Grammars*	
Chapter 1	Conceptualising Identities: Anthropological Alternatives to Essentialising Difference and Moralizing about Othering *Andre Gingrich*	3
Chapter 2	Grammars of Identity/Alterity: A Structural Approach *Gerd Baumann*	18
Step II:	*From a Repertoire of Grammars to Hierarchies and Power*	
Chapter 3	Othering the Scapegoat in Nepal: The Ritual of *Ghantakarna* *Michael Mühlich*	53
Chapter 4	German Grammars of Identity/Alterity: A Diachronic View *Anne Friederike Müller*	63
Chapter 5	Alterity as Celebration, Alterity as Threat: A Comparison of Grammars between Brazil and Denmark *Inger Sjørslev*	79

Step III: *From Power to Violence – when Grammars Implode*

Chapter 6 Completing or Competing ? Contexts
of Hmong Selfing/Othering in Laos 101
Christian Postert

Chapter 7 'Out of the Race': The Poiesis of Genocide
in Mass Media Discourses in Côte d'Ivoire 112
Karel Arnaut

Chapter 8 Dehumanization as a Double-Edged Sword:
From Boot-Camp Animals to Killing Machines 142
Jojada Verrips

Step IV: *From Testing Grammars to Widening the Debate*

Chapter 9 Between Structure and Agency: From the *langue*
of *Hindutva* Identity Construction to the *parole*
of Lived Experience 157
Christian Karner

Chapter 10 Encompassment and its Discontents:
The Rmeet and the Lowland Lao 173
Guido Sprenger

Chapter 11 Debating Grammars: Arguments and Prospects 192
Gerd Baumann and Andre Gingrich

Notes on Contributors 205

Subject Index 209

Name Index 215

List of Figures

2.1	The Grammar of Orientalization or Reverse Mirror-Imaging	20
2.2	The Segmentary Grammar of Contextual Fission and Fusion	22
2.3	The Grammar of Encompassment by Hierarchical Subsumption	25
2.4	Grammars of Encompassment in Southall, London, ca. 1986–92	26
2.5	Three Grammars of Selfing and Othering	27
2.6	Myth as a 'Staggered' Semiological System, after Barthes (1973: 115)	39
2.7	Ternary Staggering of the Orientalizing Grammar	39
6.1	Contexts of the Encompassment Grammar: Interaction with Supralocal Officials	103
6.2	Contexts of the Segmentary Grammar: Formal Hmong-Hmong Interaction	105
6.3	Contexts of the Orientalizing Grammar: Informal Hmong-Hmong Interaction	106
10.1	Contrasting Examples of Encompassment	175
10.2	The Three Grammars in Rmeet Usage	183
10.3	Two Schemata of Models for Anti-Grammars	188

Foreword

Grammars, identity, structural: each key word in the title of this book in some ways represents a provocation, but perhaps a justifiable one.

The word 'grammars' has become a nigh-impossible term to use in anthropology, sociolinguistics, cognitive psychology, philosophy and, latterly, artificial intelligence. No one knows one when they see one, no one dares use the word for fear of evoking anything between yesteryear's ideas of grammar from the Humanists to Jakobson and more recent ideas from Chomsky's 'generative grammar' to Derrida's 'grammatology'. Grammar, one of the most imaginative discoveries we know and perhaps the most potent hypothesis about anything from a baby's mind to that of a philosopher, has become a truly taboo word, placed on the *Index Verborum Prohibitorum* by a fear of being so polysemic that it might easily be misunderstood. One may borrow the Freudian term *überbesetzt*, or 'overcharged', to diagnose this fear of a word not simply overused, but successively endowed with so many different meanings or 'levels' of signification. These successive uses have never been cumulative and have never added up to one defineable core idea. We simply do not know what a grammar 'is', be it ontologically, epistemologically, phenomenologically or otherwise.

Why, then, this strange awe of using the word and at the same time the seemingly absurd inflation of an astonishing variety of usages ? The word seems to echo so well with the most varied forms of our desire to see 'sense' or 'order' in people's capacities and failures to deal with their worlds. It is the almost metasocial lure of the word, coupled with its polysemy acquired by dozens of incommensurable usages, that may have something to do with it. (The word wears at the same time the robe of a prescriptive language teacher and the outfit of a cunning spy in sociolinguistics and studies of cognition.) What, then, is the word supposed to signify in our title ? We use the word as a simple shorthand for certain simple classificatory structures or classificatory schemata that we argue can be recognized in a vast variety of processes concerned with defining identity and alterity. Such social processes of classifying identity/alterity are intrinsically related to social conceptions which, of course, are always shaped and influenced by their respective historical and sociopolitical contexts. We call these social conceptions classificatory schemata or classificatory structures because they are not defined by their content, but by the way in which they arrange whatever content of self and other they are used to structure.

If there were a convenient plural for the term syntax, that might have been an alternative to 'grammars', but syntagmata evokes the wrong association, contrasted as it is to paradigmata. Other terms we considered, such as 'cognitive maps' or 'classificatory pathways' or 'logics' or 'operations' or 'models' with their various adjectives were again excluded one by one, sometimes to avoid terminological border skirmishes with other fields ranging from social and cognitive psychology via 'culture and personality' to artificial intelligence.

The choice for the term 'grammars' is informed by pragmatic considerations in three ways. First, it is based on a process of negative exclusion of various alternative terms, in order not to fall prey to those unproductive terminological border skirmishes. Secondly, it is pragmatic in that it makes only a heuristic claim. We do 'as if' there were grammars that structure the ethnographic contents we describe, and we see where it gets us. Thirdly, this choice is concerned with pragmatics in that we use the term not to postulate prescriptive rules, but to paraphrase empirical ethnographic data concerned with people's constructions of identity and alterity. We shall, however, return to this question after reviewing our working definition of identity and the three grammars in the first two chapters.

Our working definition of identity designates social subjectivities as persons and groups of persons. These subjectivities are multidimensional and fluid; they include power-related ascriptions by selves as well as by others; and they simultaneously combine sameness, or belonging, with alterity, or otherness. This anthropological working definition therefore rejects any essentialist or moralist connotations by embracing a 'soft', or in the philosophical sense 'weak', concept of identity, and by relating them to social context and social processes. We need hardly repeat that they can only be studied in their contexts and with due attention to agency. We do wish to restate, however, that these are relatively simple classificatory structures or schemata that may be recognized in seemingly incomparable processes of selfing and othering. We distinguish three of these, although we readily admit, of course, that others may think of more in due time. The three grammars upon which we have based our work are freely adapted from classic works in the anthropological canon, namely Edward Said's *Orientalism*, Evans-Pritchard's *The Nuer*, and Louis Dumont's *Homo Hierarchicus*.

The first grammar, orientalization, constitutes self and other by negative mirror imaging: 'what is good in us is lacking in them,' but it also adds a subordinate reversal: 'what is lacking in us is (still) present in them.' It thus entails a possibility of desire for the other and even, sometimes, a potential for self-critical relativism. The second grammar, segmentation, works by context-dependent and hence sliding scales of selfings and otherings among parties conceived as formally equal. It thus allows fusions and fissions of identity/alterity in a highly context-sensitive manner, but is also always subject to disputes about the right placing of the apex. The third, the grammar of encompassment, works by a hierarchized sub-inclusion of others who are thought, from a higher level of abstraction, to be really 'part of us'. It thus includes some others, but never all others, and it tends to minimize the otherness of those it includes.

By crossexamining these grammars ethnographically and theoretically, we aim at three things: first, to go beyond the unproductive, and essentially moralist, truism that every selfing involves an othering, secondly, to distinguish different modalities of identity formation and dialogical inclusion or exclusion, and finally, to move beyond the false opposition between an assumed primacy of structures or cognition on the one hand, and on the other, the helpless reduction of all social processes to agency and contextual contingency. As we hope to show, such a structural and comparative approach to the articulations of identity and alterity has immediate implications also for an understanding of extreme forms of collective and genocidal violence.

As a counterpoint to genocidal violence we must raise the question of how our grammars relate to hybridization or, as we prefer to call it, creolization. Very often, ambiguous categories are, of course, denied, denigrated, or evacuated into 'special' classificatory slots. This was the case, for instance, with the 'coloureds' of Apartheid South Africa or the 'half-breeds' of the nineteenth-century U.S. West. These cases are easily accommodated within the ternary versions of the three grammars as unfolded by Baumann in this volume. There are, however, social, cultural and political projects by which elites encourage and privilege 'mixed' forms such as *métissage* or *mestisaje*. Two grammatical operations appear to be at work here. The first is a special version of orientalization in which the positive values associated with both self and other are normatively amalgamated, creating ideal representations of 'the best of both [of indeed more] worlds'. Remaining a hegemonic operation, the second process then involves a self encompassing its former other. In the contemporary world, the role of encompassment by elites may be less visible, but where it is absent, 'hyphenated identities' continue to be kept in such 'special' categories as are called 'halfies' by some and 'mixed race' by others.

To return now to the question asked above, namely why one might call these classificatory schemata or structures 'grammars', the intuitive counter-argument to the pragmatic choice we have made is that a grammar is expected to be to some degree prescriptive, rule-orientated, or at least vaguely normative. Does this intuitive expectation hold in any way for the three classificatory structures we have called 'grammars' ? The argument is that it does. Just as linguistic grammars offer a set of rules which allow sentences to be formulated, so these social grammars offer a set of rules which allow otherings to be articulated. Furthermore, grammars are assigned a normative status by the social and cultural contexts that privilege, or indeed demand, one or another grammar to be used. Those who use an orientalizing grammar to define others normatively expect these others to recognize themselves as the non-contemporaneous negative mirror images of the orientalizers, and orientalists normatively expect other orientalists to use the orientalist grammar, rather than the grammar of segmentation or the grammar of encompassment in given contexts. An 'oriental' *is not to be* treated as a segmentary partner or an encompassed part of the self. By the same token, segmentary grammars are ascribed normative force in other contexts by other users and for those they are used about. A Freemason is normatively expected to view all the world's religions as a shifting scale of contextual fission and fusion, a federalist is not to voice ideas of encompassing a partner who *is to be* seen as a federal equal. In the same way, the cultural hegemony of a grammar of encompassment is endowed with normative force. Hindus who state that 'Sikhs are Hindus' not only expect of Sikhs that they accept this encompassment, but they also measure 'good' Hindus by whether they subscribe to this project of encompassment or are 'exclusivists' using the grammar of orientalism.

The final indication that all three grammars are endowed, in different sociocultural contexts, with some normative authority is alluded to with the term 'anti-grammar' or 'non-grammar'. Whether we deal with propagators of the orientalizing, the segmentary, or the encompassment grammar, they all have normative expectations that their grammar is the correct one and that it is incomparably better than the non- or anti-grammar of systematic violence annihilating the other. The classificatory schemata or structures, in other words, are grammars also in that they are endowed, within given sociocultural constellations, with a certain normative force. Needless to add, norms can neither determine nor render predictable any particular social action in its manifold contexts; nonetheless, norms are a force that *may* inform and standardize language, behaviour, and even conceptions of agency. In that sense, our collective exploration of grammars in action follows a general direction that will lead readers right through the creative tension zone between structure and agency.

This exploration is the result of a somewhat unusual experiment in that we addressed an open invitation to any participants of EASA's Sixth Biennial Conference in Copenhagen to subject the grammars proposed to their own ethnographic tests. The proposition was circulated early on and then discussed in detail; the ethnographic tests, however, were to be open-ended. Each contributor was to act, so to speak, as an independent test pilot: fly the model and let us see which aspects of your ethnography are thrown into starker relief or are rendered comparable in time or space, and what of your ethnography indicates the limitations of a grammars approach which must inhere in this analytic technique as it does in any other. The questions and debates that arose have been worked into the structure of the book itself which traces four steps.

Step one starts with Andre Gingrich presenting a critical anthropological review of some major transdisciplinary debates on identity/alterity. Assessing some major forms of essentializing 'othering' in these debates leads to the rationale of this volume. Several interdisciplinary 'strong' versions of conceptualising identity as opposed to difference are critiqued as essentialist and moralist. Instead, it is suggested here to employ 'weak' notions of social identity by further differentiating them in the form of grammars. These are then presented and discussed by Gerd Baumann as a theoretical and methodological proposition and illustrated by way of examples.

Step two then departs from this proposition of a repertoire of grammars, in order to explore it in those specific fields of action that are primarily informed by hierarchies and power relations. Michael Mühlich's analysis of ritualized forms of 'othering' scapegoats in Nepal provides a first case in point, while Anne Friederike Müller's analysis of political discourses in Germany throws into relief the historical transformations in the use of the grammars. This use of the grammars for diachronic comparison is followed by Inger Sjørslev's exploration of the grammars' uses for comparison across *prima facie* incomparable social fields, namely by examining Brazilian and Danish conceptions of identity/alterity in their contexts of power, hierarchy, and contested forms of creolization.

Step three takes us from power in its heterogeneous variants to the more troubling forms of exerting power through violence. This helps to reflect on the limits imposed on the use of the grammars. In the theoretical and methodological exposition of Step one, it was suggested that one of these limits could be seen in constellations where the grammars are made to 'implode' and give way to an 'anti-grammar' that accompanies, legitimizes, and prepares violence. This point is now tested out, first by Christian Postert's analysis of interethnic relations in Laos, then by Karel Arnaut's study of implicitly genocidal discourse in mass media discourses in Côte d'Ivoire. Finally, Jojada Verrips shows how the dehumanizing language as instrumentalised in certain Western armies effects not only violent exclusions, but also violent inclusions into groups prepared to act as 'killing machines'.

Step four combines other ethnographic examinations with an attempt to widen the debate in two ways. Guido Sprenger's case study from Laos leads to scrutinizing the distinction between grammars and anti-grammars, whereas Christian Karner's reflections upon Hindu nationalism result in the productive suggestion to further differentiate between grammars and situational utterance. The editors' final chapter will then pull together three strands of argumentation: questions answered by the project, questions raised about the project itself, and reformulations that the project can offer to such abiding problems as extreme violence and the relation between structure and agency.

Having outlined the premises, the dialogical methods, and the goals of this endeavour may now also help us to clarify the third provocation contained in the subtitle: 'A Structural Approach'.

'Nothing could be more unfashionable in anthropology right now than a structural approach,' so most contributors agreed at one stage or another. Yet when discussing the age-old division between a purported primacy of structures and the fashionable but helpless reduction of all social facts to contextual contingency, we saw room for a pragmatic solution to bridge the two extremes. This project works with the concept of 'structure' not in the sense of any 'elementary' mechanism of thought, but rather in the sense of flexible classificatory models employed in, and for, social interaction. By proposing a 'weak' conception of identity and by then differentiating three classificatory models or grammars, we thus operate with a profoundly anti-essentialist concept of structure. Needless to add that our usage of the term is not beholden to any sectarian subvarieties of structuralism, but it is certainly indebted to several variants of structuralism whose worth has been proven by ethnography over time, and it has been further inspired by some of the more recent anglophone and francophone work in this field. One conclusion from our exploration through the creative tension zones between structures and forms of agency highlights the heuristic pursuit of grammars traced and observed in contextual action. We see this as a possibility to bridge that divide between structure and agency not only theoretically, but also with attention to the subtleties of ethnographic context.

In following this structural approach to grammars of identity, this volume has, to some extent, privileged a focus on ethnic and national identities. Nonetheless, some contributors have opened up other fields, at least three of which seem to be worth pursuing further. They include gender and sexuality, aesthetics and arts, and finally, macrolevel and globalized interactions such as international and postcolonial relations. In all these fields, a contextually sensitive examination of grammars and anti-grammar will invite the merging of fieldwork with comparative endeavours. We shall return to these possibilities and projects, too, when surveying the prospects of the argument in the final chapter.

Acknowledgments

Tracing the ideas for this book is like reconstructing an air traffic controller's map of criss-crossing flight lines that eventually converge to land on the same runway. The first idea concerned a critique of the dominant 'strong' conceptions of identity excluding difference, and the alternative proposal of a, philosophically speaking, 'weak' conception of identity/alterity forming a dialogical pair (hence the slash in our title). This approach emerged from a Wenner Gren Conference on 'Time and Temporalities in the Anthropological Record', for which thanks are due to Sydel Silverman.

The second idea, that of distinguishing different 'grammars of identity/alterity', originated at a seminar series on 'Multiculturalism and Gender', for which thanks are due to Mary Nash and Diana Marre at the University of Barcelona. The impetus to put together the two ideas emerged at the 2001 Socrates Intensive Programme, a summer school at the University of Vienna for which we thank Thomas Fillitz. To try out this fusion of ideas, we were able to convene a panel at the Sixth EASA Conference at the University of Copenhagen, for which our thanks go to Inger Sjørslev. Thinking together with colleagues coming from very different flight paths again, there developed quite new moments of convergence as well as differentiation. The time to pull these together was given us by the Austrian Science Fund and its award of the Wittgenstein Prize to Andre Gingrich, and by the International Research Centre Cultural Sciences (IFK), Vienna, which awarded a three months' fellowship to Gerd Baumann.

The map as outlined is populated by many colleagues and friends who have sustained our joint effort with their openness, helpful critique, and good humour. We want to thank with particular appreciation our colleagues and friends at the Research Centre Religion and Society, University of Amsterdam, the Amsterdam School of Social Science Research, the Austrian Academy of Sciences, and the Department of Social and Cultural Anthropology, University of Vienna. They will forgive us for not singling out individual names, and some indeed would not wish us to. Finally, but crucially for the endeavour of course, we are most grateful to our contributors who have cooperated so willingly and often enthusiastically, to the readers of the EASA Executive Committee, to Andreas Dörr for the Indices, and to Berghahn Books who have improved our joint result and have seen it into print with the patience and skill of true professionalism.

Gerd Baumann and Andre Gingrich
Amsterdam and Vienna, January 2004

Step I

From an Essentialised Use of 'Othering' to a Differentiation of Grammars

Chapter 1 Conceptualising Identities: Anthropological Alternatives to Essentialising Difference and Moralizing about Othering
Andre Gingrich

Chapter 2 Grammars of Identity/Alterity: A Structural Approach
Gerd Baumann

Chapter 1

Conceptualising Identities

Anthropological Alternatives to Essentialising Difference and Moralizing about Othering

Andre Gingrich

From an anthropological perspective, debates on identity/alterity in the early twenty-first century face an increasingly clear dilemma. On the one hand, various notions of identity/alterity (or difference) inform vast segments and fields of the humanities and the social sciences. By consequence and at least partially as an adaptation and reaction to that situation, references to identity/alterity (or difference) have proliferated in major anthropological works as well. In one way or another, these 'imports' from wider interdisciplinary fields inform a wide range of recent debates inside anthropology, primarily among junior scholars. On the other hand, a closer inspection of more established usages of these terms by senior anthropologists reveals sobering results. In a recent study, Boston-based Brazilian anthropologist Paulu Pinto (2002) examined a wide spectrum of such conventional usages by anthropologists and other social scientists. Although that spectrum includes works by authors such as Frederik Barth, Abner Cohen, and Pierre Bourdieu, Pinto concludes quite convincingly that in practice, the ensuing concepts of identity are few, and moreover, they do not relate well to debates outside anthropology, or for that matter sociology. Inside anthropology, such accumulated conceptual reflections and elaborations by senior scholars on 'identity/alterity' therefore are dispersed and somewhat isolated from wider debates and from their more recent 'import' into the field.

If the recent wave of these notions' usage in anthropology is largely due to transdisciplinary inspiration, I will argue that this requires now more stringent theoretical reflections about these notions by anthropologists themselves: reflections about how this field may in fact substantially benefit from, and also how anthropology may creatively contribute to these concepts. Whenever that recent, widespread usage of notions of identity is due to creative transdisciplinary cross-fertilization, then this represents a potentially positive development, of course. Certain interdisciplinary and anthropological debates about identity, however, are still dominated by one of two tendencies that are inclined to restrict and impede these positive potentials.

One tendency discusses identity primarily, if not indeed exclusively, in terms of difference. This logic often overrates and essentialises 'difference'. Sometimes, it represents identity only in terms of difference while at other times, it represents difference as something altogether external to identity. A fair share of the debates on 'identity *and* difference' has more or less unwillingly become part of this first tendency. Yet othering and belonging are mutually constitutive components of identity. By contrast, a position that would regard alterity as being external to identity would thus necessarily tend to essentialise difference.

A second tendency is oriented towards doing almost the opposite. It is inclined to criticise and condemn nearly any reference to difference/alterity/other by denouncing it, more often than not in moralist terms. If othering and belonging are indeed mutually constitutive components of identity, then this second tendency is inclined to ignore 'alterity' altogether. The outcome then may easily become one-sided towards a direction to the opposite of the first tendency, i.e. by putting too much of its emphasis upon belonging.

Remarkably, both of these tendencies mutually maintain and encourage each other by virtue of their shared dichotomous arrangement. One tendency views difference as an absolute, whereas the other is inclined to rely on what, philosophically speaking, may be called a 'strong' concept of identity. In this volume, we posit a 'weak' vision of identity precisely to stress its inherently dialogical relationship with alterity. This chapter[1] therefore discusses and assesses some of the epistemological and textual backgrounds of both tendencies, and it argues for a more nuanced anthropological alternative. One such alternative can be found in the more nuanced and differentiated classificatory schemata or structures proposed in this volume as 'grammars' of identity/alterity.

Working Towards an Anthropological Definition of Identity

This chapter represents a reflexive exercise in that it deals with the categories of 'self' and 'other' in a dialogue between anthropologists (selves) and wider fields of transdisciplinary studies (others). The premise that anthropologists' widespread usage of notions of 'identity/ alterity' largely relies on borrowing these terms from wider discourses helps us to focus, first, on some of those key concepts in wider debates. Simultaneously, such a critical examination of 'other' concepts will help to bring out the potentials and the strengths of what anthropology itself has to offer in this field.

From where, then, did anthropologists usually borrow their understandings of 'identity/alterity or difference' over the past decade or so? The preferred fields were philosophy, literary criticism, and generally, that wide conglomerate which, for better or for worse, has come to be known as Cultural Studies. Debates and elaborations on ' identity/alterity or difference' represented a central activity inside Cultural Studies throughout the late 1980s and 1990s. In a very detailed and self-critical review of these activities, Lawrence Grossberg, one of Cultural Studies' key representatives, even argued that debates on 'identity' had perhaps attracted too much theoretical attention at the price of sometimes ignoring other topical fields (1996). Simultaneously, Grossberg argued, this had seduced many to overrate the significance of the concept. After all, not each and every research topic could be reduced to 'issues of identity'. Grossberg went on to criticize a related tendency emanating from Cultural Studies, namely, to discuss 'issues of identity' primarily as topics of 'difference' (which is why I have put the term 'difference' beside 'alterity'). Accepting this critical self-assessment by a top representative of Cultural Studies as a healthy warning signal might indeed help anthropologists to put the whole matter into appropriate contexts. Some of these very fields from where anthropologists often borrowed their notions of identity have meanwhile reached the self-diagnosis that they focused too much on 'identity', and that they did so with inadequate means, that is, by overemphasizing 'difference'.

Grossberg 's constructive and stimulating conclusion proposes to move away from binary dichotomies in this field, and he wants to drop any exaggerated or 'strong' notion of difference. Instead, he proposes a, philosophically speaking, 'weak' notion of difference, such as 'other'. Unlike the emphasis on difference that characterizes the 'strong' notion of identity, this would then not exclude the identification of commonalities among various forms of 'other'.

This interim summary from Cultural Studies highlights three points. First, it formulates a welcome but careful scepticism towards those enthusiastic priorities for singular identity politics that lose sight of wider civil and global contexts. Academic intellectual support for militant ethnic minority chauvinism, e.g., of the Basque ETA variety, would be a case in point. Second and instead, Grossberg's interim summary argues for multidimensional notions of 'identity/other – alterity'. Thirdly, it relates them back to agency. In any given context, one or several of these dimensions of identity may or may not inform agency, and likewise, unprecedented forms of innovative agency my in turn become part of one 's identity. The haunting example that Grossberg uses on this point concerns participation in the 1991 Tien 'anmen demonstrations in Beijing, which became decisive for the biographies and identities of these participants.

None of Grossberg's three conclusions are far removed from the near-consensus reached by anthropologists during the 1990s. The relevant entry in the Routledge 'Encyclopaedia of Social and Cultural Anthropology', for instance, argues along similar lines. It points out that – among several other important factors – identity simultaneously *includes* 'sameness' (e.g., belonging to a group) as well as 'differing' (e.g., from other groups and/or persons), oscillating between ascription by oneself and by others, and being accorded significant content. 'These include evaluative and emotional characteristics from which the individual derives self-esteem, or a sense of knowing or belonging. These features are highly variable in intensity and salience, as are any associated normative expectations which may furnish individuals with guides to their social behavior. Individuals' identities are, then, emergent properties of their categorical memberships' (Byron 1996: 292).

Grossberg's argument and Byron's entry thus delineate a convenient epistemological working definition for the present endeavour, which is based on an inherently dialogical relationship between sameness and differing, belonging and othering, identity/alterity (Taylor 1994: 32–34). Following this subject-centred sense, I will therefore use a working definition of such personal and collective identities as simultaneously including sameness and differing. These identities are multidimensional and contradictory, and they include power-related, dialogical ascriptions by selves and by others which are processually configurated, enacted and transformed by cognition, language, imagination, emotion, body and (additional forms of) agency.

On this basis I will therefore critically examine, in the next two sections, two of these concepts of identity/alterity which anthropologist have more or less intentionally 'borrowed' from wider fields. These concern, first, what may be called a specifically philosophical tradition in conceptualising identity by separating it from difference. Second, I will turn to what may be called a specifically postcolonial tradition, one which posits identity against alterity. After this interdisciplinary trajectory, a subsequent section will then move on to retrieve specifically anthropological traces and elements of conceptualising identity/alterity. Retrieving these traces and elements will in turn lead up to identifying some of anthropology's present potentials in this field.

A Philosophic Discourse on Difference: Heidegger

The influential works of philosophers Jacques Derrida and Paul Ricoeur have had a tremendous impact on a large spectrum of postmodernist and cultural studies, as well as on the anthropology of the 1980s and 1990s. My focus here, however, is upon one philosopher who profoundly influenced the works and the present-day legacies of both these authors: Martin Heidegger. Unsuspected as this family resemblance or possible *Wahlverwandschaft* may be, I submit that it needs to be explored anew.

One generation before Derrida and Ricoeur, Martin Heidegger was that key philosopher whose work, disseminated in different ways and variable forms, influenced both of them. In particular, some of Derrida's reasoning about *différance*, and some of the 'anti-logocentric' thrust in his criticism of modernist 'grammatology' are owed to Heidegger (Derrida 1967; Wiegerling 1991). Regarding Ricoeur, Heidegger's own phenomenological appreciation of literature influenced Ricoeur's hermeneutic approach (Ricoeur 1986: 43, 225; Capurro 1991: 245) and from there, had its impact upon important aspects of the so-called 'literary turn' in parts of anthropology of the 1980s and 1990s.

Both Ricoeur and Derrida acknowledged Heidegger's strong influence upon major areas of their respective works. In a general sense, Heidegger's conservative criticism of enlightenment and subjectivity had offered inspiration to this younger generation and their own philosophical critique of modernity. Through their critique, an increased intellectual awareness was promoted, among other aspects, about the limits of hegemonic rationalities and about the scope of cultural diversity. While my own assessment of a Heideggerian approach to identity will not deny these and other achievements by Derrida and Ricoeur, I will argue, however, that this particular aspect of Heidegger's legacy tends to stimulate an upgrading of essentialising notions of difference.

Less directly, Heideggerian influence upon anthropology can be traced to Gayatri C. Spivak's work. A major inspiration for Spivak's writing stems from Lacan's variety of psychoanalysis, which will be the focus of the next section. To a somewhat smaller extent, however, Spivak's work also builds on Derrida's theories, particularly on his 'Of Grammatology', which Spivak translated into English (Spivak 1996: 75).

As indicated, my point here is not a critical examination of Ricoeur's or Derrida's existing impact, *per se*, upon anthropology. Furthermore, I do not deny at all that phenomenological approaches may indeed substantially contribute to anthropological insights. The work of Christina Toren (e.g., 2002) on childhood and the formation of personhood, 'ontogeny' in Toren's terms, represents a very imaginative and fertile case in point.

What I want to do in this section, however, is to question whether anthropological conceptualisations of identity/alterity might receive any positive inspiration from Heidegger's views on identity, or from such views on identity which would primarily situate themselves in this particular tradition of Heidegger's legacy. My basic argument is that a Heideggerian concept of identity has to be based on essentialising difference. For this reason, I suggest that anthropologists should reject it. Heidegger's heterogeneous legacy for the humanities and the social sciences is a highly contested field. This is why I wish to emphasize from the outset that, first, I discuss only a few aspects of that legacy here, namely those pertaining to identity. The results of my discussion will not imply any necessary conclusions for other aspects of that legacy. By consequence, I regard it as a fairly unrelated question whether some of those other aspects might be regarded as relevant or interesting for anthropologists. I am certainly not implying that Heidegger 'should not be quoted' when I emphasize my specific point about his concept of identity, and how it might relate to the history of his work in Germany between the 1930s and the 1950s.

Heidegger's philosophical and political role before, during, and after the Nazi period, of course, have been researched and debated in much detail (e.g., Rockmore and Margolis 1992; Wolin 1993). The possible interrelation between his work and his biography during the Nazi years have convinced many scholars, including myself, to treat his work with utmost care and profound scepticism. Those problematic biographical elements include Heidegger's support for the Nazi movement during the 1930s, his anti-Semitism, his NSDAP membership from early on, including his notorious 1933 speech as university director, in which he called upon German students to bring out the truly authentic in them (Heidegger 1990:16; Leaman 1993), and after 1945, his apologetic attitude about his own role during the Nazi years. It was, first of all, Hanna Arendt's problematic exculpation of her former teacher (Ettinger 1995) and second, Heidegger's gradual 'de-Nazification' (Young 1997: 1, 214) by several French and anglophone philosophers of subsequent generations, which made his work acceptable again in some circles after it had been upgraded by postmodernist admiration for Heidegger's anti-modernist mysticism. This is why Heidegger's work continues to serve as one key referent for current debates on 'identity', and a central text in this regard is his *Identität und Differenz* (1957).

This small booklet is part of Heidegger's later work, a period in which his writing is preoccupied with the *Kehre* (the 'turning'). On the one hand, the *Kehre* designates Heidegger's search for a 'turning' away from modernity – which made his later work so attractive for some postmodernists; on the other hand, the *Kehre* also designates the 'transformation' in his own thinking – which, according to him and to his more sympathetic readers (Trawny 2003; Young 1997) dates back to the second half of the 1930s. By contrast, his critics argue that his thinking was 'turned' only by Nazi Germany's defeat in and after 1945. At any rate, *die Kehre* indicates Heidegger's move towards what he called fundamental ontology, and what a critical account might prefer to label as an objectivist-idealist philosophy of being, a philosophy fascinating to some for its increasingly mysticist orientation.

This is the intellectual and historical context in which *Identität und Differenz* was published. For that purpose, Heidegger put together the texts of two different lectures: one lecture, or chapter of the book, deals with 'identity', while the second discusses 'difference'. This spatial and temporal separation of identity from difference already reveals a great deal – a point, in fact, which was not lost upon Heidegger: he found it necessary to add a few lines on his own separation of the two topics, in his preface to the book. It still needs to be thought through, he indicated in that preface (1957: 10), that identity and difference belong together, but whether difference originates from identity, readers would have to find out for themselves. In this way, Heidegger attempts to poetically attenuate a separation that the main text itself does nothing but emphasize. The first chapter treats identity as tautology, as unity, and as togetherness or belonging. In a way, this chapter echoes Heidegger's conviction of a (collective or single) elementary solitude of human beings, supplemented by their occasionally being available for someone else.

The second chapter then treats difference as a concept of quite another dimension. By contrasting his own work to Hegel's, Heidegger (45) treats difference, in this context, as the 'onto-theological constitution' of metaphysics, that is, as the central condition that separates (and connects) the universal and the particular (in Heidegger's terms *Sein* and *Seiendes*), which he identifies as the central topic of (his) philosophy (61).

In short, Heidegger separates identity from difference not only formally, i.e., by juxtaposing two separate chapters that never refer to each other. More substantially, this is a separation based on contents and on conviction. For Heidegger, 'identity' is primarily a subject-centred concept, which is partly informed by existential solitude. Difference, by contrast, is something completely external to 'identity' (notwithstanding the preface's attenuation): it is, first and foremost, a fundamental condition of universal and particular being. To condensate his point even more, identity is primarily (though not exclusively) a subject-centred concept, whereas difference is an ontological category.

Before summarising the findings so far, one may well think of an ironic aside to paraphrase Heidegger's position. It 'still needs to be thought through' why Heidegger attributes such great ontological and metaphysical weight to 'difference' among humans. Does this perhaps represent the soft post-1945 version of a supremacist and racist legacy, or to put it differently, the cornerstone of a nationalist ideology in the guise of a 'democratic' philosophy? Readers will 'have to find out for themselves ...'.

In summing up so far, a Heideggerian tradition of viewing difference as separate from and external to identity exemplifies a particularly 'strong' notion of difference. Heideggerian notions of identity and difference do not allow much room for thinking commonalities together with (more or less important) differences. In this legacy, therefore, difference always tends to remain more important than, and separate from, identity. Moreover, such Heidegger-inspired approaches will tend to transform any 'weak' notions of 'other' and of 'alterity' towards their own priority for a 'strong' notion of difference.

A Postcolonial Discourse of Identity: Spivak

A contrasting tendency can be identified across the 1980s and 1990s in the field of discourses known as postcolonial studies, notably in the work of Gayatri Chakravorty Spivak (1996) and of Homi K. Bhabha (1994). Among the diverse intellectual influences that have informed these two authors' impressive body of work, the writing of Jacques Lacan represents one common key referent for both. It goes without saying that Spivak's and Bhabha's work differ from each other in emphasis and orientation, and that Lacan's work has also influenced a wide range of other authors in these fields. Yet from an anthropological perspective on identity debates in wider and interdisciplinary fields, Lacan's impact on the work of these two authors is particularly interesting for the three following reasons.

First, anthropology's own relationship with psychoanalysis has a somewhat torn and unhappy history, dating back to the period before the First World War and remarkably short moments of great achievement or success. Given this historical experience, it is somewhat puzzling for many anthropologists how Bhabha or Spivak might find any new approach that would not end up in, say, the more excessive forms of cultural relativism displayed by Margaret Mead or by some authors of the 'culture and personality' school of the mid-twentieth century. Personally, I do not want to hide my own scepticism in this regard, particularly in view of Lacan's attempts to transfer analogies from the personal to the socio-political and cultural level. Bhabha and Spivak have pursued that line of reasoning even more extensively.

Second, the postcolonial approach – whether this contested term is accepted or not – has asked a number of new questions about public representations and about the subjective experience of life under 'subaltern' hierarchical conditions that were formerly colonial. It is in pursuit of these questions about experience and internalised lived hierarchies, that Bhabha and Spivak have each made use of Lacan's work. I have already indicated that in Spivak's work, a somewhat attenuated Heideggerian influence through Derrida represents a minor element of her inspiration, whereas a major source of inspiration is derived from Lacanian psychoanalysis, turned into cultural critique.

Third, Spivak's influence upon anthropological writing seems to have been stronger than that of Bhaba for two reasons. On the one hand, her gender-sensitive considerations have been especially attractive to some feminist scholarship in anthropology. On the other hand, her further elaborations on Lacan's various versions of 'other' led her to coin the widely popular notion of 'othering' (Spivak 1985). This notion was gratefully taken over by many anthropologists as a somewhat moralist shorthand formula for how not to do research. Because of these more influential repercussions among anthropologists, I will confine myself here to Lacan's work in relation to that of Spivak. It has already been indicated that the notion of 'othering' is central to Spivak's work and to her academic popularity, and that this represents the most direct relation between her work and Lacan's.

In his vast and prolific writing over several decades, Lacan (e.g., 1968) elaborated a perspective on the formation of subjectivity and identity that distinguished 'other' (with a lower case 'o') from 'Other' (with a capital 'O'). Lacan's famous 'mirror' example (Lacan 1966: 93–100; Eden 1991) designates that 'other' who resembles the self, as it is discovered when a child looks into a mirror and becomes aware of itself as a separate being. Simultaneously, this results in the very young child's narcissistic wish to be one with the mirror image, an 'imaginary identification'. Language then offers the symbolic representation of the absent 'other'. Subjectivity, according to Lacan, thus cannot be reduced to the reflexive identity of self awareness; it is also, and more fundamentally, marked by the unconscious, which is non-reflexive and ordered in ways that are analogous to language. In Spivak's variant of postcolonial theory, Lacan's 'other' is then transformed into a referent for colonized others, marginalised by imperial discourse and identified by their 'difference' from the centre.

By contrast, Lacan's 'Other' (with a capital 'O') is the 'great other' in whose gaze the subject gains identity (Ashcroft, Griffiths and Tiffin 1999: 169–71). That Other can be embodied in close subjects, such as father or mother, or it can refer to the unconscious itself. Obviously, then, this 'Other' tends to be more powerful, which is why in Spivak's theories, the 'Other' is compared to the imperial centres and their discourses. It provides the terms in which colonized subjects gain a sense of their identities as being dependent. Simultaneously, this becomes the ideological framework in which colonized subjects may come to understand the world (Spivak 1985, 1996). These are the 'others' that typically represent Spivak's colonial and postcolonial subjects, who only exist through, or against, the powerful gaze of colonial discourse.

This brief outline permits us to step back and assess the conceptualisation of 'identity/ alterity (difference)' in this postcolonial variant of a Lacanian tradition. Quite evidently here, difference and identity are *not external* to each other, with difference as the ultimately superior category, as was the case in Heidegger's ontology. With Lacan, by contrast, difference can always be *part of* identity, and vice versa – at least *prima vista*.

Identity is part of difference insofar as its own formation is subject to the basic relation with a powerful and distinct 'Other' whose gaze defines the terms. By the same token, with Lacan, difference is also 'part of identity' in subjectivity's contrast to the other in the mirror image, and in the interplay and difference between the self-reflexive conscious and the non-reflexive, unconscious Other.

This first result of our examination, therefore, indicates a kind of dialectical, mutual inclusiveness in both Lacan's and Spivak's perspectives on the relationship between identity and difference. This said, the question nevertheless arises whether this relationship really is as balanced as it appears at first sight. After all, Lacan's preoccupation with psychoanalysis led him towards a priority focus upon the contradictory processes of personal *identity* formation. And if we carefully inspect the various forms of mutual inclusiveness in Spivak's work, it is also *identity* which tends to subsume everything else in the end. Moreover, Spivak's influential argument does not open up enough substantial intellectual space for any independent or alternative existence to her postcolonial subjects *outside* the powerful gaze of dominant forces and agencies. Although the colonizing and the colonized are fundamentally different from each other, Spivak sees them as intrinsically linked to each other through reciprocal identity formation. To my mind, this comes very close to what one may call psychoanalytical fatalism in critical disguise.

In fact, Spivak' s constant shift of positions between identity and difference, one becoming part of the other in different constellations, displays a definite, long term priority for identity. This becomes visible in her claim that such fundamentally contradictory and different opponents as colonisers and colonised are seen as mutually defining each other's basic identities. By consequence, it is now 'identity' that appears as a quasi- ontological category which conditions and informs, in the final analysis, global confrontation as much as personal contradictions. One may conclude that in this variant of a Lacanian tradition, some basic notion of identity is pervasive if not ubiquitous, with some variant of other and of 'othering' as its eternal companion.

Assessing the Impacts of Heidegger and Lacan on Anthropology

Before moving on to examine some conceptual contributions from anthropology to the subject of identity/alterity, it may be useful to summarise the main results of our previous sections. It has been crucial to examine the Heideggerian and the Lacanian legacies because they are encoded in one way or another in the wider transdisciplinary debates of the humanities and the social sciences that anthropologists consult to find inspiration for their own work on identity. As we have seen, the Heideggerian legacy tends to essentialise difference and to subordinate identity to it. This paradigmatic emphasis on difference can lead to a revitalization of strong variants of cultural relativism, or it can lead to more dangerous pro-chauvinist or pro-nationalist tendencies. On an analytic level, the Heideggerian legacy will privilege the description of existential conditions of particular 'being' and will encourage connecting these with paradigmatic antimodern universals. Either way, this legacy will invite authors to introduce 'difference' as the fundamental dividing line among humans, be it on the particularist or on the universal level of analysis. In assessing this particular aspect of the Heideggerian legacy, it cannot be combined in any meaningful way with anthropological perspectives on identity, unless one wishes to enhance an explicit version of cultural relativism that must, by definition, give priority to differences between cultures.

Our review of an important Lacanian legacy in postcolonial studies yielded a less negative result. If anything, this tradition tends to overemphasize 'identity', but it does so even when there is no specific common identity (universals left aside), or when identity is not the central question at all. At least in the long run, a Spivak-inspired approach therefore might run into the danger of essentializing identity and of assimilating variants of 'other' unto a conception of the self that equates identity with 'sameness' or 'unity'. The potentials of such an approach range from intellectually inspiring various forms of strong 'identity politics' on to limiting and narrowing the intellectual space for alternatives. I shall return below to this amalgamation of identity with 'unity' and 'sameness'. On an analytic level, this legacy will tend to emphasize an appreciation for (personal and emotional) experience in a Freudian terminology, but it will then attempt to metaphorically relate it from the personal to the social level. For those anthropologists who follow it, a Spivak-Lacanian inspiration provides strong moralist warnings against 'othering' as a profoundly neocolonial activity, often without recognizing how, by definition, most social scientists – in one way or another – unavoidably have to write about 'others'.

Connecting these assessments back to our starting point, this paper began by outlining a working definition that was based on self-criticism inside Cultural Studies as well as on anthropology's minimum consensus on identity/alterity. That subject-centred working definition of personal and collective identities must include multidimensional and contradictory forms of sameness and differing, based on dialogical and confrontational, power-related agency and ascription through selves and others. If we now apply that working definition to our intermediate results, then the outcome is differentiated.

As for the Heideggerian legacy, the assessment of its anthropological potential is clearly negative. This legacy ontologically separates a 'strong' version of difference from identity, it essentialises difference, and we had to ask whether it might not be a nationalist ideology in the guise of a democratic philosophy. Our working definition had, after all, suggested to conceptualise difference not in an ontological but in a subject-centred manner as part of identity.

As for the Lacanian legacy in Spivak's work, by contrast, we merely saw some sceptical doubts emerging about the conception of identity. These doubts about Lacan's legacy in Spivak's work have raised the question of whether her juxtaposition of identity and other comes close to psychoanalytical fatalism in critical disguise. Yet at first sight, this form of a Lacanian legacy seems to be much closer to our working definition. At least it integrates some variants of otherness into its own, albeit heavily loaded, subject-centred concept of identity. That inclination to heavily load and to essentialise 'identity', however, is the highly problematic core element in this tradition. First, essentialising identity has its necessary counterparts here in an almost helpless, moralist condemnation of 'othering'. Spivak's version of Lacan's heritage seems to find it very difficult to accept any multidimensional, 'weak' forms of 'other/alterity' at all, not to speak of writing about them. Second, the essentialising notion of identity in Spivak's variant of a Lacanian tradition tends to conflate identity with 'sameness'. Our working definition, by contrast, suggests that multidimensional forms of sameness are part of, but not identical with, identity. If I am not mistaken, it is this blurring of the distinction – perhaps seductive for psychoanalytical reasoning – and a binary rather than a multidimensional approach, which lie at the root of Spivak's notion. The fertility of just such an alternative approach emphasizing multidimensional forms of sameness as 'partial connections' was clearly demonstrated by Marilyn Strathern (1991). Third, the result of Spivak's reasoning tends to permanently keep confined any alternative visions, and forms of agency, within the boundaries of binary asymmetries of identity. Judith Butler's emphasis (1993) on multidimensional female identity constructions, as well as Chandra Talpade Mohanty's focus (2002) on transcending dichotomies between (post-)colonial and (post-)colonized, both represent creative alternatives to Spivak's reasoning and its reliance on a 'strong' version of identity accompanied by a moralist stand against othering.

To go beyond 'strong' and binary versions of identity/other (difference) and to explore the 'soft' and multimensional conceptions of identity/alterity, it will be most productive now to review some of the earlier contributions of anthropological scholarship to understand identity/alterity as mutually constitutive categories.

Conceptual Contributions from Anthropology to Debating Identity/Alterity

Among these anthropological contributions, three successive phases appear to be particularly important. In one way or the other, these earlier phases have influenced and informed anthropology's current minimal consensus on identity/alterity.

As alluded to above, some of these earlier contributions were represented by authors who were close to the 'Culture and Personality' direction of the mid-twentieth century. Studies such as Ruth Benedict's *The Chrysanthemum and the Sword* (1946) and related research on 'national characters' pursued an explicit focus on (stable, coherent, almost homogeneous) collective identities. For anthropology, I regard the main legacy of that tradition as too restrictive and one-sided, since it tended to codify 'strong' versions of cultural relativism. Its failure to integrate psychoanalysis with anthropology was perhaps unavoidable. Yet this line of thought did also have some positive impact upon anthropological conceptualisations in the field. To an extent, these works were important for emancipating debates about identity, moving them away from the exclusive realm of individual psychology whose monopoly they had been before. They enabled a new openness to consider not only personal, but also socio-cultural and collective identities, and they fostered a certain appreciation of emotional components in them: this can be seen as the somewhat ambivalent legacy left by Benedict, Mead, and some others of the 'Culture and Personality' authors.

A second phase of these earlier contributions was opened up by the neo-Marxist turn in anthropology after 1968. This refers to Maurice Godelier's epistemological critique of the German philosophical tradition (Godelier 1973: 158, 168). From his own materialist and neostructuralist perspective, Godelier criticized the continuous confusion between identity (*Identität*) and unity (*Einheit*) in the German tradition, which he convincingly traced back to Hegel, whose idealism necessarily integrated both as universal identity. Neostructuralist anthropology thereby helped to sort out a conceptual confusion that had haunted the humanities – not only in Germany – from Hegel to Marx, from Husserl to Heidegger, and of course from Freud to Lacan. 'Unity' of opponents in interaction, or in mutual ascription, does not necessarily entail any common 'identity' among them (universals left aside), but only – at best – a potential for mutually exclusive (dimensions of) identities. The point becomes even more evident if applied in a subject-centred manner to topics such as slavery, mass rapes, or the holocaust.

A third, and the most recent of these contributions in anthropology, originated with Johannes Fabian's assessment of anthropology's own legacy (1983). Fabian (personal communication, 1999) wrote *Time and the Other* as an attempt to elaborate and apply for anthropology the critical insights gained by Edward Said's *Orientalism* (1978). Although I find that Fabian's study somewhat underrates the cumulative achievements by anthropological reasoning, the main thrust of his argument is a valid one. Anthropology itself has been engaged too often in creating hierarchical distances of time (history) and of place (location) by featuring the peculiarities of distanciated 'others'. Far from displaying any resemblance to Spivak's moralism, Fabian's critique of anthropological othering is empirically and analytically well grounded. In fact, it has opened up the roads for creatively elaborating anthropological alternatives today.

These short reviews of explicit earlier contributions thus indicate key phases of anthropological thinking on identity/alterity. The first of them concerned a phase of hegemonic, distanciated, 'strong' cultural relativism, which nevertheless allowed anthropology explicitly to pose the question of identity/alterity in sociocultural terms. The second, with its structural neo-Marxist turn, de-subjectified and thus somewhat attenuated the notion of identity, thus clarifying its limits. The third, the critical phase, produced an internal anthropological self-reflection (which also considered the first phase of explicit cultural relativism) and thus began to empirically specify the modalities of othering.

These elements of a legacy *inside* anthropology may be dispersed and may seem to be discontinuous. Nonetheless, they are important when compared to the two tendencies from transdisciplinary debates that have been assessed earlier on in this paper. They have never confined themselves to persons as seen trough an existentialist or individual psychological perspective, but from the outset included multiple sociocultural identities. By transcending 'strong' cultural relativism, they then transformed anthropology's own 'strong' notions of difference into weaker ones, and by outlining the limits of identity construction, they also pointed out the limitations of the identity concept seen in isolation. Finally, this legacy used its own reflexive auto-critique to achieve an empirical specification of 'othering' instead of moralizing about it. These moves can thus help to critique, and to overcome, some of those dominant tendencies in wider transdisciplinary discourses which either promote substantial problems, or at least lead the analysis astray.

They provide an apt basis for the present volume to suggest discarding any essentialised notion of difference, eschew any overemphasis on identity as sameness, and resist any temptation to moralize about 'othering'. As I have argued, both the tendencies from wider transdisciplinary discourses not only oppose each other in the foreground from extreme sides of a spectrum, but they also share some common grounds behind the scenes. Some of this meeting ground behind the scenes is indicated by Spivak's own intellectual proximity not only to Lacan, but also to Heidegger through Derrida. In the Heideggerian legacy – transformed, among others, by Derrida – an ontological emphasis on 'strong' difference is quite obviously bound to single out particular identities, too. It is less obvious, but unavoidable, that in a Lacanian tradition, a more implicit priority for a 'strong' notion of identity, in turn, is bound to indirectly emphasise whatever makes that strong identity 'different' from others. This logical necessity to indirectly upgrade difference then can only be contained in moralist terms. This is why the anthropological working definition, which we used and tested throughout this text, offers a 'weak' and non-binary, a multidimensional and fluid approach to identity/alterity.

On this basis, then, the present volume sets out to identify and specify certain classificatory schemata, structures, or 'grammars' of identity/alterity. Identifying and specifying such concrete modalities promises an 'exit strategy' from unwarranted and dangerous reifications by way of a multidimensional and non-essentialising approach. The working definition as used throughout this chapter may be usefully combined with Baumann 's pragmatic and heuristic proposition. That proposition suggests that there are at least three such classificatory structures or grammars by which sociocultural group identities are conceived and enacted in different, modified manners. In this volume, a number of scholars enter into debate and dialogue with this proposition through the analysis of rich ethnographic material. This opens up a dialogue and a debate that have been long overdue.

Note

1. For helpful comments on various aspects of this chapter, I thank Gerd Baumann (Amsterdam), Thomas Fillitz, Sylvia Haas, Alice Pechriggl, and Sabine Strasser (Vienna).

References

Ashcroft, Bill, Gareth Griffiths, and Helen Tiffin. 1999. *Key Concepts in Post-Colonial Studies.* London, New York: Routledge.
Bhabha, Homi K.1994. *The Location of Culture.* London: Routledge.
Benedict, Ruth. 1946. *The Chrysanthemum and the Sword: Patterns of Japanese culture.* Boston: Houghton-Mifflin.
Butler, Judith. 1993. *Bodies that Matter. On the Discursive Limits of 'Sex'.* New York, London: Routledge.
Byron, Reginald. 1996. 'Identity', in *Encyclopaedia of Social and Cultural Anthropology*, eds. Alan Barnard and Jonathan Spencer. London, New York: Routledge, 292.
Capurro, Rafael. 1991. 'Heidegger' in *Philosophie der Gegenwart. In Einzeldarstellungen von Adorno bis Wright*, ed. Julian Nida-Rümelin. Stuttgart: Kröner, 229–46.
Derrida, Jacques. 1967. *De la grammatologie.* Paris: Editions de minuit.
Eden, Tania. 1991. 'Lacan' in *Philosophie der Gegenwart. In Einzeldarstellungen von Adorno bis Wright*, ed. Julian Nida-Rümelin. Stuttgart: Kröner, 309–314.
Ettinger, Elzbieta. 1995. *Hanna Arendt/ Martin Heidegger.* New Haven, London: Yale University Press
Fabian, Johannes. 1983. *Time and the Other. How Anthropology Makes its Object.* New York: Columbia University Press.
Fox, Richard G. and Andre Gingrich. 2002. 'Introduction' in *Anthropology, by Comparison*, eds. Andre Gingrich and Richard G. Fox. London, New York: Routledge, 1–24.
Gingrich, Andre 2002. 'When Ethnic Minorities are "Dethroned". Towards a Methodology of Self-Reflexive, Controlled Macro-Comparison' in *Anthropology, by Comparison*, eds. Andre Gingrich and Richard G. Fox. London, New York: Routledge, 225–248.

Gingrich, Andre and Richard G. Fox, eds. 2002. *Anthropology, by Comparison*. London, New York: Routledge.
Godelier, Maurice. 1973. *Ökonomische Anthropologie* [German trans. of: *Horizons. Trajets marxistes en anthropologie*]. Reinbek/Hamburg: Rowohlt Verlag.
Grossberg, Lawrence. 1996. 'Identity and Cultural Studies: Is that all there is?' in *Questions of Cultural Identity*, ed. Stuart Hall and Paul du Gay. London, New Delhi: Sage, 87–107.
Heidegger, Martin. 1957. *Identität und Differenz*. Pfullingen: Neske.
Heidegger, Martin. 1990. *Die Selbstbehauptung der deutschen Universität. Das Rektorat 1933/34*. Frankfurt/Main: Klostermann.
Lacan, Jacques. 1966. *Ecrits*. Paris: Le Seuil
Lacan, Jacques. 1968. *The Language of the Self. The Function of Language in Psychoanalysis*. Baltimore, MD: Johns Hopkins University Press.
Leaman, George. 1993. *Heidegger im Kontext. Gesamtüberblick zum NS-Engagement der Universitätsphilosophen* [German trans. of: *Conceptual Misreadings: The U.S. Reception of Heidegger's Thought*]. Hamburg, Berlin: Argument
Mohanty, Chandra Talpade. 2002. '"Under Western Eyes" Revisited: Feminist Solidarity through Anticapitalist Struggle'. *Signs: Journal of Women in Culture and Society* 28: 499–535
Nida-Rümelin, Julian, ed. 1991. *Philosophie der Gegenwart. In Einzeldarstellungen von Adorno bis Wright*. Stuttgart: Kröner 1991
Pinto, Paulu. 2002. 'Mystical Bodies: Ritual, Experience, and the Embodiment of Sufism in Syria'. BostonUniversity: Ph.D. dissertation.
Ricoeur, Paul. 1986. *Die lebendige Metapher*. München: Fink
Rockmore, T. and J. Margolis, eds. 1999. *The Heidegger Case*. Philadelphia: Temple University Press
Said, Edward. 1978. *Orientalism: Western Conceptions of the Orient*. London: Penguin
Spivak, Gayatri C. 1985. 'The Rani of Simur' in *Europe and its Others*, vol. 1, ed. Francis Baker et al. Colchester: Uessex 1985.
Spivak, Gayatri C.1996. *The Spivak Reader*, edited by Donna Landry and Gerald MacLean. New York, London: Routledge
Strathern, Marilyn. 1991. *Partial Connections*. Savage, Maryland: Rowman and Littlefield.
Taylor, Charles. 1994. 'The Politics of Recognition' in *Multiculturalism: Examining the Politics of Recognition*, ed. Amy Gutman. Princeton, N.J.: Princeton University Press, 25–74.
Toren, Christina. 2002. 'Comparison and Ontogeny' in *Anthropology, by Comparison*, eds. Andre Gingrich and Richard G. Fox. London, New York: Routledge, 186-203.
Trawny, Peter. 2003. *Martin Heidegger*. Frankfurt/Main: Campus
Wiegerling, K. 1991. 'Jacques Derrida' in *Philosophie der Gegenwart. In Einzeldarstellungen von Adorno bis Wright*, ed. Julian Nida- Rümelin. Stuttgart: Kröner, 138–143.
Wolin, R., ed. 1993. *The Heidegger Controversy: A Critical Reader*. Cambridge, Mass.: MIT Press.
Young, Julian. 1997. *Heidegger, Philosophy, Nazism*. Cambridge: Cambridge University Press

Chapter 2

Grammars of Identity/Alterity

A Structural Approach

Gerd Baumann

This chapter will propose in more detail the three grammars of identity/alterity with which our volume is concerned.[1] To do so as clearly as possible, it makes three moves. The first of these introduces each classificatory model on its own and then exemplifies the grammars as they are employed, often in competition with each other, in the realms of politics, religion, and aesthetics. Having affirmed that the grammars can be recognized in the most diverse social processes, the second and third moves ask two critical questions, one theoretical, the other primarily methodological. Theoretically, the three grammars must face what I have called 'the ternary challenge' as part of the age-old question whether classificatory structures are binary or ternary. I will propose that all three grammars are ternary, but each in its own way. This further increases the analytical potential of the grammars, but it also raises a methodological question. Since the grammars seem to work almost too well for comfort, the third move will face Karl Popper's (1972 [1935]) time-honoured question of falsification: if a proposition works well, then what are the criteria for it not working ? The answer to this question will be sought in language and language use, or *langue* and *parole* to be precise, and it will address the question of violence. In particular, it will focus on genocidal violence, that is, killing the other at the cost of killing one's own former self. After this short guide through the argument, let me now return to where we are so far.

If it is true that claims to identity, collective or individual, are inevitably tied to exclusions of alterity, that every 'us' excludes a 'them', then there is little more to say: we can only specify the historical circumstances or the ethnographic peculiarities in any one case. But as Andre Gingrich has shown, there is not much point in declaring selfings into universal necessities and their corollary, otherings, into wicked propensities. If, on the other hand, one opts for philosophically 'weak' interpretations of the concept of identity, this can create a space which allows for alternative approaches, namely, to differentiate between different modalities of selfing/othering and put these differentiations to analytic use.

Such a framework of distinction and comparison will offer itself most readily perhaps in the shape of socially shared classificatory structures or, as I have called them here, 'grammars' of attributing identity and alterity to whomever. One of these grammars is well-known to anyone: the binary grammar of 'we are good, so they are bad'. The categorical divide can be filled in at will: we hunt, they gather; we farm, they herd; we are pure, they pollute. The permutations need not always be as tangible: we are tolerant, they repressive; we serve, they are selfish; we discuss propositions, they scream dogmas. Nonetheless, the simplicity of this binary grammar is obvious, and I shall return to it later under the heading of an 'anti-grammar'. The question is, however, whether we cannot identify rather more complex grammars of selfing and othering.

Three Structures, Freely Adapted to Serve as 'Grammars of Us and Them'

The task of the next three sections is to introduce the three grammars that, I propose, underlie processes of selfing/othering. I divide the words 'selfing/othering' by nothing more than a slash because they describe two faces of the same process. To introduce the grammars is a tricky task for, although they are based on classic social theories, they are by no means self-evident as grammars to systematize the ubiquitous processes of selfing/othering. I need to apologize to the three 'ancestors' whose work has been used and adapted here quite ruthlessly: Edward Said (1978), E.E. Evans-Pritchard (1940), and Louis Dumont (1980) would each of them have protested against their different insights being combined in the way I propose. But that combination is the whole point now, and classics stand strong enough to survive a certain amount of re-interpretation, adaptation, and even 'cannibalizing'. Transformed into grammars, these classic models do not, of course, describe how social systems work, even if two of the authors have made this claim (Dumont 1980, Evans-Pritchard 1940). Rather, they are used as guides as to how different discourses order the relationships between self and other.

Orientalizing: From Binary Classification to Reverse Mirror-Imaging

Taking for granted the black-and-white grammar of binary opposition mentioned above, a great step forward was made by Edward Said (1978) who recognized the binary grammar at work in the long historical process of Westerners representing 'the Orient' to themselves. Admittedly, even Said's version of orientalism may look, at first sight, like a baby grammar, a framework that only uses the simplest of oppositions and exploits them to maximum contrast. Just like the baby who blabbers 'me and not-me' to distinguish two poles of its egocentric sociality, so orientalism seems to blabber 'us' and 'them' to articulate the crudest differentiation of all. Yet the similarity is deceptive, and what is at stake in orientalism is not merely a binary opposition, I argue, but a binary opposition subject to reversal. This is not always as clear as it could be, but it seems to be implicit in Said's recognition that Westerners not only denigrated that which they called 'oriental', but also desired it. Orientalism as Said analysed it, was not some primitive technique of reversal favoured by the stupid or the vicious, but on the contrary, a sophisticated discipline developed by academic and artistic elites, and the grammar of orientalism is not limited to: 'we are good, so they are bad.' The intellectual and creative elites who established orientalist discourses in political theory and economics, poetry and novels, philosophy and music would never have fallen for such placcative nonsense. What made the caricatures intellectually interesting and aesthetically challenging for such elites, many of them tired of and estranged from their own cultural milieus, was also the cultural self-critique that an orientalizing of the other made possible and, as importantly, communicable. Let me use a diagram to show both the negative mirroring and the positive reversals of the orientalist grammar.

Occident Positive	Orient Negative
rational	irrational
enlightened	superstitious
technological	backward
Occident Negative	Orient Positive
calculating	spontaneous
sober	luxuriant
materialist	mystical

Figure 2.1 The Grammar of Orientalization or Reverse Mirror-Imaging

Orientalism is thus not a simple binary opposition of 'us = good' and 'them = bad', but a very shrewd mirrored reversal of: 'what is good in us is [still] bad in them, but what got twisted in us [still] remains straight in them.' One may note in passing that the bracketed insertions ('[still]') recall the denial of contemporaneousness that Fabian (1983) has analysed as a crucial strategy in othering others. At the same time, however, the sense of Western superiority entails also a sense of loss: 'we' are 'no longer' so spontaneous, luxuriant, or mystical. The distancing from the self-created other is also a distancing from an uncomplicated idea of the self.

Notably, some of the orientalist oppositions (calculation vs. spontaneity, rationality vs. mysticism, society vs. community) are not between good and bad in any simple sense. Far from being a stupid reversal, the grammar of orientalism can implicate self-critique, albeit under the auspices of a self-invented other. This observation may shed some light on both the excesses of cultural self-seeking. The xenophobic version is to seek superiority for whatever merits one calls one's own; the xenophiliac one is to search for redemption from an equally self-counter-mirrored Other. The xenophiliac who searches for some special wisdom in Tibetan monks or rainforst Amerindians, and who discoveres a special 'natural grace' in children of colour or Third World athletes is no less orientalist than the xenophobe who sees the West as democratic, reasonable and secularist and the Orient (wherever it may be) as despotic, fanatic, and fundamentalist. Simplistic as this grammar may seem to be, it is anything but stupid, and its intellectual as well as political dangers are all the more visible when academic and communalist discourses of othering converge on this syntax of mirrored reversals (van der Veer 1994). The baby grammar of 'us is good and them is bad' is thus transformed, in orientalism, into a double-edged, potentially subtle, and at times even dialectical way of selfing one's own and othering the alien. Without this double-edged potential of critiquing one's own while still finding the other strange and inferior, this grammar would hardly have satisfied orientalizers like Flaubert or Verdi or Gide. What we find in the grammar of orientalizing the other is thus an operation of reverse mirror-imaging: selfing and othering condition each other in that both positive and negative characteristics are made to mirror each other in reverse.

Segmentation: From 'Ordered Anarchy' to Federal Disorder

Although it comes second here for reasons of exposition, the oldest grammar of alterity to rise to the status of an anthropological theory was Evans-Pritchard's (1940) model of the segmentary lineage system. Evans-Pritchard studied the Nuer, a people numbering a million or so that was spread out across the vast swamplands of the Southern Sudan. Every Nuer person is part of a pyramid of identifications ranging across four to six genealogical levels from minimal lineages to maximal clans and, finally, a shared tribal identity as the Nuer. This segmentary grammar of identity thus determines identities and alterities according to context. While in the context of a lineage-level blood feud a Nuer must 'other' an implicated neighbour to the point of threatening a revenge killing, the same neighbour is an ally in the context of a clan-level conflict or, as in Evans-Pritchard's days, a threat of colonial conquest. This is why Evans-Pritchard coined the paradoxical term 'ordered anarchy'.

To understand the discovery of this system, or better perhaps its invention by the anthropological analyst, it is helpful to know one of the paradoxes that it was meant to resolve: the Nuer people seemed constantly to be at war with each other, especially in blood feuds from the smallest scale to the largest, and yet they pulled together to resist British interference for nearly forty years. Unfortunately, the model was applied, from the 1950s to the 1970s, to an incredible range of societies purported to be based on divisions of lineages and clans. This indiscriminate application was too much of a good thing, for the model came under sustained ethnographic critique from the 1970s on (Kuper 1988). What was at stake in these critiques, however, was the use of the model to predict actual political decision-making; and in this regard, it is no more reliable than a first-year management student's model of organizational decision-making structures when compared with the actual deals concluded in the backrooms and corridors of power. Evans-Pritchard, too, was perfectly clear about this: no Nuer ever told him about a segmentary lineage system that projected genealogical segments upon territorial units. The model of segmentary fission and fusion, that is, identification and othering, is no more than that: the postulate of a 'logic as if', that is, a grammar which, if it were applied to decisions on the ground, would confer upon these decisions a certain logical consistency conspicuously invisible in the daily flow of political mannoeuvring and manipulation.

Interpreted for present purposes, the social grammar of a segmentary system is a logic of fission or enmity at a lower level of segmentation, overcome by a logic of fusion or neutralization of conflict at a higher level of segmentation. In the following diagram, we represent four levels of segmentation, called 1 to 4. Each level produces its own, decreasingly smaller, segments, called 1.1 and 1.2, 2.1 through 2.4, 3.1 through 3.8, and so on.

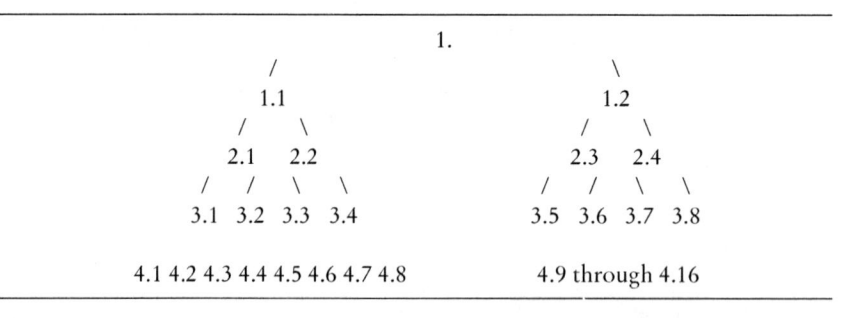

```
                            1.
              /                           \
             1.1                          1.2
          /      \                      /      \
         2.1     2.2                  2.3      2.4
        /   \   /   \                /   \    /   \
       3.1 3.2 3.3 3.4             3.5 3.6  3.7 3.8

   4.1 4.2 4.3 4.4 4.5 4.6 4.7 4.8        4.9 through 4.16
```

Figure 2.2 The Segmentary Grammar of Contextual Fission and Fusion

The resulting structure resembles that of a football league, or rather, the football fans, for while clubs do not usually merge or split up, fans do. At the lowest level of segmentation, it is the fans of two little village clubs that pitch their enthusiasm against each other. At the next higher level, the losing fans cheer with their erstwhile rival club's fans when faced with the district championship. Whichever team wins the district championship can be sure of all the district's fans when it faces the province championship; and finally, the team of province 1.1 will attract the loyalty of all villages 4.1. through 4.8 when fighting against the team of province 1.2 which, in its turn, is cheered by all the fans of the village clubs 4.9 through 4.16. The crucial difference to this football league metaphor is that the matches at all levels are played concurrently and simultaneously. It is thus entirely a matter of context who is one's foe and who one's friend at what classificatory level. The Nuer, so explains Evans-

Pritchard, actually live 'as if' this model described their selfings and otherings: if they did not, then blood feuds between lineages would burst asunder all their settlements, where maximal lineages or even clans must co-reside.

Tellingly for this grammar, we have left out the 'national' championship of the Nuer Football League: in an acephalous system such as the Nuer's, a system where there are no formalized offices of coercive power over a delineated territory. The highest level of sameness, that is, ethnic identity as Nuer pure and simple, is not filled in. It is left blank, that is, unless there appears a contender of equal or greater force, in the Nuer's case the British Empire and its military machine. When the British troops invaded Nuerland, so the model says, Nuer people were pursuing different rivalries and alliances in different games at different levels of segmentation. Only when all Nuer interests came to be pitched, at the highest level of segmentation, against a British threat to all, internal fissions were fused in a united resistance.

The intellectual beauty of this segmentary grammar of identity/alterity lies in its contextual awareness. The Other may be my foe in a context placed at a lower level of segmentation, but may simultaneously be my ally in a context placed at a higher level of segmentation. Identity and alterity are thus a matter of context, and contexts are ranked according to classificatory levels. Fusion and fission, identity and difference are not matters of absolute criteria in this grammar, but functions of recognizing the appropriate segmentary level. In the segmentary grammar, people can thus selve themselves, and can other others according to context, that is, according to the structural level of the conflict or contest, coalition or cooperation that is at stake at any one given moment.

This, however, is impossible in a system that is not, as the Nuer's was, acephalous, that is, without institutionalized political and territorial power structures and without formal political offices. In a world of power centres and territorial states, the closest one can come to a segmentary system of selfing and othering is a federal system: one contestation or election asks me to take sides as a citizen of my city; another asks me as a citizen of my federated state; a third asks me as a citizen of my nation-state; a fourth perhaps as a citizen of the European or African Union. Admittedly, such federal politics represent a rather impoverished version of the segmentary grammar, for it usually falls to one or another power centre to tell us which level of our identity is being addressed at any one moment. On the other hand, federal orders can work quite well to help people realize their unity at a higher segmentary tier and acknowledge each other's diversity at a lower tier of segmentation. When power centres, however, push for centralization and monopolies of power, instead of tiered levels of governance and self-governance defined according to context, the intellectual beauty of the segmentary grammar disappears, and the subordinated tiers will rebel.

Sixty years after Evans-Pritchard's analysis, the Nuer and all other people of the Southern Sudan are victims of a genocidal war, waged by the unelected government of the Northern Sudan and called a 'civil war' by the perpetrators and most of the world's media. The very word: 'civil war' is a lie in such a case. After several centuries of Northerners enslaving Southerners in the Egyptian-ruled precolonial Sudan, there followed the so-called 'Anglo-Egyptian Condominium of the Sudan', a uniquely absurd construction by which the British claimed political power and Northerners continued to exercise their exploitative economic power. When the Northern Sudanese succeeded, in 1956, to preside over 'Independence for All of Sudan', the British hastily abandoned all their previous plans to separate the two unequal halves of their semi-colony into two separate postcolonial states. It only needed the American-led discovery of oil in the Southern Sudan around 1980, for the Southerners to wage a war of independence in response to the centuries of precolonial slavery, colonial exploitation, and post-independence suppression and theft by the Northern Sudanese authorities and ruling class. The events since then have been horrendous; but can the grammar of segmentation help us perhaps to understand this non-'civil war' ?

The first question is whether there is, or is not, one state called Sudan. The Nuer and the other Southerners demand their own apex in a segmentary ordering of identity/alterity: a Republic of South-Sudan independent from the 'Islamic Republic' of the Northern Sudan. Why, then, can they not get it? After all, the Republic of Eritrea, which even happens to border present-day Sudan, managed in the 1980s to secede from the Republic of Ethiopia and is now a fully-recognized and sovereign member of the United Nations. The tragedy of the Southern Sudanese problem, however, lies at the classificatory levels below the apical point. The rival liberation armies of the Southern Sudan have failed, at their own and each other's detriment, to define the federal sublevels by which they would organize their, regionally desirable and internationally manageable, new Republic of South-Sudan.

Following the Nuer and their South-Sudanese compatriots into the present-day politics of national identity/alterity, one can see more clearly the trouble with the impoverished federal version of the subtle segmentary grammar. The Nuer, after all, were the past masters and proven experts at playing the contextually sensitive game of segmentary identities: 'who I am at what moment, is a question of context; and defining the context is a question of knowing the right, contextually appropriate, classificatory level'. This knowledge, however, is no longer as subtle and supple, or as intellectually beautiful, as it was in Evans-Pritchard's day. Yet even when the existence of power centers reduces the grammar of segmentation to its impoverished version of federalism, we have not entirely unlearned its skills of contextualising our definitions of self and other. Much of the politics we perform is, in fact, a silent dramatization of these different segmentary levels of creating identity and insisting on otherness. All arguments for de-centralization and federal orders, as opposed to monopolies of power or so-called globalization, are arguments in favour of the segmentary grammar of selfing and othering. The crucial question, however, is posed all the more acutely now: who is to have the power to define the ultimate apex of the pyramid, and who defines which intervening classificatory levels ? We shall return to this power-loaded question as soon as we have introduced the third grammar on its own terms.

Encompassment: From Indian Castes to Co-opting Outcasts

If the orientalist grammar was remarkable for its double-edged play between exclusion and exoticized appreciation, and the segmentary grammar of alterity impresses by its contextual flexibility and subtlety, then the third grammar is seductive by its sheer universalizing rigour. It was worked out by Louis Dumont in his analysis of the Indian system of caste. The Chicago edition of his *Homo Hierarchicus* (1980) contains an eight-page appendix that abstracts a purely formal logic that, Dumont argues, describes the essence of the caste system. Just as with Evans-Pritchard, it is beside the point here whether Dumont's analysis does or does not adequately theorize the workings of the social system he studies: anthropologists have of course developed alternative approaches and will continue to do so (Galey 1991; Quigley 1993). What matters for our purposes here, however, is the formal operation of encompassment as a grammar of identity/alterity. Encompassment means an act of selfing by appropriating, perhaps one should say adopting or co-opting, selected kinds of otherness. This grammar of encompassment, too, is based on distinguishing levels, much like the grammar of segmentation. But rather than contextualizing difference by recognizing a multitude of levels, this grammar works on two levels only. The lower level of cognition recognizes difference, the higher level subsumes that which is different under that which is universal. To put it somewhat polemically: 'you may think that you differ from me in your sense of values or identity; but deep down, or rather higher up, you are but a part of me.' Seen from below, woman is the opposite of man. Seen from above, that is, the level of man as defining the generic term, woman is but part of mankind. Your difference, in other words, is not situational or contextual, as it would be in the grammar of level-conscious segmentation; rather, it is a fiction caused by your own low horizon: '*Your* low level of consciousness may need *my* otherness to define itself, but *my* heart is big enough for *both* of us.' An amusing example may be seen in Thomas Aquinas, an admirer of pagan antiquity who could not reconcile himself to the thought that he might go to heaven when Socrates and Plato and Aristotle would burn in hell, just because Christ had come a little late for them. *Anima naturaliter Christiana*, 'the human soul is Christian by nature', so the *Doctor Ecclesiae* decided, and thus the virtuous pagans were encompassed into a Christianity *avant la lettre*.

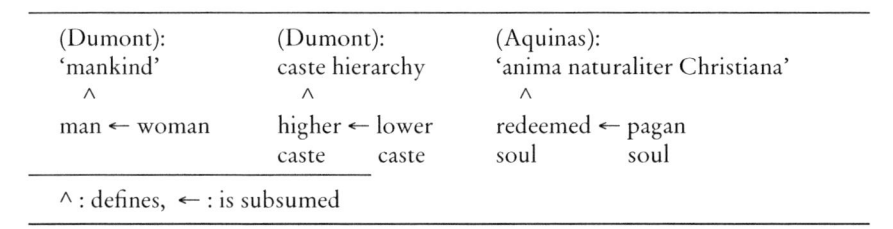

(Dumont): 'mankind'	(Dumont): caste hierarchy	(Aquinas): 'anima naturaliter Christiana'
∧	∧	∧
man ← woman	higher ← lower caste caste	redeemed ← pagan soul soul

∧ : defines, ← : is subsumed

Figure 2.3 The Grammar Encompassment by Hierarchical Subsumption

In the grammar of encompassment, the putatively subordinate category is adopted, subsumed or co-opted (←) into the identity defined and, as it were, owned by those who do the encompassing. Encompassment is thus always hierarchical: it needs the higher caste to encompass the lower, the Christian to encompass the pagans.

For an application to present-day debates, let me first turn to Southall, the multi-ethnic suburb of London where I did seven years of research (Baumann 1996). Here, one could observe palpable tensions between immigrants of Hindu backgrounds and their neighbours of Sikh backgrounds. These reflected the violent conflicts in the Punjab, home to both groups, which culminated in the murder of Prime Minister Indira Ghandi, the siege of the Sikhs' Golden Temple, and the terrorist campaigns of fundamentalist Sikhs against Hindus and nationalist Hindus against Sikhs. Yet amidst all this strife and its transnational reverberations, most of Southall's Hindus insisted that the violence was about nothing: 'Sikhs are Hindus', so I was told time and again, 'and the only trouble is: they don't know it.' Christians, too, were Hindus, so I was told on several occasions, for Christ was but a reincarnation, after all, of Brahma, the Creator of All. The logic of encompassment is as flexible as it is imperious: from a lower level of consciousness, minorities (or even majorities, for this is what Sikhs are in Southall and Christians are in Britain) may think themselves different; but from a higher level of consciousness, these differences are but fictions of identity politics: in reality, or rather viewed from higher-up, the self-styled others are but a subordinate part of an encompassing Us.

A second example taken from London concerned the claim by, mostly, Afro-Caribbean political activists that their own designation of colour, 'Black', applied as much to people of Asian descent as to people of African descent. 'Black', so the argument went, is a 'political colour', as opposed to a description of skin colour. Predictably, most of Southall's South Asian-descended people were bewildered, and many of them outraged, by being called political 'Blacks' by skin-colour 'blacks'.

(Hindus:)	('Anti-Racists'):
Hindus:	'Black People'
∧	∧
Hindus ← Sikhs	Afro-Caribbean People ← Other People of Colour

Figure 2.4 Grammars of Encompassment in Southall, London, ca. 1986–92

The brief and necessarily anecdotal exposition of the three grammars has alluded to different examples for different grammars. It is crucial, however, that the same social situations of selfing and othering can make use of several grammars at the same time. The grammars then appear as competing or rival versions of constructing identity and alterity. Before the next section turns to this simultaneity of different grammars in social use, it may be useful briefly to recall the basic structure of each of the grammar in a diagram:

Orientalism:	Segmentation:	Encompassment:
Self + | Other –	∧	Self as Whole
———————	/ \	∧
Self - | Other +	/ \ / \	Self ← Other as
	/\ /\ /\ /\	as Part Sub-Part

Figure 2.5: Three Grammars of Selfing and Othering

If the three grammars can help to distinguish and systematize three different ways of performing selfings and otherings, then the next task must be to see how far they can enable comparison. For this, the best starting point is comparison within the same ethnographic context. It will be useful, therefore, to trace the different grammars in constellations of selfing and othering where the crucial problem ('who are we ? who are they ?') is the same, but where there are different parties chosing different grammars to make their points. It is probably safe to say that there are very few constellations of selfing and othering in which different people would not make different choices as between one grammar or another. Let it be tried, therefore, to see the grammars in some situations of grammatical contestation, that is, situations in which different grammars offer different solutions to different people, or indeed, as may happen, to the same people in different contexts. The next two sections will try this in the domains of politics, religion, and aesthetics.

The Grammars in Competition and Interaction: Examples from Politics and Religion

Political examples for the three grammars being engaged in mutual competition and rivalry can be observed in contests person against person, party against party, country against country. Each of these must construct his or her or its 'other' and has a choice then, whether to declare this 'other' into an orientalized mirror image, a segmentary ally or adversary in one or another specified context, or an other who exaggerates his difference while he is 'really and deep-down' just an encompassable part of 'us'.

Let me briefly take the example of post-World War Two Germany to show this competition of grammars. During the first two decades (ca. 1948–1969) of there being two German states, West German governments claimed a 'Right of Sole Representation' known as the Hallstein Doctrine. This represented a grammar of encompassment: although de facto there were two German states, the argument ran that 'deep down', *de iure* and morally, the citizens of communist East Germans were really West Germans deprived of their 'true' citizenship and nationality. Over the next two decades (ca. 1969–1989), the segmentary grammars long proposed by the East German state elites were slowly recognized by the West German *Ostpolitik*: Chancellor Brandt and his successors never recognized the Eastern version of segmentation ('two nations on German soil, one capitalist, one socialist'), but conceded the realities of the situation by the segmentary doctrine of: 'one German nation, two sovereign German states.'

When the two states were united in 1989, many East German citizens wished for a segmentary solution: two German states fusing what was best in each of them into a newly created apex, a Germany that was democratic as well as socialist. The actual and historical solution, however, effectively annexed the former East Germany to the powerful Western state, re-affirming the Western constitution and political culture, laws and civil society as the sole legitimate order. Ironically, this blatantly Western solution looked so unrealistic and imperialist that the capital of the unified state had to be transferred from Bonn in former West Germany to Berlin, formerly divided between West and East. Just as ironically, former West Germans and former East Germans continue to think about each other in an orientalizing grammar. Most Westerners see themselves as enterprising, self-reliant and tolerant, but also as materialistic, egotistic and anomic; they see the Easterners as lacking in initiative, as being reliant on the state and intolerant, but also as more sociable, more solidary, and less anomic. Most Easterners, needless to add in such a mutually orientalizing constellation, reciprocate with similar negative mirror-imagings: 'we', the people of social values and solidarity against 'them', the materialistic egoists; but also 'we', the somewhat inexperienced provincials, against 'them', the well-travelled cosmopolitans.

To turn to tracing the present-day political applications of the segmentary grammar, we have already cast a sideways glance at how the 'inventors' of the segmentary grammar, Evans-Pritchard's Nuer of the Southern Sudan, fared against the pseudo-federalist perversion of the segmentary grammar imposed by a genocidal Northern Sudanese government. The Nuer had little choice but to rebel against this perversion, but they and the other South-Sudanese were unable to agree on how to subdivide their new pyramid of power. The crucial point of contention, namely who defines the ultimate apex of the pyramid and who defines which intervening classificatory levels is equally clear in the politics of Europe.

In structuring the European Union, one may perhaps contrast two possible versions of the segmentary grammar. One, the presently existing one, is a 'Europe of Nation-States', and it segments power structures by the level of nation-state capitals. The other, envisaged as a 'Europe of Regions', would skip that nation-state level and segment power structures by regional metropolitan cities. By skipping the classificatory level of nation-state capitals, a 'Europe of Regions' would, on the one hand, remove problematic nation-state constellations. One may think here of the Flemish and Walloons in Belgium; the Catalans, Basques, and other nations in 'the State of Spain'; or of the Scots, Welsh and Northern Irish who would no longer access Brussels via Westminster. There is thus something to be said for this rewritten version of the segmentary grammar. On the other hand, it would of course rewrite the grammar of European identities according to potentially repressive ethnolinguistic criteria. It would no longer be up to Madrid to decide who is a

Spanish citizen, but up to Barcelona to decide who is a Catalan citizen and to Cardiff to decide who is Welsh enough to be Welsh. Nor would the rewriting need to stop at the present-day nation-state borders. By skipping the level of the nation-state, there might as well be a Basque Region of Europe, straddling the former border between ex-Spain and ex-France or a Tyrolian region across the Austro-Italian border. The example may show that segmentary systems can only work within institutionalized power structures, as opposed to the acephalous system of the Nuer, when there is consensus about the classificatory levels. This consensus would have to define not only the apex of the segmentary structure, but also any and all of the criteria that define the intervening levels of segmentation. Contesting grammars of identity/alterity, or even just contesting the application of one of these grammars, is thus far from a classificatory pastime. It implies mutually incompatible, sometimes even incommensurate modes of selfing and othering. The stakes are equally high when we trace the contest of grammars in contexts called 'religious'.

Since it is misleading to cordon off 'religious' discourses from other 'authorizing discourses' (Asad 1993), I will only use the term here as a common-sense shorthand for those selfings and otherings that are articulated 'in the name of' one or another hierarchy or conviction that calls itself 'religious'. Most commonly, such religious claims to authority or truth are argued by way of the orientalizing grammar. Many Catholics, to take an old example, value their own ritual splendour and 'otherworldly depth' above the sobriety and 'superficiality' that they ascribe to Protestants; at the same time, they admit that 'Protestant' liberal individualism has something to recommend itself when compared to 'Catholic' hierarchical thinking. This orientalizing grammar of negative mirror-imaging may be found just as easily between many Christians and Muslims, Sufi and anti-Sufi establishments in Islam or, for that matter, competing tendencies in Judaism, Hinduism, Buddhism, and whatever religious –ism one may wish to cite. Academic –isms are no exception, by the way: orientalizing the other is easy, whether the other is known or not known, defined or undefineable.

When, however, the selves and the others thus constituted through the grammar of orientalization come under shared pressures from the outside, let us say by a groundswell of secularism or agnosticism around them, then their mutual differences are often relativized by means of a segmentary grammar. These new versions of the segmentary grammar are most often implicit in processes aimed at 'ecumenical initiatives' or a 'dialogue of faiths'. Here, too, it is the choice of the apex or the intervening classificatory levels which specifies the inclusiveness or exclusiveness of selfings and otherings. If you take the highest apex available, you can sing along with Mozart's last *Masonic Cantata*, KV 618:

> You who revere the Creator of the immeasurable universe,
> [whether you] call him Jehova or God, Fu or Brahma,
> harken the words of the Universal Lord ! (Mozart 1791: 1, transl. mine)

This is a fine example of the segmentary grammar being applied to all convictions recognized as 'religious'.

Not surprisingly, most religious uses of the segmentary grammar are a little more selective in defining identity with, and alterity from, the other. Then, instead of placing a super apex at the top of the segmentary pyramid, they insert an intervening classificatory level. One can recognize a well-known example in the Muslim idea of 'The People of The Book' (*ahl al-kitab*) which postulates a close kinship between Jews, Christians and Muslims by virtue of recognizing a common source in what Jews call the Torah and Christians call the first books of 'The Old Testament'. The idea was taken up in the U.S.A. under the name 'Abrahamic religions', and there it was even used by moderate politicians after the World Trade Center massacre of September 11 to assuage populist anti-Muslim hysteria and hatred. Unfortunately, the public invocation of the segmentary grammar did not prevent the many wanton arrests of foreign or American Muslims. When orientalism reigns supreme, segmentary grammars have a hard time in arguing for equality under one apex or sub-apex.

A new version of the segmentary grammar has been propagated over the past few decades by the cross-faith initiatives that identify themselves as 'People of Faith'. These are people of different religions who share each other's symbols and rituals to worship together. Much as with Mozart, these people of their own faith regard all other people of other faiths as the same, and they even regard all non-believers as others to be converted into selves.

Here, however, the religious uses of the grammar of segmentation raise a most arresting problem in the form of grammatical ambiguity. If the 'People of Faith' were to engage in strong strategies of proselytism to convert nonbelievers, then the grammar of segmentation preached could easily turn into a grammar of encompassment practiced. The question is: are religious others recognized as segmentary partners in a concert of faiths, or are they being encompassed by an elite that calls itself 'The People of Faith'? Looking back at the segmentary grammar of classic Free Masonry professed by Mozart, we can see the same ambiguity. Listened to from outside the Masonic lodge, it sounds like an invitation to join a segmentary grammar of all religions being of equal worth. When sung within the Masonic lodge, however, it may implicitly invoke the grammar of encompassment: deep down, so it says, it does not matter then whether you are Jewish or Christian, Confucian or Hindu: the Masonic 'Architect of the Universe' is your god, too, and the super apex of Free Masonry encompasses all of you as virtual members of our lodge. This is not a new problem by any means. Anthropologists jokingly call it: 'Malinowki's Law: people say one thing and do another', or even: 'people say one thing and mean another'.

With these considerations of ambiguity, however, one can see all the more clearly that the grammars always depend upon agency. In the end, even the most inclusive religious selfings and otherings can equally plausibly switch off the grammar of segmentation and turn to the grammar of encompassment to lay stress on their own superiority without entirely delegitimizing those whom they claim to encompass. We have already mentioned the statement of Hindus in London who, when feeling threatened by Sikh religious nationalism, claim that: 'Sikhs are Hindus' (Baumann 1996: 116–22). Similar strategies of encompassment could be observed in London when a Hindu explained that: 'Jesus is but a reincarnation of Brahma' or when a Muslim cleric stated: 'More than half of England's Anglican Bishops say that Christians are not obliged to believe that Jesus Christ was God. […] It is indeed just reward for the tireless efforts and thorough positive and rational propagation of Muslim theologians […] that we see today the endorsement by prominent [Christian] clergymen as regards the real status of Jesus Christ' (Bana 1988: 2).

It is evident in all these cases that the different selves and others need by no means agree on one or another of the grammars. On the contrary, it is the asymmetries in the use of the grammars which make these grammars into argumentative tools. When one party argues that it encompasses the other, the other party will often respond by postulating a grammar of segmentation; when one party wants to exclude another from a potentially shared segmentary order, it will often fall back on the orientalizing grammar to emphasize the alterity of the other. The grammars provide a repertoire of structures through which to put forward arguments about self and other; but it is crucial to stress that all grammars are always at the disposal of all social actors, and it is precisely the constantly shifting invocations and revocations of each grammar that matter in the social processes of selfing and othering as we can observe them empirically. What happens, however, when we trace the grammars in highly formalized productions or 'finished' social processes, such as we find them in works of art or, for that matter, works of popular culture ? This question opens up the most complex field of enquiry for the social sciences: aesthetics.

The Grammars in Competition and Interaction: Examples from Aesthetics

Aesthetic productions, be they operas or soap operas, leaflets or novels, folk songs or fashion magazines, must all create two things at once: a self that the reader or viewer or listener can identify with, as well as an other that the consumer, or de-coder, of the work can comprehend as the self-defining counter-pole. So-called 'classic' opera and drama, novels and poetry appear to be classic precisely in that they lay out the poles of self and other in its classic orientalizing form. Mozart's misguided Don Giovanni needs the counter-pole of his down-to-earth servant Leporello, just as Cervantes' Don Quixote needs the counter-pole of his servant Sancho Panza. Their initial characterization stresses the orientalizing juxtaposition with headline clarity: 'Title Hero Astonishing' versus 'Servant Predictably Naive,' but the development of the dramatic story line opens the listener's or reader's eyes to the reversal of this orientalist contrast: it is Don Giovanni who ends up in hell and Leporello who lives to tell the tale of divine punishment; likewise, it is

Don Quixote who finally succumbs to his illusions and Sancho Panza who lives to proffer the final wise commentary on the vicissitudes of following one's Quixotic phantasies.

Built into these unfoldings of an orientalist structure, we often find a diverting or exciting play with segmentary orders. Its classic form is the Comedy of Errors, when one person is mistaken for another and vice versa, when the expected love match of the hero with the heroine and the man-servant with the girl-servant threatens to turn into an erroneous match between hero and girl-servant, man-servant and heroine. The fissions and fusions of the segmentary structure are played out in their most plausible as well as their most implausible form, in order finally to return to a joyful re-affirmation of the socially plausible love matches or fusions.

These structures, both the slow unfolding of an orientalizing grammar and the play with the possibilities of a segmentary grammar, are of an astonishing spread. Whether operas from Monteverdi through Verdi to Berg, novels from Cervantes through the Brontë Sisters to Thomas Mann, dramas and comedies from Calderón through Racine to Tshechow, popular or mass culture from English detective stories through Brazilian *fotonovelas* to global soap operas: the range seems infinite. It is quite possible that pornographic sequences, too, do nothing other than that: play with the slow unfolding of an orientalizing grammar, be it about male/female, black/white, strong/weak, willing or unwilling, and then provide all manner of expected or unexpected segmentary fissions and fusions. But let us turn to a chaster example from conventional literature to see the play of grammars at work. Love poetry offers itself quite immediately as an aesthetic negotiation of identity with, and alterity from, an other. Following the lead of friends (Gingrich and Fox 2002), I take the most famous exemplar, Shakespeare's Sonnet 18:

> Shall I compare thee to a summer's day ?
> Thou art more lovely and more temperate:
> Rough winds do shake the darling buds of May,
> And summer's lease hath all to short a date:
> Sometime too hot the eye of heaven shines,
> And often is his gold complexion dimmed;
> And every fair from fair sometime declines,
> By chance, or nature's changing course, untrimm'd;
> But thy eternal summer shall not fade
> Nor lose possession of that fair thou ow'st,
> Nor shall Death brag thou wander'st in his shade,
> When in eternal lines to time thou growest:
>   So long as men can breathe or eyes can see,
>   So long lives this, and this gives life to thee.

May it be tried to approach this sublimely crafted text by way of the three grammars ? The intention is not, I should add, to 'solve' the poem's mystery or to dissolve its aesthetic quality and emotional impact. Rather, the aim is to test the three grammars against the best there is in a particular aesthetic tradition, and what we shall see is that it is not only sublimely crafted, but also pretty crafty.

Asking whether the beloved can be fused, symbolically, into the segmentary order defined by the apex summer ('Shall I compare thee ?') the answer is no, and the explanation is given by a series of orientalizing oppositions: summer lacks the perfection of the beloved which appears timeless ('thy eternal summer'). This timelessness, however, does not reside in the beloved, but in the poem itself ('eternal lines') which, by encompassing the alterity of the loved one within its own timeless identity, imparts its timeless life upon the person thus encompassed. This may not be everybody's idea of love, and the lover, or rather the poet, is certainly pushing the limits of immodesty. Yet this makes it all the more puzzling why it should have fallen to Sonnet 18 of the 154 sonnets to become Number One of the world's Pop Classics in English love literature. The grammars may have something to say about the question.

Note how only the first line plays with the fusion and fission of segmentary identity/alterity, while thousands of love poems exhaust themselves and the reader in endless comparisons of the 'you are like' kind. The next ten or eleven lines proceed to excite the reader by playing at length with the game of orientalizing oppositions so familiar in Shakespeare. The symbols used may be difficult to decipher at first sight ('summer's lease', 'eye of heaven', 'fair from fair', 'fair thou ow'st'), but even a reader with a modest command of English can intuit the structure of the argument: summer thought perfect, summer found deficient, humans thought imperfect, beloved truly perfect. The grammar of orientalizing oppositions allows the reader to classify the symbols' mutual relations even if the symbols themselves have not been deciphered yet. Then comes the crafty crunch: the beloved is immortal because – his lover's poem is immortal. This sudden change to the grammar of encompassment throws an entirely new light on the poem which now asks to be read again. Two of the grammars, usually orientalizing followed by segmentation, can be easily recognized in each of the 154 sonnets. Yet perhaps the special intensity of Sonnet 18 owes something to its dramatic progression through all three grammars: from questioning segmentation through a voluptuous play with orientalizing oppositions to a shocking act of encompassment. If proof were needed that Shakespeare was not the lover, but quite simply a client of the patron 'Mr W.H., ... the begetter' of the sonnets, this artful twist of grammars might contribute to it.

In reviewing the aesthetic uses of the three grammars, it may, however, fall to music to provide the most subtle examples of the playing with grammars. Consider as a first example the relationship of Western Music with 'Other Musics' such as it was worked out in the musical aesthetics of, successively, primitivism, exoticism, and, most recently, 'World Music.' Musical primitivism views Western Music as sophisticated, 'Primitive Music' as raw. By the orientalizing reversal, however, Western Music is also seen as over-cultured and cerebral, 'Primitive Music' as refreshingly primordial and elemental. The result is an aesthetic of composition that is typically characterized by the shrill and angular quality of the 'primitive' sounds that are pitched to interrupt and contradict, to threaten and sometimes question, the harmonic and *cantabile* lines of the Western elements.

Musical exoticism, as found in the work of Ravel or Debussy or in the countless 'Spanish Rhapsodies' written by French, German and American composers, aims at leaving behind the stark orientalist dividing lines and seeks a mutual fusion between the familiar and the exotic sound worlds. It can be construed as the attempt at a segmentary grammar combining different musics. Classic results are, for instance, Bartók's or Kodaly's fusions between Western scales and exotic rhythms, often of peasant origins; alternatively, Debussy's play with exotic Chinese or Javanese scales contained within the traditional Western ideas about rhythm and form; or indeed George Gershwin's infusion of Jazz elements into his self-declared aim of creating a 'truly American music.' Similar solutions can also be heard in what has since been called 'World Music'. Here, too, the underlying idea is a segmentary grammar in which each musical tradition of the world can be fused with many or selected others, but the results often show a rather predictable division of labour: Western scales combined with African cross-rhythms, Western rhythms combined with Eastern vocal techniques, or non-Western rhythms or timbres poured into stiff Western A-B-A forms. The permutations are numerous, but the results from Dvorak's 'Bohemian Dances' to Paul Simon's South African-inspired inspired 'Gracelands' usually share the same dilemma: Western composers criticize their lack of aesthetic unity, the non-Western musicians criticize their lack of authenticity. Can the grammars help to clarify this conondrum?

Exoticist, 'Americanist' and 'World' music share the same grammatical dilemma, and that is the dilemma between a segmentary fission and fusion of still-recognizable styles and an encompassment grammar which forces exotic or 'other' elements to 'fit into' aesthetic frameworks that are alien to them. Let us be concrete at the risk of gainsaying 'other' musicians' reactions. It would be hard to think of a Bohemian peasant recognizing 'himself' in the musical borrowings of Dvořak and impossible to find a Jazz musician who would not accuse Gershwin of 'stealing and using *our* music'; it will take an overdose of cultural hegemony to find a South African or an Indian musician who applauds the way in which *we* are represented in *'their* World Music'. At the same time – and here comes the beauty of the three grammars approach, – you will find no Russian folk musicians protesting about Stravinsky stealing their aesthetic integrity and no Hungarian folk musicians chiding Bartók for his working with, rather than using, folk music aesthetics. The transformation from using the others, that is, encompassing them, towards working with them, that is, redefining oneself in a new segmentary order, seems crucial here. On the one hand, we find a selfing and othering that claims the grammar of segmentation, but then subsumes its exoticized 'other' by means of a hierarchical or hegemonic encompassment. On the other hand, we find a new form of selfing, the creation of a new aesthetic apex ('real Bartók', 'real Stravinsky'), which achieves its integrity by redefining self and other in an ever-changing oscillation between fission and fusion.

If this test of the grammars argument seemed to work so well in the realms of politics, religion and even aesthetics, then the argument itself is in trouble: an argument that works all the time is no argument at all. Let me try, therefore, to reverse the tables by submitting the grammars to two more stringent challenges.

The first of these challenges is well-known to anyone who has read their structuralism: structures look binary on the surface, but at root, they are ternary. This is a serious challenge (Benveniste 1971 [1966]; Douglas 1966; Lévi-Strauss 1968; Turner 1969; Leach 1976; Mróz 1984) for our grammars seem to look stubbornly binary at first sight. The second of the challenges is well-known to anyone who has read the principles of theoretical and methodological self-critique (Popper 1972 [1935]; Kuhn 1962; Luhrmann 1989): if you cannot specify the conditions or the contexts that render your theory inapplicable, then your whole theory is useless. In other words, so this challenge demands, we must pre-specify the conditions under which the grammars will cease to work. In facing the ternary challenge, I shall argue that all three grammars are indeed ternary, but each in its own way. In proceeding to the challenge of self-falsification, I will address the question of exceptional violence, that is, violence that does not maintain a system of inequality between selves and others, but destroys that system itself and thus destroys both the others and the former selves as they used to define themselves.

The Ternary Challenge Posed: Benveniste, Lévi-Strauss, Mróz

The three grammars look, at first sight, like being binary grammars that create a Self and an Other as mutually exclusive poles: 'what is mine cannot be yours, and what is yours cannot be mine.' This observation, if correct, opens up an old 'can of worms': the oldest challenge to structuralist modes of thinking. Structuralism, so this old challenge said, is a manner of viewing the world in white-and-black: 'Draw a line down the middle of the page, and you can play Lévi-Strauss,' as one of my undergraduate teachers confided in me at the height of Lévi-Straussian structuralism. But even Lévi-Straussian structuralism was aware, at the time, that binary divisions of the world had little chance of capturing the richness and sophistication of 'other' people's taxonomies. Three examples may summarize this ternary challenge here.

Arguably, construing the world in terms of binary structures is the oldest classificatory toolkit of men and women, juniors and seniors, and maybe even early hominids from this side as opposed to that side of the river. At the same time, a division-in-two will intrinsically raise the awkward question of what may be in the middle. Binarisms inevitably raise the possibility of tripartition, and anthropologists have a long tradition of recognizing this. One may think of van Gennep's (1909) classic, the discovery that all rites of passage insert right into the cleavage between 'before' and 'after' a transitional phase, a threshold or liminal phase. Later anthropologists, best-known among them Mary Douglas (1966), Victor Turner (1969) and the great Edmund Leach (1976), have elaborated a veritable school of recognizing tripartitions behind, or rather between, seemingly binary structures.

Between the uninitiated and the initiated, life-cycle rites of passage insert the neophyte; or between life and death they insert the liminal presence of the no-longer-animate but also not-yet-dead, already ancestor but not yet pure spirit. Seasonal rites of passage similarly elaborate the liminal period between springtime and Lent with an anti-structure of Carnival, or the dry season and the rainy season with a, usually three-day, Rain (-Making) Festival. Even the shortest-term rites of passage insert a liminal period between the 'before' and the 'after', witness the now near-ubiquitous modernist custom of inserting an official 'Minute of Silence' between a collective confrontation with death (be it a Head of State's or a World Trade Center massacre) and the need to resume daily and workaday routines. The matter gets even more interesting, however, when the third part is not a liminal in-between, whose definition relies on the two seemingly self-defining stages before and after, but assumes an equal definitional status.

This definitional autonomy of the third part is difficult to achieve in temporal sequences, since we tend to structure our temporal orders in terms of 'before' and 'after', with the 'in-between' but a fleeting moment, be it a year of mourning, a forty-day observance, a three-day dispensation, or even a minute's silence or, in Leach's words, 'timelessness' (1976: 34–5. The grammar of tripartition is even more visible and more autonomous when we order the social world not by time, but by interactive relations. Two of these orders are of special interest here. One is the ordering of interaction by linguistic structures, the other is the ordering of interaction by marital structures. Surprising as this may sound, the evidence is simple enough in both cases. For the first, linguistic structures, it is most instructive to turn to the structuralist linguistics of Emile Benveniste (1971 [1966]) and apply them with the help of the sociologist Lech Mróz (1984). For the second case, it is most interesting to turn to the structuralist anthropology of Claude Lévi-Strauss and apply it with a view to discovering the tripartite implications of each of the three binary grammars gleaned so far.

Emile Benveniste (1971 [1966]) pursued the understanding of language, not as a signal system operated between a sender and a receiver, but as a practice of discourse that always involves or at least implicates a third party. Saying 'I love you' seems the obvious example of a two-party statement. Yet it would be utterly meaningless as a dialogical signal if there were not a third party who is excluded as the un-loved by the speaker of the message. Similarly, the well-worn phrase 'Can we talk ?' entails an exclusion of a third party, and so it implicates that there is a third party that is part of the seemingly dialogical signal system. Every use of the pronouns 'I' and 'you' thus implicates a third party, a 'he' or 'she' or 'it', and every use of the pronouns 'we' and 'you' makes silent use of a 'they' or 'them' who are present, but not addressed in the dialogue. Benveniste's theory of pronouns is thus, in effect, a postulate that all binary grammars are, at root, ternary grammars.

To take this insight outside linguistics and apply it to the domain of lived social relations, the sociologist Lech Mróz (1984) chose the ethnographic example of Gypsies in Poland. Mróz was dissatisfied with the age-old binarism of: 'we are Poles, they are Gypsies', and so he determined to look at this binarism from the Gypsies' side. What came out was a call-to-arms for all ternarists as opposed to all binarists. To sum up the argument, Mróz took the Gypsies' point of view and designed their ethnic world with the help of three concentric circles. The inner circle describes ourselves or our own: the *cacó Roma*, that is, 'the Real Roma' of the subgroups known as Lovara, Kalderasha, and Polska Roma: all of these are nomadic, as it befits a 'real Roma'. The middle circle describes 'other' Roma: among them are the Roma settled in the villages of the Carpathian Mountains and even in the industrial city of Nowa Huta. The outer circle, the non-dialogical third party in Beneviste's terms, are the strangers, the people one cannot dialogue with, and whom one certainly should not intermarry with: that is, the non-Gypsy Poles and all other *gadjos*, that is, non-Gypsies. It may be worth noting here that the settled Roma may not represent an independent category by themselves, but rather a category of creolization between 'real' nomadic Roma and non-Roma sedentary Poles. Yet Mróz's point is clear: to understand the selfings and otherings of Gypsies in Poland, so he argues, one needs a ternary grammar, precisely as postulated by Benveniste, and not a binary grammar. Yet is there such a stark choice between one or more binary grammars and one single, all-encompassing ternary grammar?

The answer proposed by Lévi-Strauss would seem to be different and rather more dialectical. It would absolve us from the binary choice between 'either binary or ternary' and open up the way toward an integrated solution. As it happens, both Mróz and Lévi-Strauss see the limits of marriageability as the crucial borderposts that cordon off Benveniste's three categories of an 'us', a 'you', and a 'them'. So let me briefly survey Lévi-Strauss' argument as against that of Benveniste and Mróz.

Even though Lévi-Strauss is often portrayed as the binarist *par excellence*, he devoted one of his most ingenious structuralist analyses to the ternary implications of binary structures. The question he asked was almost provocative: 'Dual Organizations: Do they Exist?' The argument requires a great deal of technical detail about marital exchange systems which may seem arcane at first sight,[2] and few of us will take exception to them remaining so; but the upshot in the present context could not be more compelling: Dual organizations, so Lévi-Strauss' elegant answer to the question of his title, can only exist by virtue of their ternary implications. This is a good starting point in order to resolve the problem of binary versus ternary grammars. Each binary grammar, so I propose alongside all the authors just reviewed, is a ternary grammar, be it intrinsically, implicitly, or deeper down than their proponents will admit. At the same time, however, each of the three binary grammars here proposed has its own way of going ternary.

The Ternary Challenge Answered: All Three Grammars are Ternary, but Each in its Own Way

Answering the challenge for the segmentay grammar, we can be brief here. All the examples we have seen, from the Nuer original through the European, the German and the Spanish examples of federal orders to the segmentary grammars in religious and aesthetic fields, all the data showed how shifting the apical point up or down creates a different delineation of the Third Party, that is, a party that forms no part of the segmentary ordering of self and other, a party of 'them' who, as Mróz has expressed it following Benveniste, is not part of the dialogue between the 'us' and the 'you'. They are not partners within the segmentary grammar of selfing and othering, but precisely those who fall outside, or are kicked outside, the limits of applicability of that grammar.

With the grammar of encompassment, likewise, the ternary implication is evident. To say that 'Sikhs are Hindus' implies that Muslims are not, and are excluded as partners in this dialogue or, as the case may be, monologue. The encompassing notion of caste hierarchy does not apply to the third party, the casteless, just as the encompassing notion of 'Black' as a political colour excludes whites. Encompassment is always selective, and it thus by necessity excludes a category of 'them' who are neither 'us' nor 'you' and who cannot participate in the dialogue of who is who. The only case of doubt about the ternary implications appears to lie with the orientalist grammar, for its operation of negative mirror-imaging seems to be restrictively binary. This doubt, however, is easily resolved by consulting the proven master of applied structuralism, Roland Barthes (1973 [1957]) when he analysed the semiology of what he called 'myths'.

Roland Barthes analysed the 'way of speaking', – today we would call it discourse – of 'myth', a discourse that uses seemingly taken-for-granted commonplaces to insinuate and propagate ideological messages. Barthes gives the most lucid example by analysing the 'signification' of the cover illustration of a copy of *Paris-Match*. On this cover, he writes, 'a young Negro in a French uniform is saluting, with his eyes uplifted, probably fixed on a fold of the *tricolore*. All this is the *meaning* of the picture' (Barthes 1973: 116). To put this picture on the cover of a popular and patriotic weekly, however, establishes a second level of meaning, which Barthes calls 'signification' and which he here decodes as the mythical message: 'that France is a great Empire, that all her sons, without any colour discrimination, faithfully serve under her flag, and that there is no better answer to the detractors of an alleged colonialism than the zeal shown by this Negro in serving his so-called oppressors' (Barthes 1973: 116).

According to Barthes, this step from the self-evident sign to the ideological signification can be theorized as a 'staggered' semiological system: 'It can be seen that in myth there are two semiological systems, one of which is staggered in relation to the other: a linguistic system, the language (or the modes of representation which are assimilated to it), which I shall call the *language-object*, because it is the language which myth gets hold of in order to build its own system; and myth itself, which I shall call *metalanguage*, because it is a second language, *in which* one speaks about the first' (Barthes 1973: 115).

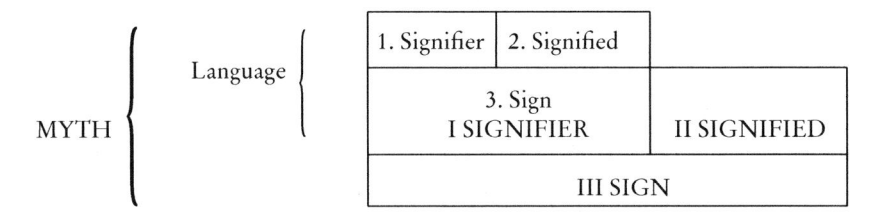

	1. Signifier	2. Signified
Language	3. Sign I SIGNIFIER	II SIGNIFIED
MYTH	III SIGN	

Figure 2.6 Myth as a 'Staggered' Semiological System, after Barthes (1973: 115)

Let us now look for the technique of 'staggering à la Barthes' in the orientalizing grammar, the one that seemed restricted to being a simple binary structure, and let us again start with a commonplace example. Most Dutch people, like so many natives of all European states, define the alterity of their 'immigrant' populations by a very predictable orientalizing grammar: 'we function much better than they do; although they [still] have some good old-fashioned values (like strong family structures, lavish feasts and generous hospitality) which we ourselves have lost.' The more, however, that longer-settled immigrant groups are joined by more recent arrivals, the collective 'they' applied to 'the immigrants' in their entirety gives way to a staggered structure of the orientalizing grammar which may be indicated in the following diagram.

Self +	Old-Others -	
Self -	Old-Others +	New-Others -
	(Old-Others -)	(New-Others +)

Figure 2.7 Ternary Staggering of the Orientalizing Grammar

Typically, the negative characteristics ascribed to the longer-settled immigrants are relativized by an idea that, ultimately, it will be possible to assimilate or integrate them, whereas the negative characteristics of the newly-arrived immigrants are emphasized all the more sharply as they are contrasted to the longer-settled ones. Sometimes, the combination: 'Old-Others - / New-Others +' is underemphasized by the native-national Selves, which is why I have placed it in brackets. In all cases, however, the ternary staggering of the orientalizing grammar allows the natives, ideologically to play out one group of immigrants against another. In the Dutch case, the line of distinction concerns long-settled versus recently arrived migrants; in other cases the line of distinction concerns immigrants from the former colonies versus immigrants without historic bonds to the new country of residence; in yet other cases, the line of distinction concerns religion and then places 'assimilable Christian' immigrants versus 'unassimmilable Muslim' immigrants.

This staggered version of the orientalizing grammar indeed establishes what Barthes (1973: 114) calls 'a three-dimensional pattern' in that it distinguishes three categories: an unquestionable 'us', in this case the nationalist natives who do the talking, a category of 'the tolerable immigrants' with whom they are prepared to talk, and a category of 'the bad immigrants,' who are excluded as mere problem objects. To translate this into the terms used by Benveniste and Mróz, this staggered racism creates a 'we' who speak, a 'you' who are potential partners in dialogue, and a 'they' who are excluded from any dialogue.

One can hear, behind these staggered versions of orientalization, an echo of the tragicomic folk versions of folk evolutionism that turned 'normal' people into 'selective' racists. The well-known cases of people making individual exceptions from collective prejudices fit just as easily into the ternary staggered structures of the orientalizing grammar. 'I don't like Jews, but my neighbour Abraham is OK', was their motto. 'We are advanced', so they claimed, 'they are our obstacle, but you, the exceptions, are on the way to becoming "us"'. One may conclude, thus, that all three grammars of selfing/othering represent ternary structures, but each of the grammars achieves its ternary potential in its own way.

For analytic purposes, this is an encouraging conclusion, for if we want to distinguish different grammars within the ubiquitous common-place of 'every selfing is an othering', then each of the grammars should give its own answer to the ternary challenge. It appears that each of them does, and that even in complicated situations, the simplest grammar will lend itself to multiple and staggered uses.

The proposition of the three grammars seems to have braved the first two moves. First, it could be recognized in the realms of politics, religion, and even aesthetics. Then, it could face up to the classic challenge of binary versus ternary classifications. The final move, however, has to face the crucial challenge of self-falsification: if the grammars seem to work in so many contexts with such a degree of complexity, then what are the limits, and when do they cease to work ?

The n+1 Challenge Posed: Hume, Popper, and the Need for a Cognitive Answer

No matter how many thousand cases we adduce to 'prove' our theory, the sceptical reader will always ask for one more case to be convinced. This problem is known as 'Hume's problem' after the Scottish Enlightenment philosopher David Hume (1711–1776), whose 'Enquiry concerning human understanding' (1957 [1774]) asked a question that would dog the philosophy of science for two-hundred years: no matter how many times (n) you inductively confirm your hypothesis, how can you be sure that there is not one further case (n+1) which disproves your hypothesis ? A hypothesis, in other words, cannot be scientifically proven by piling one inductive corroboration upon the next, for the sceptic will always ask for the next case, the 'n+1' case that will falsify the hypothesis. How, then, can we evidence anything at all in a rational manner ?

Hume's problem was answered most famously and simply by the philosopher of science Karl Popper, for the answer was the reversal of the question. It is not its endless corroboration that makes a theory scientific, but its falsifiability on pre-specified criteria. The scientist, so Popper points out, differs from the prophet or the ideologue in that she pre-specifies the circumstances under which the hypothesis proposed will be admitted to be false. Admittedly, there are a large number of cogent critiques that have shown Popper's simple reversal to be itself normative and ideological. Firstly, his own applications of the theory (Popper 1945) were marred by an ideological bias against Marxism, psychoanalysis, most schools of psychology, and all social sciences. Secondly, the natural sciences, too, were shown by Thomas Kuhn (1972) and later sociologists of science not to follow Popper's injunctions: instead of revoking their hypotheses as soon as they encountered falsifying instances, they reformulated and requalified the conditions under which their hypotheses would work, as opposed to abandoning them altogether. Popper's evidence had been taken from a few great 'scientific revolutions' as opposed to 'normal science' as it is practised within ruling 'paradigms'. Thirdly, the anthropologist Tanya Luhrmann (1989) showed how seemingly 'irrational' people, in this case English middle-class women who in their spare-time practised 'witchcraft', were able to forge rational and even predictable lives out of combining mutually contradictory and mutually exclusive paradigms. The question of rationality, by the way, was tackled first by the same Evans-Pritchard to whom we owe the segmentary grammar (1940), though this time in his earlier work (1937).

There is, thus, much to be said against Popper's philosophically rigorous, but in too many ways overly normative test of scientific credibility. Nonetheless, if Popper's test is the most rigorous, then let us apply it to our own hypothesis: the idea that we can resolve the impossible moral aporia (that every selfing is an othering, and every othering is equally bad) by distinguishing three very different grammars of selfing-and-othering. In facing Popper's challenge, we cannot withdraw to invoking 'exceptional and extraneous circumstances'. We cannot say that the three grammars 'work all the time except when….' there is a Hitler or a Stalin or Pol Pot in power. For Popper, these incidental and contingent exceptions would not do, for we have to pre-specify our criteria of falsification within the very same theory that we propose. Since our theory of the three grammars is, in the last analysis, a cognitive theory, we must face the challenge of giving a cognitive answer to the n+1 question, that is, the question of pre-specifying ourselves the criteria of our own falsifiability. The answer to Popper's challenge must thus be cognitive and structural, and where better to look for such an answer than in the practice of language?

The n+1 Challenge Answered: When Language Fails, Grammars Implode and Violence Explodes

If the three grammars are truly useful in distinguishing the different starting-points and consequences of selfings-and-otherings, then we must look for cases in which our three grammars hypothesis can pre-specify its own criteria of falsification and defeat. Everyone knows such examples, and they are easy to find under key words such as genocide, ethnocide, political, racial or religious extermination or annihilation. Each of these spells a breakdown of all three grammars and a return to the anti-grammar of: 'we are good, so they are bad' with the genocidal conclusion: 'we must live, so they must die'. All three of the grammars, so it must be admitted, depend upon a certain measure of violence for the privileged people to continue defining the 'people below' them as 'others'. The only truly pacifist grammar that we have is the transcendent grammar of love, where the self *is* the other and the other *is* the self, but this exceptional grammar transcends the remit of any empirical social science and usually even of aesthetics.

All three grammars are thus kept in place, reasserted and reproduced by the infusion of a certain, though sometimes minimal, amount of violence. Genocides, ethnocides and similar processes, however, are qualitatively different. They not only dominate the other, but they destroy him and in the course destroy the previous self, too. This difference between system-immanent violence and system-destructive genocide has deeply philosophical reasons as well as offensively banal practical reasons. Among the deeply philosophical reasons, we may think back to the start of the argument: if every selfing implies an othering, then the annihilation of the other implies an annihilation of the self. Among the offensive practical reasons, we need only think of the universal failure of every project of annihilating the other. Whether Hitler's or Pol Pot's survivors, Native Americans or Tutsi Rwandans, it is impossible, among Homo Sapiens, to annihilate the other completely. Either people will physically survive as others, or else their memory will be made to survive within one's own cultural tradition: after all, it was 'we' who did 'this' to 'them'.

Both the philosophy and the practicalities of annihilating the other are thus impossible on their own terms. The problem, however, remains: we need a cognitive, as opposed to a historically contingent, answer to Popper's challenge. We cannot say that 'grammars rule OK until genocidal violence will suddenly explode', but instead we must look for cases in which the three well-rehearsed grammars of selfing-and-othering are made to implode. It is the uses of language that are most important here, and we should look for these not at the level of *langue*, but at the level of *parole*.

The most famous and infamous example of all grammars of selfing-and-othering imploding into an anti-grammar of 'we are good, so the others must die' is, of course, the Nazi Holocaust. Hundreds of social scientists and historians have filled whole libraries to explain it, but for present purposes we can limit ourselves to two or three key points in their important debates. The first was Adorno's and Horkheimer's sociological classic (1949) arguing 'The Dialectics of Enlightenment.' The Enlightenment and its intrinsic stress on rationality and efficiency, so their position goes, bore within itself the dialectic seeds of its own destruction. This is a great and elegant theory, but it fails to explain why genocides were practised long before anyone had even heard of 'The Enlightenment'. It also fails to explain why some policy-sponsored genocides found popular support (let us say in sixteenth-century Latin America, the subsequent centuries of slave-trade, nineteenth-century colonization, and twentieth-century Jews), just when other campaigns of state-sponsored genocide did not meet popular support. A better approach, in my view, is that of the late Eric Wolf (1999). His book, too, deals with the Nazi regime and its ideology, but it does so in an astonishing comparative perspective. Wolf (1999) compares the Nazi terror with the Aztec cult of human sacrifices and the Kwakiutl ideology of ruining yourself to impress your neighbours and rivals. This is an interesting constellation: it implicitly compares the annihilation of the other with the annihilation of the self!

One emphasis chosen by Wolf's account is especially fertile for the present argument: his detailed attention to language use. Even Eric Wolf, however, shares the principal limitation of all the comparable sources (Sternberger et al. 1989 [1957], Forgacs 1994). He focuses on the language use of the perpetrators of the genocide themselves, notably the Nazi leaders and their speeches, books and press, rather than on the language use among the originally innocent people whom they succeeded in turning into accomplices. There is no need, for our argument here, to prove that the Nazi bosses wilfully misused and abused the German language: we know that the Nazi bosses never had any intention of othering Jews, Slavs or homosexuals in grammatically recognizable terms. Instead, what we need to show here is how patterns of language use may have contributed to otherwise 'normal' people acquiescing in, or collaborating with, a project of mass annihilation. This poses a different question, namely: how were millions of people who had previously used grammatical models of defining identities and alterities between 'Germans' and 'Jews' now suddenly seduced into abandoning these grammatical otherings? The best source to trace this process are thus not Hitler's *Mein Kampf* or even the rantings and ravings of Dr. Goebbels, his chief propagandist. Rather, we would need a careful empirical record of how 'normal' Germans lost their ability of othering 'their' Jewish others grammatically by means of changing their language use.

Astonishingly, such a record exists. It was written as a diary by Victor Klemperer from the early months of 1933 and was first published in 1957 (Klemperer 1999 [1957]). Klemperer, a German philologist of Jewish ancestry, worked as the Professor of Latin Languages at Dresden University until his forced emeritation by the Nazis. The astounding thing about Klemperer's evidence is his immediate grasp of how a perverted language use will seduce even the initially innocent into complicity with genocidal policies and a politics of language that de-humanizes the other – until there is no grammar left in which the other can be construed as a legitimate other. Well before the genocidal violence started, Klemperer's diary recorded 'the very first word that forced itself upon me as specifically Nazi, not because of its morphology, but because of its new usage'. This usage, first heard from a student whom Klemperer had, in effect, adopted into his household, concerned the word: 'punitive expedition'. For once, Klemperer's prose is tight:

> It was shortly after Hitler's accession to power. [...] 'How are things at the firm?', I asked [my adoptive son]. 'Very good !' he answered, 'yesterday we had a really great day. In the Okrilla [club] there were a few insolent communists, so we carried out a punitive expedition.' – 'You did what ?' – 'Well, making them run the gauntlet under [the blows of] rubber batons and [we used] a little castor oil [a popular laxative]: nothing bloody, but quite effective at least. Well: a punitive expedition as I say.'[...] 'Everything', so Klemperer comments, 'that I could ever imagine in terms of a brutal arrogance and a despising attitude against an alien kind of human being was crystallized in this word 'punitive expedition': it sounded so colonial that one could see an African village surrounded by enemies and could hear the lashes of hippopotamus whips. (Klemperer 1999 [1957]: 60-61, transl. mine)

In noting how the colonialist and racist term 'punitive expedition' was now applied to fellow-citizens of the same state, Klemperer could see precisely what was happening even to his adopted son through adopting Nazi language into one's own *parole*. By means of calling a political brawl a 'punitive expedition', political enemies are reduced to 'savages', that is, people who must be subjugated as objects, no longer seen as subjects, and indeed, by means of the castor oil, are reduced to self-soiling savages.[3] Note, in this case, that this first observed Nazi-inspired misuse of language is not directed against 'aliens' or even Jewish Germans, but against fellow German nationals who happened to be communists.

This application of colonialist language to one's own fellow nationals was also marked in the term 'concentration camp'. Klemperer recalled how he had 'only heard the word as a boy, and then it had an entirely exotic-colonial and entirely un-German sound to my mind. [After the] Boer War [of the 1890s] the word had disappeared entirely from German usage'(1999 [1957]: 51–2, transl. mine). What is at stake in both cases, it seems, is the exclusion of political enemies from the fold of the nation: they are turned from citizens, endowed with at least minimal rights, into conquered savages.

The same exclusion from the nation is visible as early as April 1933 and, remarkably, among educated people who tried to defend their Jewish colleagues. 'Pathetic, that Conference of Physicians at Wiesbaden!', notes Klemperer's diary entry of 20 April 1933, as the doctors insisted that 'the racial question had not been fully thought out yet [and] "the aliens" such as Wassermann, Ehrlich and Neisser had attained great achievements' (1999 [1957]: 45, transl. mine). If even the well-meaning defenders of Jewish colleagues classify these professional exemplars as 'aliens', then the Nazi patterns of language use have managed, long before the genocide started, to exclude a whole population from the body of the nation and thus from the status of people with civil rights. A similar exclusion from any grammar of difference within the same population had already been evidenced by the neologisms that Klemperer noted in his diary entry of 27 March 1933:

> New words emerge or old words acquire new special meanings, or new combinations are formed which soon coagulate [*erstarren*] into stereotypes. [...] The Jews of foreign countries, especially the French, English, and American ones, are now time and again called 'the World Jews.' Just as frequently one uses the term 'international Jewry', presumably the model of which 'World Jews' and 'World Jewry' are the German translation. This is an ominous translation: [so] right across the world, Jews are only found outside of Germany? In that case, where are they found within Germany ? (1999 [1957]: 43–44, transl. mine)

The subtlety with which Victor Klemperer was able to analyse the implications of Nazi language use, long before the genocide had even started, is remarkable even today. The implosion of all legitimate grammars of othering, for which the Holocaust remains the most potent example, must have had something important to do with the brutalization of the language (*langue*) and especially of its daily usages (*parole*). One might adduce other examples. When the former Yugoslavia exploded into a civil war fought by Serbs, Croats and Bosniacs in Bosnia, such an implosion of language had already taken place. One example may suffice. When Serbian media reported the destruction of Croat or Bosniac houses, they reported the destruction of 'houses'; when they reported the destruction, by Croat or Bosniac fighters, of Serbian houses, they spoke, not of houses, but of 'hallowed hearths' (*vekovna ognjista*, lit. 'centuries-old hearths') which would be avenged by 'Our God' (*nas Bog*) of 'the Heavenly Serbia' (*nebeska srbija*). One can see how the language itself is being made ready for a genocidal war.

These connections between language and exceptional violence by means of the grammars may have something to say about the problem of violence. I call violence a problem, for although there is a current trend in the social sciences that violence represents nothing more than the continuation of social negotiation by other means, I am sceptical of the point. For one, it has a bad ancestry: it was the fanatic warmonger von Clausewitz (1780–1831) who invented this line in order retrospectively to justify a nationalist 'war of liberation' for, *nota bene*, the monster state of Prussia. Needless to add, he deserted when violence suddenly threatened his life, rather than the lives of his soldiers. More importantly perhaps, the benefit of the view of violence as communication is paid for by a serious cost. True, it may help us move beyond a point where violence is defined only by what it is not. At the same time, however, it diminishes our chances to deal with exceptional and extreme forms of violence such as genocides and ethnocides. These cannot, I submit, be regarded as 'normal' pursuits of 'normal' societies unless one endorses the absurdity of either a value-free social science or a cultural relativism devoid of any reflexive potential. To say it somewhat polemically, I have yet to see an academic not frightened of violence and a book that declares exceptional violence into a normality, but does not market its topic as a moral problem. The line that all violence is quite simply a special sort of communication is thus neither as original as it looks, nor is it reflexive. Andre Gingrich and I will return to the point in the final chapter of this book.

Importantly, however, a certain amount of coercion and violence is involved in probably all processes of othering the other in the terms of the three grammars. Orientalism, after all, suppresses its orientalized; segmentary and federalist systems depend on unequal distributions of power; and encompassment, too, is a strategy to dominate, rather than emancipate the other. It is evident, however, that there is a world of difference between suppressing the other to maintain a system of inequality and annihilating the other to create a system based on so-called 'pure' sameness. In situations like these, the other is no longer construed grammatically, be it as orientalized counterpart, as segmentary partner or as an encompassed part of a hegemonically defined whole. Instead, the other is construed in the anti-grammar of genocide: 'For us to survive as ourselves, the others must die.' How, then, are grammatical otherings/selfings sidelined to give way to ungrammatical otherings/selfings?

By the word 'ungrammatical' I do not, of course, mean to adjudicate somebody's language command: Hitler, Stalin and the Rwandan *Radio Mille Collines* all followed the grammatical conventions of their languages. What they did not follow were the conventions of othering the other by one or another of the three grammars and thus to define identities and alterities as mutually constitutive and at least residually dialogical. Just as linguists' grammars make the difference between sentences meaningful to others and sentences unintelligible to others, so the grammars of identity/alterity spell the difference between otherings that are meaningful to the others and the ungrammatical otherings that are unintelligible to the othered. To stretch the metaphor, the anti-grammar of genocide is not only unintelligible to its victims, but self-destructive for its advocates. Where exactly we place the distinction between violence and genocide, is not a problem for statisticians in that case, though it is often treated as such in the media and in daily commonsense. But how many dead bodies does a genocide require in what situation; who should count the dead bodies when, and should the statisticians perhaps work out proportional victim quotas within a region, a country, or across the globe ? Clearly, one would prefer a qualitative answer that is contextually sensitive and takes account of the gradations of agency observable in all empirical cases. Perhaps, distinguishing different grammars, plus their collective distinction from the, ultimately self-destructive, anti-grammar of genocide, might help here.

Summary and Outlook: Are there Better and Worse Grammars ?

The aim of the argument was to differentiate the notion of 'othering' used as a blanket term for defining alterity and excluding difference. This differentiation was possible by distinguishing different processes of selfing/othering according to three grammars. These were based on, or rather freely adapted from: orientalism (Said 1987), segmentation (Evans-Pritchard 1940) and encompassment (Dumont 1980). Orientalizing creates self and other as negative mirror images of each other; segmentation defines self and other according to a sliding scale of inclusions/exclusions; encompassment defines the other by an act of hierarchical subsumption.

These grammars could be recognized, usually in mutual interaction and as rival logics, in the most varied processes of othering and selfing in the realms of politics, religion, and aesthetics. A first challenge to the grammars problematized their seemingly binary character in the face of ternary classifications. In response to the challenge, it appeared that each of the grammars was implicitly ternary, but, – as one would hope, – each in its own way. Segmentation goes ternary by injecting or ejecting levels of classification. Encompassment is implicitly ternary as every hierarchical adoption also defines a category of unadoptables. Orientalizing goes ternary by a technique first exposed by Roland Barthes' (1973 [1957]) idea of 'staggering'.

A second challenge lay in the vast variety of ethnographic examples that could be construed in the terms of the three grammars. To tackle Hume's problem, the n+1 problem of endless corroboration, one could follow Karl Popper and ask: what has to happen for the three grammars not to work ? In situations of genocide, the Other is turned from being a necessary, if undervalued, partner in the processes of collective selfing into an obstacle to selfing that must be removed by indiscriminate violence. The denial of the right to be different turns into a denial of the right to be. Yet how does it happen that grammatical selfings/otherings are forced to give way to ungrammatical ones? One answer may lie in the cognitive role of language. The three grammars, so it may be argued, are made to implode by those fatal reductions of language which reduce the complex uses of each grammar to the blatancy of an ungrammatical binarism: 'for us to live, they must die'.

Thinking of such breakdowns of all grammatical selfings and otherings, one cannot but ask the question: are some grammars better than others ? This is a value-laden question, and some readers of previous drafts have indeed charged me with being a Western humanist for raising it. I happily plead guilty as charged, but will add that I have yet to see a single instance of value-free social science. Moralizing about othering is boring and useless, I agree, and precisely that was the starting point of this chapter. Yet when one differentiates different grammars of selfing/othering, then the moralizing, too, may perhaps be a little more differentiated.

The ethnographic and historical analyses of relatively peaceful, relatively violent, and potentially genocidal situations in the light of the three grammars may possibly combine to a useful comparative foothold. They may help to show up the ways in which different grammars articulate different ways of dealing with others in specific circumstances and constellations. While the answer to the value-laden question must of course be sought in each context, some speculations may thus be admissible here. One might hypothesize some possible comparative statements in the form of three preliminary hunches.

Orientalist selfings/otherings can work relatively peacefully, but only when the orientalizers recognize that the orientalized contribute something very different but equally necessary. One may think here of the Hungarian peasants and 'their' alien Gipsy musicians and perhaps even the pre-World War II Germans and 'their' Jewish scientists, intellectuals or rural cattle-traders, as much as of Said's intellectual orientalists from Flaubert to Gide who all desired 'the Oriental'. Orientalism can lead to ideas of complementarity, but does not usually lead to ideas of equality.

The idea of equality is most strongly enshrined in the segmentary grammar, and it can even be recognized in its impoverished form of the federal contract, not least because any foe in one situation can be classified as a friend in another. Segmentary constructions, however, are inherently unstable unless compressed by an outside enemy, real or imagined. One may think here of the Anglo-Egyptian colonial regime that motivated the Nuer all the more strongly to resist their conquest under a shared apex as united Nuer. When power concentrations or power centers usurpe the apical point of a segmentary pyramid in its empoverished federalist form, then people will, where possible, dispute, or rebel against, this apex. Alternatively, they will often insert new intervening classificatory levels into the segmentary order which allow them to claim special alliances with others.

Encompassment does not, *pace* Dumont, enshrine ideas of equality, but nonetheless it can help maintain peaceful co-existence for long stretches of time. Examples that come to mind are the Punjabi Hindu villages with 'their' Sikh craftsmen in the status of 'village serfs' or of the countless African villages with 'their' minorities of non-ethnics or ex-captives or 'new people' descended from former slaves. It stops working, however, as soon as either the encompassers want 'real power' or, probably more often, the encompassed want 'real equality'. The only apparent solution then is a segemtary reordering, for instance by establishing a multiparty, multi-ethnic or otherwise pluralist village council. – But as indicated already, these hypotheses are speculative at this stage, and we need further research to corroborate, refine, or discard them.

Notes

1. The ideas here presented first arose in the seminar series 'Multiculturalismo y genero' organized by Mary Nash and Diana Marre at the University of Barcelona, and I am grateful to my colleagues for their generous permission to let me elaborate, question again, and expand in the following, the ideas first tried out in their book (Nash and Marre 2001).
2. The argument was based on a comparative study of marriage classes in South America and Indonesia. In the South American cases, binary organizations were combined with a system of restricted marital exchange (technically speaking, a symmetrical form of endogamy), while in the Indonesian cases, binary organizations were combined with a system of generalized marital exchange (technically speaking, an asymmetrical form of exogamy). For either of these systems to work, it must define, on the one hand, the classes and, on the other hand, the mutual relations that pertain between them. The South American variety could use the binary structure to define its classes, but required a ternary structure to define their mutual

relations; the Indonesian variety could use the binary structure to define the set of relations, but required a ternary structure to define the classes in the first place (Lévi-Strauss 1968: 132–63).
3. Klemperer was aware, even at the time, that the new use of the colonial word followed a model set by the Italian Fascists (p. 60), a derivation which is confirmed by Forgacs (1994). Forgacs writes that 'the ritual aggression at once humiliated the victims and subjected them to a symbolic purgation: the drinking of castor oil was associated both with the cleansing of the body and with the administration of corrective punishment to naughty children by parental authority' (Forgacs 1994: 6). There is much to be said for Forgacs's larger analytic hypothesis, namely that 'all manifestations of [the Fascist] imaginary have a displacement in common, through a sort of inversion or negation of the violent act from a hurting to a healing one' (5). 'Ultimately, all [...] components of [the Fascist] rhetoric of 'just' violence can be seen as converging on the notion of Fascist violence as therapy, as designed to heal and make whole the imagined body of society and the state' (8–9). But in the particular case reported by Klemperer, this interpretation of a forced purgation as an act of cleansing and healing seems to me rather to miss the point.

References

Adorno, Theodor W. and Max Horkheimer. 1947. *Dialektik der Aufklärung: Philosophische Fragmente.* Frankfurt: Querido.

Appiah, K. Anthony. 1994. 'Identity, Authenticity, Survival: Multicultural Societies and Social Reproduction', in *Multiculturalism: Examining the Politics of Recognition*, ed. Amy Gutmann. Princeton: Princeton University Press, 149–64.

Asad, Talal. 1993. 'Anthropological Conceptions of Religion: Reflections on Geertz', in *Genealogies of Religion*, ed. Talal Asad. Baltimore: Johns Hopkins University Press, 27–54.

Bana, Mohamed. 1988. *Jesus – as Only a Messenger.* Durban: Islamic Propagation Centre International.

Barthes, Roland. 1973 [1957]. *Mythologies*, trans. Annette Lavers. St Albans: Paladin.

Baumann, Gerd. 1994. '"The Lamps are Many, but the Light is One"? Processes of Syncretization in a Multi-Ethnic Part of London', in *Syncretism and the Commerce of Symbols*, ed. Goran Aijmer. Gothenburg: Institute for Advanced Studies in Social Anthropology, 102–118.

———. 1996. *Contesting Culture. Discourses of Identity in Multi-Ethnic London.* Cambridge: Cambridge University Press.

Benveniste, Emile. 1971 [1966]. *Problems in General Linguistics*, trans. Mary Elizabeth Meek. Coral Gables, Fl.: University of Miami Press, Miami Linguistics Series No. 8.

Douglas, Mary. 1966. *Purity and Danger. An Analysis of Concepts of Pollution and Taboo.* London: Routledge & Kegan Paul.

Dumont, Louis. 1980. *Homo Hierarchicus: The Caste System and its Implications.* Chicago: University of Chicago Press.

Evans-Pritchard, E.E. 1937. *Witchcraft, Oracles and Magic among the Azande.* Oxford: Clkarendon Press.

———. 1940. *The Nuer.* Oxford: Clarendon Press.

Fabian, Johannes. 1983. *Time and the Other: How Anthropology Makes its Object.* New York: Columbia University Press.

Forgacs, David. 1994. 'Fascism, violence and modernity', in *The Violent Muse. Violence and the Artistic Imagination in Europe, 1910-1939*, eds. Jana Howlett and Rod Mengham. Manchester: Manchester University Press.

Galey, Jean-Claude. 1991. *Kingship and the Kings*. London: Routledge.
Gingrich, Andre and Richard G. Fox, eds. 2002. *Anthropology, by Comparison*. New York: Routledge.
Gennep, Arnold van. 1960 [1909]. *The Rites of Passage*, trans. M.B. Vizedom and G.L. Caffee. London: Routledge & Kegan Paul.
Heidegger, Martin. 1957. *Identität und Differenz*. Pfullingen: Neske.
Hume, David. 1957 [1774]. *An Inquiry concerning Human Understanding*. New York: The Library of Liberal Arts
Klemperer, Victor. 1999 [1957]. *LTI: Notizbuch eines Philologen*. Leipzig: Reclam.
Kuhn, Thomas. 1962. *The Structure of Scientific Revolutions*. Chicago: University of Chicago Press.
Kuper, Adam. 1988. *The Invention of Primitive Society. Transformations of an Illusion*. London: Routledge.
Leach, Edmund. 1976. *Culture and Communication. The Logic by Which Symbols are Connected*. Cambridge: Cambridge University Press.
Lévi-Strauss, Claude. 1968. 'Do Dual Organizations Exist ?', in *Structural Anthropology*, trans. Claire Jacobson and Brooke G. Schoepf. Harmondsworth: Penguin, 132–63.
Luhrmann, Tanya. 1989. *Persuasions of the Witch's Craft: Ritual Magic in Contemporary England*. Cambridge, Mass: Harvard University Press.
Mozart, Wolfgang Amadeus. 1791. '*Die Ihr des unermesslichen Welltalls Schöpfer ehrt.*' Cantata for solo voice and piano, KV 619.
Mróz, Lech. 1984. 'People and Non-People. The Way of Distinguishing One's Own Group by Gypsies in Poland', *Ethnologia Polona* 10: 109–28.
Nash, Mary and Diana Marre, eds. 2001. *Multiculturalismos y genero*. Barcelona: Edicions Bellaterra.
Popper, Karl. 1945. *The Open Society and its Enemies*. London: Routledge & Kegan Paul.
———. [1935]. *Conjectures and Refutations*. London: Routledge & Kegan Paul.
Quigley, Declan. 1993. *The Interpretation of Caste*. Oxford: Clarendon Press.
Said, Edward. 1978. *Orientalism*. New York: Vintage Press.
Sternberger, Dolf, G. Storz und W.E. Suesskind. 1989 [1957]. *Aus dem Wörterbuch des Unmenschen*. Frankfurt: Ullstein.
Taylor, Charles. 1994. 'The Politics of Recognition', in *Multiculturalism. Examining the Politics of Recognition*, ed. Amy Gutmann. Princeton: Princeton University Press: 25–74.
Turner, Victor. 1969. *The Ritual Process. Structure and Anti-Structure*. London: Routledge & Kegan Paul.
Veer, Peter van der. 1994. *Religious Nationalism. Hindus and Muslims in India*. Berkeley: University of California Press.
Wolf, Eric.1999. *Envisioning Power. Ideologies of Dominance and Crisis*. Berkeley: University of California Press.

Step II

From a Repertoire of Grammars to Hierarchies and Power

Chapter 3   Othering the Scapegoat in Nepal: The Ritual
            of *Ghantakarna*
            Michael Mühlich

Chapter 4   German Grammars of Identity/Alterity:
            A Diachronic View
            Anne Friederike Müller

Chapter 5   Alterity as Celebration, Alterity as Threat:
            A Comparison of Grammars between
            Brazil and Denmark
            Inger Sjørslev

Chapter 3
Othering the Scapegoat in Nepal
The Ritual of *Ghantakarna*

Michael Mühlich

This chapter will examine the role of scapegoats and the process of scapegoating in society. This role and process may be discerned in terms of the three grammars proposed in this volume, that is, orientalization, encompassment and the revitalization of segmentary social groups and interests. While these terms have their own history in anthropology, my usage will be interpretational, rather than strict in is application.[1] I will primarily focus on a ritual in Nepal, namely the *Ghantakarna* ritual held at the peak of the monsoon season by Newars of the Kathmandu Valley. The term scapegoat needs, however, to be defined more exactly if we are to succeed in gaining a global view on a subject which may and should give rise to opposing views, touching as it does on hierarchy and its encompassment in one type of society and on marginalisation in others.

Scapegoats and Scapegoating: How Orientalization May Produce Social Cohesion

Ambiguity may be the main reason for the lack of the term scapegoat as an analytical category in anthropological textbooks and dictionaries, though one may suppose that as a global term it evokes some common understanding of the meaning of certain rituals in a variety of cultures. In what René Girard has called the scapegoat mechanism, that is, the societal tendency to collectively transfer guilt onto a sacrificial victim, it may be conceived as a main trait of all rituals that are concerned with preserving an ideal form of society. Recently, Declan Quigley (2000) has taken up Frazer's comparativist perspective in order to elucidate the central meaning of scapegoating for the continuation and structuring of society. Starting with the paradigm of royal ritual, he shows that the continuation and preservation of the core of society is firmly linked to the process of scapegoating, even though it may be concealed under forms of seemingly permanent social distinctions as, for instance, the Hindu caste order. In other words, while scapegoating appears to leave its traces on a ladder-like structuring of society, its main aim and focus is to recreate the core of society, or to preserve the ideal society at large. Thus, as Quigley (2000: 237) states: '[E]ven in those cases where scapegoats are actually killed, they must first be killed symbolically, to be made to appear as non-human in some sense.'

In contributions to Tibetan studies, for example, such as Nebesky-Wojkowitz's (1993 [1956]) monumental study of *Oracles and Demons of Tibet*, or Paul's (1982) study of the Sherpa pantheon and rituals, the term scapegoat is introduced both as a translation of the Tibetan term *glud* and as a metaphor. This is proposed in order to understand those rituals that aim at the eviction of sin and harmful forces by sending them off and away from the community, that is, by means of expulsion rather than by sacrifice or (ritual) destruction. Such rituals may occur in the context of healing ceremonies on the one hand, and in the context of seasonal festivals on the other. In global terms, scapegoat rituals as a form of othering seem to serve the function of revitalizing relations of social cohesion.

Now, our present-day Western concept of a scapegoat has hardly anything to do with such instrumental and socioritual contexts, or with those embedded in an unfragmented experience of ritual processes. When 'we' think of scapegoats, we will rather encounter them in the form of the unconscious stigmatization of outsiders, as being responsible for the defects and conflicts in our own society. According to Freud's psychoanalytical theory, a scapegoat is someone who is the victim of aggression without having actually provided any actual reason for such aggression. A deviant or lowly esteemed feature of a person or group is turned into a prejudice or social stigma against the group as a whole, by an unconscious identification of peripheral social groups as representing negative social traits as such. Thus acts of aggression within groups or the society at large are projected onto the members of peripheral groups who are turned into scapegoats. Such projections of negative or even xenophobic feelings onto outsiders have always been observed by anthropologists in indigenous societies – for example, indigenous groups that consider themselves as 'the humans', while designating neighbouring groups as 'cannibals' or as possessed by witchcraft. In our own society, as the theologian Norbert Lohfink (2001) has recently pointed out, such projections, though irrational by nature, apparently have a subservient function of preserving social cohesion in times of internal crises. As an example, he points out how after the collapse of the global confrontation between capitalist West and communist East, new forms of local violence escalated in many parts of the world, which included the emergence of new scapegoats.[2]

My observations in Nepal in 1991 could provide some evidence to support this hypothesis: when the revolution in Nepal was still being fought out, rebellious students sometimes turned their violence against anybody who earned his livelihood from the government. In Jiri (Ramechap), teachers were chased through the streets and stigmatized as a source of evil by hanging what is called a *kalo mala* around their necks, an object made of old shoes. In Germany in recent years, refugees were pushed into the role of scapegoats. According to Lohfink, this was even tolerated by the state or regional governments in order to compete with a rising rightist movement of violence which might otherwise have turned against the state itself.

These examples may lead us to infer some qualifications for the first of our grammars. Orientalism as an 'imaginative geography' has been defined by Said (1995 [1978]: 72) as a 'form of radical realism; anyone employing Orientalism ... will designate, name, point to, fix what he is talking about with a word or phrase, which is then considered either to have acquired, or more simply to be, reality'. This comes very near to the common notion of stereotyping. However, Said's account of Orientalism not only includes this power-driven perspective of managing the other but also the reflective attitude of consciously identifying 'us' versus 'the Orient'. Or, in more abstract terms, as Baumann phrases it in this volume, the Orient was also imagined to be a source reflecting 'what is good in them as compared to us'. My interpretational usage of Orientalism as 'orientalization' thus applies to a form of othering which includes both the possibility of stigmatization and of consciously reflecting the other. In our present-day Western projections of the 'dangerous' other, the process of scapegoating seemingly reduces the process of orientalization to a one-way street: there is no reflection of what is good in them as compared to us.

Even in the past, however, the original meaning of our present-day emic concept of the scapegoat did not merely focus on the transfer of aggression and frustration onto a (sacrificial) victim. Indeed, a meaning similar to that of a scapegoat in Tibetan cultural contexts can be found in the Old Testament, which says in Leviticus (16:6–10, 21–22 and 26):

> And Aaron shall offer his bullock of the sin offering, which is for himself, and make an atonement for himself, and for his house.
>
> And he shall take the two goats, and present them before the LORD at the door of the tabernacle of the congregation.
>
> And Aaron shall cast lots upon the two goats; one lot for the LORD, and the other lot for the scapegoat.
>
> And Aaron shall bring the goat upon which the LORD'S lot fell, and offer him for a sin offering.
>
> But the goat, on which the lot fell to be the scapegoat, shall be presented alive before the LORD to make an atonement with him, and to let him go for a scapegoat into the wilderness. [...]
>
> And Aaron shall lay both his hands upon the head of the live goat, and confess over him all the iniquities of the children of Israel, and all their transgressions in all their sins, putting them upon the head of the goat, and shall send him away by the hand of a fit man into the wilderness:

> And the goat shall bear upon him all their iniquities unto a land not inhabited: and he shall let go the goat in the wilderness. [...]
> And he that let go the goat for the scapegoat shall wash his clothes, and bathe his flesh in water, and afterward come into the camp.

Within the ritual process, the man charged with the burden of accepting a leading role in the scapegoat ritual was thus originally linked with strong personality traits rather than being reduced to negative ones. Similar features are attributed, as indicated in Tibetan and Sherpa traditions of persons acting as ritual scapegoats, who are thought to take away with them the sins of the community in the course of dance festivals. The stigmatization or marginalisation of those accepting such roles is balanced out by highlighting their leading roles in the ritual process. This feature will also come to light in the ritual context of *Ghantakarna*.

The Ritual Context

Given these contrastive, though not exhaustive remarks on the concept of scapegoating, I would now like to map out a framework for understanding the ritual context within which scapegoat rituals may occur.

The ritual of *Ghantakarna* may be described briefly in a few lines. It revolves around a myth, described in detail by Anderson (1988) and Véziès (1981), according to which a demon, night by night, captured and devoured the farmers' women. Receiving notice of the demon's evil-doing, Vishnu, the lord of the universe, proclaimed him his enemy.[3] He appeared in the form of a frog. Offering himself to the demon, the frog led him into a swampy area near the river where he drowned. Recalling the story, groups of farmers will construct effigies of reed depicting the demon at the crossroads of several city quarters in Kathmandu and in villages elsewhere. Sexual joking accompanies the whole process of construction, the figures indeed displaying sexually aggressive characteristics. Small puppets of cloth representing women are attached to the reed figures, which again relates to the original myth. At the same time, a boy is chosen from the low caste of Pode (sweepers). His body will be painted with sexual symbolism comprising both male and female genitals. Holding an earthen pot in his hands, he then collects alms from all passers-by and shopkeepers. It is said that these alms are collected for the cremation of the demon. Young boys shout slogans, especially 'Om Shanti, Jaya Nepal' ('May peace prevail, Nepal be victorious!'),[4] and they urge the boy to continue collecting alms, while allowing themselves to become extremely excited by the symbolism displayed.

When night falls over the valley, the reed figures are torn down. The boy, representing all the unwanted attitudes and thus figuring as a living scapegoat, takes his seat on the effigy after his body has meanwhile been cleaned. Then, a group of farmers pulls the effigy by a rope through the streets towards the river, where other groups meet and the figures are swept away. It is said that the group that manages to get to the disposal site first has achieved a feat, so that sometimes struggles over who came first may arise.

The demon represented by the boy is called *gatha muga*: in Newari, *ghanta karna* in Nepali. If translated verbatim, the following meanings emerge: *Ghantakarna* signifies 'bell ears', which may be associated with the demon's attitude of not wanting to listen to any word from his victims or the high gods. There is also an association, however, of the term with the classical Sanskrit tradition. According to Monier-Williams (1986), *Ghantakarna*, 'bell-eared', is the name of an attendant of the god Shiva as well as of a demon (Raksasa). He is thought to preside over cutaneous complaints and worshipped for exemption from them in the month of Caitra (mid- March to mid-April). Ecologically, the period of cultivation is the time of spreading cutaneous disease, and thus one may also infer that the festival of *Ghantakarna* emerged as a remedial tradition, that is, as an instrumental healing ritual., w In the course of time, however, differing meanings have been associated with the festival, which are clearly exhibited in the life-size reed figures of the demon and the body painting of the boy. The Newari term of *gatha muga*: reflects this process of adding further meanings to the festival, since it signifies 'bell clapper' and may thus invoke the additional meaning of the 'attention aroused' by the ritual, as in the phrase 'making big ears'. It could thus indicate that collective attention is drawn to something considered impure and being disposed of, and as the public treatment of the *gatha muga:* indicates, he indeed appears to be more like a scapegoat than as a demon. By collecting small donations of money from all passers-by, shopkeepers and neighbours of a given area, the *gatha muga:* are collecting this 'uncleanliness' that has to be expelled.

The donations received by them are called *jagat*. This is an Urdu loan-word, itself derived from the theological Muslim-Arabic term *zakat*, which in Nepali is used with the similar meaning of alms-giving. In the context of the ritual there are also offerings of *bali*, 'consisting of dirty husks, curdled blood and buffalo entrails [...covered] with fruits, flowers and rice [and] topped with a flaming cotton wick' (Anderson 1988: 75).[5] These are laid out at crossroads by women in order to distract evil spirits from entering into people's homes. *Bali* would thus connote an offering substituting a sacrificial victim, especially one offered to supernatural beings who may otherwise cause harm to people. By contrast, the small money donations of *jagat* collected from neighbours and passers-by may be thought of as ransom money meant to transfer one's individual sin (*pap*) to the scapegoat. Such donations are not considered as *dana* offerings aiming at the accumulation of merit (*punya*), even though *dana* may also bear the meaning of a gift for disposing of bad karma – perhaps in the form of a gift offered to a priest or some other respected recipient. The *jagat* offerings have primarily the instrumental meaning of expunging sin; that is, from the analytical perspective of othering, such offerings would indicate a process of stigmatization. However, their meaning cannot be viewed in isolation from the ritual process as a whole.

If we seek insight into how the three grammars proposed for the study of processes of othering are linked to each other in ritual processes, one approach might be by way of Maurice Bloch's (1986) ritual theory as presented briefly by David Gellner (1999: 140ff.). Accordingly, the ritual stages of the Ghantakarna ritual would adhere to the following scheme. In the initial stage, the ritual seems to focus on the aggressive domination of the forces of life, a stage during which violence is projected onto the scapegoat. In terms of our grammars, this would correspond to aspects of orientalization, though at first only in one direction: it is the boy from a low caste representing the demon's uncontrolled sexual attitudes. In the second stage of the ritual, those who participate actively in exorcicizing the demon and by disposing of his effigy separate themselves from the untamed forces of life. By taking a leading role in this ritual stage as the one who 'rides the demon', the chosen boy finds his capacity to compete with these unwanted attitudes being highlighted. As he rides the demon's reed figure while holding a torch that is burning in his right hand, he visibly displays some pride. In other words, his role as the scapegoat is encompassed and accorded acceptance within the universe of experience.[6] In the final stage, when returning to their homes with purified attitudes, the actors, that is, the farmers, return to life empowered, and may now legitimately celebrate the revitalized unity of their lineages. In terms of our grammars, the final ritual stage displays the reunification of segmented or dispersed social interests.

In terms of David Gellner's version of ritual theory, I would propose that the ritual of *Ghantakarna* stands halfway between an instrumental and a social ritual.[7] There are some indications that the ritual has been instrumentalised to an extent by the participant youth so as to display their political interests. In its total unfolding, however, it seems that it is still effectively performed in the manner it always has been: within the established universe of experience, it has little significance for the legitimation of power structures, nor does it carry any implicit devices for hierarchy and marginalisation. Instead, this ritual rather serves the function of healing or purifying society from unwanted individual attitudes.[8] These unwanted attitudes are symbolically displayed. Still, I would propose that they are not merely experienced as mythological demonic forces or beliefs related to witchcraft (even when these beliefs are embedded in the yearly ritual cycle) but also as down-to-earth, self-understood by-products of day-to-day activities.

The ritual is conducted annually at the peak of the rice-planting season, which should be completed on the day the ritual is performed. The day chosen for the festival is the fourteenth day of the waning fortnight of the month of Sravana (mid-July to mid-August), which marks the end of the cultivation period lasting for fifty-two days and starting on the sixth day of the waxing fortnight of Jyestha (mid-May to mid-June).[9] In addition to its effects on health problems due to the high level of moisture in the air during the monsoon season, the period of rice-planting is perceived as a time when social transgressions may not be held fully in check, since cooperation between neighbours during work in the fields necessitates a denial of the autonomy of households. It is also a time when sexual transgressions are constantly joked about, as I have witnessed when visiting farmers working in the fields. It seems to be this attitude that has to be held in check with the performance of the ritual. The *Ghantakarna* myth refers to this attitude indirectly by way of demonic forces. Thus, as is mentioned by Robert Levy (1992), David Gellner (1992) and Todd Lewis (1984), the ritual of *Ghantakarna* should be seen as part of people's traditional experience of the year's agricultural cycle, that is, as a ritual performed in order to purify society of those forces of untamed nature which have entered the settlements at the time of rice planting, when the autonomy of households and lineages comes into question.

The whole ritual process of *Ghantakarna* seems to demonstrate how scapegoating may be embedded in an interlinked series of steps: orientalization, encompassment, and the reunification of segmentary interests. From the vantage point of ritual theory, this series is governed by the principle of 'rebounding violence', which serves to reunite dispersed interests and produces social cohesion under some form of collective ideology. Even though rebounding violence is thus operative in the ritual process, there remains an ambiguity. The motif of the expulsion of unwanted sexual attitudes is clearly sensed by participants as an instrumental act, and thus the process of othering remains on a conscious level. I suppose that, for the Newars observing the ritual, the process of scapegoating has little effect on their attitudes regarding othering as social stigmatisation. Although the boy acting as the scapegoat is chosen from the Candal (i.e., Pode) sweepers' caste, which would thus suggest an association of unwanted attitudes with low-caste status and a stigmatization of those considered at the periphery of society, this feature becomes less obvious outside the traditional settlement pattern. In those city areas where contact with modernity is obvious, where the scapegoat is exposed to the eyes and cameras of tourists and the open public, the scapegoat symbolism has indeed been reduced. This would suggest that people are aware of stigmatization outside the traditional setting. Thus from the perspective of an outsider, it remains difficult to say whether such ritual scapegoating is indeed felt in a broader sense as a social stigma by the main actor or whether it is regarded as in some way a privileged role, highlighted as part of the logic of rebounding violence. Of course, hardly anyone from high-caste households slips into that role, even though the person acting as scapegoat earns a good income on this day for the burden he bears.

Conclusion

When harmful forces or attitudes are consciously perceived and displayed as being a consequence of day-to-day experience, scapegoating and scapegoat rituals remain on a conscious level. Under circumstances like these, othering as orientalization becomes a self-reflective process. Scapegoat rituals may indeed serve to channel aggression in society without stigmatizing outsiders and projecting aggression upon them. Their main function, then, does not lie in preserving a ladder-like hierarchy in society, which may be the first impression or likely image for the external observer when confronted with the ambiguities displayed in such rituals. Our perception of 'Oriental' societies is, however, much too strongly shaped by a radical realism of classification: for example, caste as a ladder-like order explained by reference to the original degree of purity often is associated with certain professions, and mirrored, again, in salvational concepts that legitimate the structuring of society according to such principles.

My interpretation has used the concept of 'Orientalism' in the broader sense of 'orientalization' so as to include the possibility of both stigmatization and reflective processes yielding an image of the other. By the same token, this broadening can also be applied to Dumont's concept of encompassment, that is, of divergent or opposing features contained within a holistic perspective. While Dumont's concept of encompassment has also been applied outside the 'oriental' sphere, as when he found it operative in the modern notion of individualism encompassed within Christian salvational beliefs (Dumont 1986), the basic idea behind both applications is the gradation of groups or individual traits on a ladder-like ideal scheme. Marginalised groups or individual deviations from the norm are only 'encompassed' within the system, being seen either as performing ritual duties necessary for maintaining the ideal hierarchical order or as the focus of individual grace. One may thus wonder whether the actors who slip into marginalised roles in a given social system are aware that their (ritual) roles are also instrumentalised for the sake of the ideal as such.

From an insider's perspective, scapegoat rituals and scapegoating may sometimes indeed have less to do with marginalisation per se. Paradigmatically, the *Ghantakarna* ritual displays the inversion of the role of the scapegoat boy into 'a hero riding the demon king', showing that illegitimate and untamed force and forces may legitimately be controlled even by someone from the bottom of the hierarchyperiphery of society. Thus the conscious reflection of othering implied in the ritual scapegoating process exemplifies the function of preserving the ideal core of society more than it serves that of contributing to the perception of a ladder-like hierarchy. In this context, encompassment obviously carries a different connotation: it is an expression of relative distance from or nearness incorporating those at the periphery in order to recreate, the ideal core of society. The degree and kind of scapegoating operative in any given society may thus be regarded as a qualifier for concurrent normative concepts of othering.

Notes

1. I am grateful to Declan Quigley for reading the draft of this chapter and alerting me to the difficulties of applying these concepts in an abstract sense, especially given that they are more associated with classical themes of political anthropology and the anthropology of modes of thought. The ethnographic data for this contribution were collected in July 1998, while conducting research on the uses of money and credit in Nepal (Mühlich 2001). My

thanks for information on historical sources relating to the *Ghantakarna* ritual go to Philip Pierce and Kashinath Tamot, Nepal Research Centre, Kathmandu.
2. In order to determine the plausibility of Lohfink's assumption, more research is required on the social transformations of the post-Cold War period in various parts of the world, particularly on images of enmity concurrent in society, as will also be the focus of other contributions to this volume.
3. It should be noted that Lord Vishnu is not only perceived as the lord of the universe but also as an 'ideal king', while the king of Nepal is in turn perceived as an incarnation of Vishnu. Thus the demon *Ghantakarna* may concurrently be seen as having questioned the supremacy of the king as well.
4. According to Kashinath Tamot (pers.com.) the slogan "Om Shanti Jaya Nepal" is a recent development in society. The traditional slogan is "A:ju je ha: ". It is heard differently by the listeners as "adule ha" etc.. The word is corrupted and difficult to explain . The word a:ju je may be a:ju jaya, which may mean "forefather (lit. "grand-father") be victorious". A:ju may be the masculine form of ajima: (lit. "grand-mother", mother goddess) developed from Skt. a:rya, Pkt. ajja and Skt. aryl:, Pkt. ajji. Ha: appears to carry the sense of "hurray!". A deity is the ancestor for Newars, whether he/she may be a god, man , ghost or demon.
5. Another important attribute of the ritual is the purchase of three-legged iron nails to be pounded into the thresholds of houses in order to prevent evil spirits from entering people's homes. In addition, people will wear five-coloured iron rings on that day which are thought to protect against attacks of malevolent ghosts (*bhut*). Again, in 2002, it is reported that many fewer iron nails were sold for the ritual event.
6. I shall return to the issue of encompassment in my conclusion and simply refer here to the fact that the boy is at least 'accepted' by the audience at this stage of the ritual.
7. Since the mid-1990s several years of political unrest have also apparently left traces upon the performance of the *Ghantakarna* ritual. More recently the collection of alms at crossroads may have come to be associated with the forcible collection of donations for the fight of the Maoists, since money is asked for primarily from those shopkeepers and passers-by who appear to be more wealthy.
8. In one case I observed in 1998, however, the body painting also included the national flag of India. This would, of course, appear to be insulting to people of that nation, since a parallel was being drawn between tabooed sexual attitudes and people of a certain cultural background. This example may indicate that the ritual of *Ghantakarna* is not entirely free of political instrumentalisation.
9. The *Ghantakarna* festival is first mentioned in the Gopalarajavamsavali of the fourteenth century AD (Vajracarya and Malla 1985: 117, 163; Kashinath Tamot, pers.com). The reference appears in the context of the Crown Prince Dharma Malla (1384 AD) who, in the year of his marriage, introduced the tradition to exhibit dolls at the the thirteenth day of the waxing fortnight of Sravana , an auspicious period, which may later have been shifted to the fourteenth day of the waning fortnight. The waning fortnight is considered an inauspicious, that is, *asadha*, period, hence the protective character of the ritual against harmful forces.

References

Anderson, Mary. 1988. *The Festivals of Nepal.* Culcutta: Rupa and Co.
Bloch, Maurice. 1986. *From Blessing to Violence*. Cambridge: Cambridge University Press.
Dumont, Louis. 1980. *Homo Hierarchicus: The Caste System and its Implications,* complete revised English edition. Chicago and London: Chicago University Press.
———. 1986. *Essays on Individualism: Modern Ideology in Anthropological Perspective.* Chicago and London: Chicago University Press.

Gellner, David. 1992. *Monk, Householder, and Tantric Priest: Newar Buddhism and Its Hierarchy of Ritual.* Cambridge: University Press.

——. 1999. 'Religion, Politics and Ritual: Remarks on Geertz and Bloch' *Social Anthropology* 7 (2): 135-153.

Levy, Robert I. 1992. *Mesocosm: Hinduism and the Organisation of a Traditional Newar City in Nepal,* first Indian edition. Delhi: Motilal Banarsidass.

Lewis, Todd T. 1984. 'The Tuladhars of Kathmandu: A Study of Buddhist Tradition in a Newar Merchant Community' (Ph.D. Thesis, Columbia University, UMI 8506008).

Lohfink, Norbert. 2001. 'Gewalt und Friede in der Bibel. Hinführung zum Schreiben der deutschen Bischöfe "Gerechter Frieden"' in *Steht nicht geschrieben? Studien zur Bibel und ihrer Wirkungsgeschichte. Festschrift für Georg Schmuttermayr,* eds. J. Frühwald-König, F.R. Prostmeier, R. Zwick. Regensburg: Pustet, 75–87.

Monier-Williams, Monier. 1986 [1899]. *A Sanskrit-English Dictionary,* reprint. Delhi: Motilal Banarsidass.

Mühlich, Michael. 2001. *Credit and Culture: A Substantivist Perspective on Credit Relations in Nepal.* Berlin: Dietrich Reimer Verlag.

Nebesky-Wojkowitz, René de. 1993 [1956].: *Oracles and Demons of Tibet: The Cult and Iconography of the Tibetan Protective Deities,* reprint. Kathmandu: Mandala Book Point.

Paul, Robert. 1982. *The Tibetan Symbolic World: Psychoanalytic Explorations.* Chicago : University Press.

Quigley, Declan. 2000. 'Scapegoats: The Killing of Kings and Ordinary People', *The Journal of the Royal Anthropological Institute (incorporating* Man) 6 (2): 237–54.

Said, Edward. 1995 [1978]. *Orientalism: Western Conceptions of the Orient,* reprint. New Delhi: Penguin Books India.

The Holy Bible [1988]. Authorized King James Version. Oxford: Oxford University Press.

Vajracarya, D. and K.P. Malla. 1985. *The Gopa:lara:javamsa:vali:.* Wiesbaden: Franz Steiner Verlag.

Véziès, Jean-Francois. 1981 . *Les fêtes magiques du Népal.* Paris: Editions Cesare Rancilio.

Chapter 4

German Grammars of Identity/Alterity

A Diachronic View

Anne Friederike Müller

This chapter attempts to answer two questions. First, it sets out to test whether the three grammars of selfing and othering can be used to grasp changes over time in the constitution of collective identities. In this vein, I propose to combine the synchronic structuralist view of the grammars with a diachronic approach. Second, this chapter is concerned with an ethical and political assessment of these three structural models. What is it that makes some grammars more or less peaceful or aggressive than other grammars?

To answer these questions, this study will trace the changing popular conceptions of the nation from the late nineteenth to mid-twentieth century. Germany is a particularly interesting case with regard to the two questions posed. The first German nation-state emerged remarkably late by European standards, in the last third of the nineteenth century, and it eventually turned out to be more destructive than any other state in the first half of the twentieth century. Over a short time, Germany evolved from a congeries of dozens of single states, rather hopeless from a nationalist vantage point, into a powerful, industrialised and colonizing nation-state, and then into genocidal, cynical dictatorship. What kind of grammars prepared, accompanied, or allegedly legitimated these processes in the eye of the public?

To begin with, a brief remark about the material used in this chapter: I attempt to adopt as much as possible the perspective of ordinary people and historical actors when looking at the process of nation-building and the experience of National-Socialist dictatorship. The main documents which I have chosen to use are personal diaries, memoirs and letters, as well as popular magazines and popular novels, the aim being to reconstitute what was the common cultural ground for elites and ordinary people alike (Herzfeld 1997: 3).

Segmentation and Inclusion, Traced Diachronically

German nation-building in the nineteenth century can be surprisingly well understood by applying the three grammars specified in this volume. As for segmentation/inclusion, in the second half of the nineteenth century, two wars against common 'enemies' united the many German states into one entity. In 1866, the armies of Prussia and some seventeen allied small Northern German states defeated Austria and all other German states. Immediately afterwards, Prussia and its newly annexed territories, the small Northern states, Saxony, and a part of Hessen, formed some sort of core nation-state, the *Norddeutsche Bund* (North German Federation). Only three years later, another war united this polity with the Southern states in a single front against France. The war had been triggered off, ostensibly to settle the question of succession to the Spanish throne. The German side won. All German monarchs and the army acclaimed the Prussian king Wilhelm as German Emperor on 18 January 1871. The frontiers of the German nation-state were traced almost exactly along those lines, as Austria, anti-Prussian in the 1864 war, neutral in 1870/71, remained excluded from it, for instance. This process of inclusion slides back to the other extreme only after 1945, when the German Empire is partitioned into four occupation zones, with some of the smaller German states remaining in existence, if sometimes in a slightly altered form.

Encompassment, Traced Diachronically

Thus, in the late nineteenth century, national unification took place under the aegis of Prussia. This state of affairs was congealed in the form of the future nation-state as well. According to its constitution, the Prussian king automatically became German Emperor. In practice, the Prussian Prime Minister occupied the post of Imperial Chancellor. A parliament was elected with universal male suffrage, but it shared its legislative powers with a second, federal chamber whose decisions Prussia could easily block. In practice, the power lay with the Emperor, the army under his command, the Chancellor, and the mainly aristocratic higher echelons of the Prussian bureaucracy.

Prussia encompassed the other German states. This was clearly expressed in the prevalent cultural grammars, too. One of the main examples that Dumont uses in his Postface to *Homo Hierarchicus* (1980) featured in Imperial Germany as well. Prussia, the superior German state, was seen to include the inferior ones, just as the category of 'man' includes that of 'woman' (Dumont 1980: 239–40).

Generally, Germany's transformation into a nation-state was interpreted as 'strengthening over time', as a coming of age and becoming 'male'. *Germania* had been 'violated'/'raped' by the French in 1813, but had fought in a 'strong' and 'manly' way in 1870 (Frevert 1996: 157). Similar, but critical observations were made abroad. From the British perspective, Germany had originally been characterized by feminine activities such as music and romantic poetry, embodied perfectly by Victoria's German consort, Prince Albert. From the 1870s onward, Germany appeared more and more like a masculine, militaristic bully. Cartoons in the First World War exploited this gender imagery to the full, opposing German soldiers and female personifications of other countries, such as Belgium or Britain (Firchow 1986: 78).

Inside Germany itself, there operated a similar demarcation between 'male' and 'female' regions. The whole of Germany had supposedly become 'male' by being encompassed by Prussia. Compared to Prussia, however, the Catholic South, particularly Bavaria, was considered to be emotional, traditional, and aesthetically minded. The soft Catholic 'heart' was opposed to the relentless Protestant 'conscience' (Langbehn 1890/93: 25).[1] Prussia was not only Protestant, but also a very militaristic state from its very beginnings – another element that contributed to its being 'male'. In the 'marriage between Prussia and Germany', Prussia had the 'male role' (Langbehn 1890/93: 210). These gendered comparisons were not merely decorative speech: they legitimated very real power relations. As stated above, the Prussian king became automatically German Emperor, which had originally been justified by the fact that Prussia had led the other, smaller German armies into war against France in 1870. Alleging that there were 'natural' reasons for Prussia's superiority (its rationality, its 'maleness') helped to secure its supremacy in the long term. On some occasions, Wilhelm II would state bluntly that Bavaria did not have the power or the freedom to be independent (Müller 1931: 239); alluding to Bavarian femininity made the same point more subtly. A similar gender symbolism was stressed in relation to the new province of Alsace-Lorraine; it stood under Prussia's direct rule because only Prussia was 'strong enough to tame Alsace-Lorraine' (the historian Treitschke quoted in Jeismann 1992: 259). Interestingly, the French side, too, saw Alsace as a feminine entity – but this time as a maiden captured by the enemy and happily rescued in 1914 (Jeismann 1992: 365).

Orientalism, Traced Diachronically

As for the third model, orientalism, it may appear surprising that it worked within the 'Occident' at the very same time as it it so conspicuously legitimated the colonizing of other parts of the world by the most powerful industrialised Western nations.[2]

As a matter of fact, in the phase of nation-building at the end of the nineteenth century, the (desired) German self-image comprised a move from a negative to a positive representation of the Oriental. Germans who 'improved' their national self-image in this way took their cue from a negative value-judgement: a widespread *topos* asserted that Germans were uncivilized and barbaric when compared to neighbouring nations in the West and South. This assertion sprang forth and was confirmed again and again in a series of intercultural encounters between Italians and Frenchmen on the one side, and Germans on the other. Its origins can be traced as far back as to the fifteenth century when German students in Rome were described as brutal, barbaric, unreasonable, as well as drinking heavily and eating copiously (Reinhardt 1992: 97). Whatever little 'civilization' Germans owned at all had been transmitted to them by the Roman Catholic Church, as contended Enea Silvio Piccolomini, the future Pope Pius II, in a letter addressed to a German theologian in 1458 (Werner 1994: 44–45).

By the eighteenth century, French cultural dominance had replaced Italian influences. What did not change was a sentiment of cultural inferiority on the German side. For it is a remarkable fact that, up to a certain point, Germans shared and continued to share the negative image that was projected upon them by their Southern and Western neighbours. In some diaries of the Imperial period, we find evaluations made by Germans of their compatriots that coincide with the image of the un-cultured, unrefined rustic that had been passed on since the epoch of Humanism.

For instance, a German woman living in Paris observed that her compatriots visiting the World Exhibition in 1900 made a very unfavourable impression on the French public, as indeed on herself, on account of 'their loud manners, the excessive sacrificial offerings they made to Bacchus in restaurants and bars, their vociferous bartering and their complaints about high prices in shops and places of entertainment' (Bülow 1930/31a: 401). Max Weber gave the following account of his meeting with former fellow student Otto von Gierke in Scotland in 1895:

> Incidentally, the world is a village in Great Britain, too. Would you believe that we met acquaintances from Berlin here? When we were taking the steamer to Loch Katrine, I suddenly noticed on the *peer [sic]*, among the pinched English mouths of those hurrying to get aboard, the Germanic bard's face of Gierke. We then travelled together as far as Loch Lomond, where our ways parted. Meeting a compatriot does affect one strangely. Ordinarily we have become acclimated to the point where we have adopted the general custom of speaking in a whisper. We act as if we did not see the people to the right and to the left of us. We answer only when asked, and then briefly and very politely. We always eat less of everything than we would like to, open our mouths as little as possible, and even when our stomachs rumble audibly, we splash about in the soup with our spoons as if we didn't care about the grub.
>
> But no sooner were Germans nearby than there was such an outburst of laughter while we were waiting for the *'coach'* that all the English came rushing up to see the barbarians, and in the *coach* I overheard someone say *merry Germany*. Before we parted we had a *lunch* that the waiters there won't soon forget. G. began to eat as though we were in the Teutoburg Forest [in Germanic times], and I joined in. When everything kept disappearing, the perplexed *waiters* finally brought superhuman quantities of *roast-beaf [sic]*, salmon, etc., presumably out of fear that otherwise we were going to bite people. Three of them stood around our table, and they stared aghast at the debris of their property. They were obviously relieved when a signal finally came from the steamboat and put a stop to the meal. (Weber 1926/76: 209, in a letter to his mother)

Far from being a private matter causing embarrassment, consternation or amusement, this supposedly typical national behaviour could give rise to diplomatic incidents in the international arena. Von Bülow, Secretary for Foreign Affairs from 1897 until 1900, despaired about those German diplomats who did not 'appreciate the importance of good breeding in international intercourse'. He added that '[s]ome Germans made a repellent impression abroad because of their rough manners, their aggressiveness, and their loud boasting' (Bülow 1930/31a: 426). Hardly able to hide their thoughts and feelings, credulous and naïve German emissaries easily became the laughing stock of the diplomatic corps. Bülow illustrates this constant danger with a scene that took place in Italy in 1906:

> I was passing through Berlin and on the point of returning to Norderney [a North Sea island] where I hoped to finish my convalescence, when Count Mounts, our Ambassador to Rome, asked for an interview. An annoying mishap had befallen him. There had been an exhibition at Milan; it had been opened by the king of Italy, and the whole Diplomatic Corps had been invited. At the moment when the ceremony began a slight shower of rain came on. As etiquette demands on such occasions, all the diplomats were in uniform. Now Monts was both famous as a hypochondriac, who could think of nothing else but his health, and known to be notoriously stingy. He was scared stiff that the rain would give him a cold and spoil his uniform. At last he got into such a state of excitement that he began to shout across the show-ground, which the rain had made a little worse for wear: 'Regardez-moi cette saleté!' His French colleague, Barrère, was standing near him. I have already had occasion to show how Barrère – more skilful [by] far, and better informed than Monts – could always play cat-and-mouse with him. He noticed Monts's agitation and began, in the friendliest way, to excite him further: 'Cette pluie est vraiment désagréable, nous allons tous attraper un gros rhume, vous avez l'air bien pâle. Et puis nos uniformes sont abîmés. Et ces uniformes, chamarrés d'or, coûtent très cher'. Monts, who had completely lost his head, rushed up to Count Guicciardini, the Minister for Foreign Affairs, and shouted: 'Il n'y a ici que les diplomates et les domestiques qui soient en uniforme, je vous fais là une observation très sérieuse!' He ended by creating such a scene that Count Ponti, the Mayor of Milan, said to him, 'If you used that tone to me as Count Monts I should be obliged to call you out; but since you are the German Ambassador, I shall lodge a complaint with my government'. Both Ponti and Guicciardini were justifiably considered friendly towards Germany. While this frenzy attacked Monts in the midst of a public ceremony, Barrère was saying with a smile to all the Italians who surrounded him: 'Comme les Allemands sont violents, comme ils sont mal élevés, comme ils aiment à provoquer des rixes. On a bien raison de parler de querelles d'Allemand'. As is well known, the French call any quarrelling over nothing 'une querelle d'Allemand'. (Bülow 1930/31b: 245–46)

One way of dealing with this stereotype was to reassess it and to accept 'barbarians' as an apt characterization while giving the word a positive meaning. From the 1880s onwards, one finds German texts dealing with the Ancient Germans in which they were happily called 'barbarians'. That there was a defensive slant to this use of the term 'barbarians' becomes obvious from the fact that it was always used in opposition to 'Romans' or 'Hellenes'. Every time, it was expressly stated that the barbarians outdid those supposedly superior people in terms of health, strength, purity, morality, naturalness, and goodness of heart. These ideas pervaded the expanding popular press of the second half of the nineteenth century, as one may easily see from its prototype *Die Gartenlaube*, a 'family journal' founded in 1853, attracting readers from all social backgrounds, ages, and both genders, and reaching a nationwide circulation of almost 400,000 in the 1870s (*Gartenlaube* 1888: 687; 1895: 239; 1904: 910; 1916: 175).³ One recognizes here, as in a mirror image, the reverse picture of the uncouth, uncultured German: lack of civilization becomes morality, purity, and health, inability to pretend becomes naturalness and goodness of heart, clumsiness is rephrased as physical strength. Michael Herzfeld uses the concept of 'cultural intimacy', 'the recognition of those aspects of a cultural identity that are considered a source of external embarrassment but that nevertheless provide insiders with their assurance of common sociality', to describe a comparable process in modern Greece, whereby a shameful identity is transformed into a proud self-image (Herzfeld 1997: 3).

In late nineteenth-century Germany, this kind of 'symbolic reversal' was not only applied to the alleged ancestors of the German nation, the barbarians of Ancient Germany, but in a much more generalized way this principle can be detected at the base of most German cultural and national identity of that time and the decades to follow. 'Strength' (and related concepts) as a positive feature, as an indicator of a healthy life unspoilt by civilization, was embedded in a series of initially deprecatory observations about German culture made by neighbouring peoples, subsequently turned into positive self-descriptions. Some examples may illustrate this phenomenon.

In Imperial Germany, simplicity and naturalness were looked upon as specifically German traits of character. Such qualities were a recurrent feature in eulogies of great Germans. Invariably, their external appearance mirrored their inner dispositions, which resulted naturally from the fact that 'real' Germans refused all make-belief and all form devoid of content. For example, the nationalist poet Arndt was styled into a 'German in the full sense of the word'; his appearance was plain and simple, unpretentious, without pomp; he always spoke the truth, was hostile to flattery and dissimulation, but nonetheless amiable towards everybody (*Gartenlaube* 1870: 70). The poet Freytag, one of the 'most German' men, was 'simple, but of noble appearance' (*Gartenlaube* 1871: 410). War Minister Moltke, a simple, modest, unpretentious man, was true and natural from head to toe, and did not long for popularity: 'a German in the most beautiful sense of the word' (*Gartenlaube* 1873: 664). The physician and anthropologist Virchow's obituary notice culminates in the statement that he was a truly German man: self-sacrificing, unostentatious, always prepared to fight for truth and justice (*Gartenlaube* 1891: 695).

Outer simplicity and its moral corollaries, honesty and kindliness, were also prerequisites for German rulers. Emperor Wilhelm I corresponded rather perfectly to this image (Eulenburg 1923: 129). The future Emperor

Wilhelm II was represented as a simple family-father in flattering portraits: even a politically neutral popular magazine wrote on the occasion of the Emperor's silver wedding anniversary in 1906: 'Everyone knows from so many events and incidents which have transpired into the public sphere that the relation between parents and children is most cordial, and that the relationship between the spouses is tender' (*Berliner Illustrirte* 1906, no.8: 115). Later on, there appeared critical remarks on the discrepancy between his words, advocating a return to the simplicity of the forefathers, and his deeds of a life of pomp and circumstance (Bülow 1930/31b: 200).

Like Wilhelm I, Bismarck naturally fitted into the image of the true German, leading a simple life and always speaking his mind. His dwellings reflected a complete lack of interest in decoration, pomp, or even beauty. Visitors to his manor in Friedrichsruh professed to have been 'struck by the simplicity of the house' which they qualified as a 'manifestation of the real spirit of Prussia' (Bülow 1930/31a: 21). Bismarck's funeral ceremony was generally classified as 'simple', and therefore very impressive. His mausoleum gave an impression of 'stark monumental simplicity' (*Berliner Illustrirte* 1899, no.13:4; Bülow 1930/31a: 226). At this point, the identification of 'ancient' with modern Germans comes full circle: Bismarck's mausoleum was a copy of the building in which (the 'Gothic', i.e., 'ancient German') King Theoderic had been laid to rest near Ravenna in 526 A.D.[4] Twenty-three years before Bismarck's death, a very popular novel contained a scene describing the same Theoderic on his deathbed in Ravenna. The splendidly decorated walls and ceiling of the Byzantine-Italian palace now inhabited by the 'German' (Gothic) conquerors are contrasted with the simple, unadorned bed of the Gothic king (Dahn 1884: I, 67). Given this (constructed) ancestry, it was easy to believe that exemplary Germans and great German rulers had always preferred simplicity to luxury.[5]

A comparable ideal image lay in store for German women. Just as male German protagonists of popular novels were paragons of simplicity, uprightness, and piety, an exemplary heroine such as Elisabeth in the popular novel *Goldelse* was described as a pure and childlike being, wearing simple clothes, shunning any make-up, preferring fresh roses or wild flowers picked in the forest as decoration for her hat and dresses to any ready-made and more sophisticated adornments (Marlitt 1878: 126, 234). Her character corresponds to this outer image: she is infinitely gentle, good-humoured, and honest to the point of being completely unable to lie.

True Germans valued being (*Sein*) over illusion (*Schein*), content over form, morality over manners. This cultural ideal of naturalness and simplicity was directed against specific political, cultural, and social configurations. Particularly when heralded by the middle classes, simplicity and naturalness implied a critique of aristocratic values.

To put this re-evaluation in a larger historical context, it is worth noting that, since early modern times, European aristocracies, with first the Italian, then the French courts in the ascendant, had striven for lightness in physical appearance and behaviour. This was exemplified by ballet and the desire to walk with a light step. With this softening of manners, described and analysed by Norbert Elias and other social historians, uncourtly boorishness was increasingly frowned upon. 'Civilization' was seen as superior to other stages of society, notably 'barbarism' (Elias 1939/78: 47). Elias remarked how the bourgeoisie of eighteenth-century Germany tried to check the cultural dominance of courtly, French-inspired *civilisation* with the concept of *Kultur*, i.e., depth as opposed to superficiality, thorough education and knowledge as opposed to mere manners (Elias 1939/78: 26). Elias failed to see, however, that, in a double reversal, barbarism was eventually claimed by some as part of a positive bourgeois and German identity as well.

Already in the late eighteenth and the first half of the nineteenth century, opposition against French cultural dominance had been combined with democratic and nationalist ideas, as well as with resistance against the French occupation of German soil. This called for a deprecation of French-influenced aristocratic values and an upgrading of bourgeois cultural markers, which counted for typically German at the same time.

After 1870, with the German Empire consolidating itself, the Imperial court society taking shape, and parts of the bourgeoisie amassing unprecedented wealth, German 'simplicity' ran the risk of becoming a mere phrase when used by members of the ruling classes in search of legitimacy and historical continuity. Not surprisingly, observers soon criticized the court society around Wilhelm II as 'Byzantine', i.e., prone to flattery and displaying artificial behaviour. Incidentally, at least part of the reasons for Wilhelm's loss of popularity and moral authority must be sought here. The observations of foreign visitors confirmed this change in values. Hermann Bahr, a German-born writer and art critic in Vienna who revisited Berlin in 1884, noted that despite its size, the new German capital was bathed in the atmosphere of a small provincial town. Manners were simple. In order to go to a ball, a general would use an old carriage drawn by only one horse, which would have made the most inferior lieutenant of the Austrian army ashamed. By 1890, when Bahr visited for a second time, this had changed; there was a cult of the great and the colossal (Bertaux 1962: 131). 'Culture' became a façade, a means to denounce other, 'un-German' cultural orientations (Stern 1972: 18).

At the very same time when German 'Orientality' (simplicity, barbarism) was given a positive reassessment in popular culture, 'Occidentality' was deprecated.

The values of German simplicity, natural strength and health were not only directed against aristocracy, but also against what was seen as modernity, rationality, as well as against what was believed to be the harmful consequences of 'civilization'. Again, these negative counter-foils were conflated with French culture and French politics. In an article of a popular magazine, for example, Blücher, a general allegedly deeply rooted in the essence of the German nation, with his lack of cultured manners, and his almost animal rage, is shown to vanquish 'Napoleon's icy rationality' (*Berliner Illustrirte* 1913: 222). Popular as well as scholarly discourses stressed the difference between the agile, analytical, 'rational', rhetorically oriented, French way of thinking and slower, more complicated, speculative, profound, organic German thought (*Gartenlaube* 1882: 131; Raulet 1992: 157). In the human and social sciences, Comte's positivism and Dilthey's hermeneutics are still sometimes held to illustrate the opposition between supposedly typically French and German schools of thought (Raulet 1992: 149).

Interestingly, the difference could be phrased in ways that were either flattering to the French or to the German side. Already in the eighteenth century, French voices pointed out that Northern peoples with their uncouth temperament and massive bodies could not possibly have the agility of mind that the French called *esprit*. On the other hand, *esprit* came to signify empty jingle of words, form devoid of content (Raulet 1992: 152–53). Thomas Mann would state in 1918 that French *esprit* was inseparable from modern civilisation, politicising, and rationality; he confronted it with German *Geist*, which was concerned with the 'soul' of things.

This discourse reflects the themes of German Romanticism as they were first formulated at the end of the eighteenth century: anti-rationality, harmony with nature, mysticism, and flight from society. Increased frustration with modernity ensured that these values lived on well into the twentieth century. In Imperial Germany, they became apparent in the turn-of-the-century movement of the *Wandervogel*, for instance, a youth movement that celebrated its opposition to modern urban life by a return to nature, folk music, and a 'simple' life-style.

The astonishingly erratic ramblings of the 'culture critic' Julius Langbehn that knew such an immense success with Wilhelmine readers between 1890 and 1914 advocate a cultural turn that is an exact synthesis of all the tendencies mentioned above. According to Langbehn, the German character is best described as a juxtaposition of music, honesty, barbarism, piety, childishness, and independence (Langbehn 1890/93: 27). In an anti-civilizatory and nationalist vein, Langbehn demanded that clumsiness, barbarism, gluttony, strength should find the place that is their due in German culture. Great Germans such as Rembrandt (*sic*), Luther, and Bismarck had always had a good appetite because they possessed a 'strong, innocent sensuality'. Rembrandt, the painter whom for some reason Langbehn thought to incarnate best what he thought to be Germanic, was supposed to set a model for everybody else in that he reconciled spirit with sensuality, and showed strength without brutality, delicateness without weakness (Langbehn 1890/93: 39–40).

Lack of refinement, simplicity, natural strength as specifically German characteristics, as expressions of bourgeois identity, and as remedies to modernity and rationality are perfectly expressed by the symbol of the countryside. It was commonplace to think that life in the countryside was a source of strength and health. Anton, the protagonist of the popular novel *Soll und Haben*, becomes a man and a German nationalist through agricultural work at the German-Polish border; when a friend visits him and offers him a share in his company, Anton refuses and praises life in the countryside instead (Freytag 1855/1900: I, 461). The novel demonstrates that using agricultural land for industrial purposes leads to financial ruin and physical decay. An aristocratic family encounters this fate; the bourgeois protagonist saves the remnants of their property. Again, bourgeois and anti-modernist anti-industrial values are combined in this chain of events. Unsurprisingly, the 'peasant novel' developed as a proper genre in the second half of the nineteenth century: authors like Ludwig Ganghofer described the peasant's life full of strength not yet sapped by modernity (Mosse 1980: 42).

Cole and Wolf, comparing two communities in Upper Anaunia, Italy, found that even in the 1970s, there was a distinctive attitude towards the countryside and the peasantry in 'German', i.e., South Tyrolese, nationalism. The German-speaking community of St Felix had been historically oriented towards the German cultural sphere, while Ladino-speaking Tret turned towards Italian society to the south. Cole and Wolf discovered that Felixers valued rural life positively and claimed their status as peasants as part of their cultural identity. By contrast, Italian nationalism focused more on the city as a seat of civilization, and tended to deprecate peasant life as a life without profit and honour. Tret villagers would mirror this attitude in their relations towards the neighbouring community of St Felix (Cole and Wolf 1974: 263–83). But is the appreciation of rural life unique to German nationalism?

As a matter of fact, all over nineteenth-century Europe, nationalists discovered the peasant as an expression of the intimate relation between a nation and its soil. The peasant was believed to incarnate the authentic core of the nation; he testified to its temporal continuity over centuries. Folklore studies were born out of this nationalist interest, even in Italy for which Cole and Wolf claim a deprecation of peasant life. The Florentine aristocrat Angelo De Gubernatis founded the *Società nazionale delle tradizioni popolari* in 1893; Giuseppe Pitrè launched the journal *Archivio per lo studio delle tradizioni popolari* and the series *Bibliografia delle tradizioni popolari d'Italia* in 1894. Various regional folkloric museums were set up from the beginning of the twentieth century. In 1911, on the occasion of the five-hundredth anniversary of Italian national unity, collections of folkloric items were organised all over the country (Thiesse 1998: 203). However, the peasant as described by folklorists had little resemblance to the true inhabitants of the European countryside; he was supposed to be live healthily, happily, and peacefully in harmonious small communities. These fictive peasants often played a purely symbolic role: they served to play down the negative consequences of capitalism and industrialisation, and they constituted a counter-foil to the new urban proletariate, seen as corrupted in bourgeois eyes (Thiesse 1998: 159–60).

However, there were voices within Germany which disagreed with the general national self-celebration that had become possible through the reversal of orientalist categories. While, from the 1880s onwards, the middle classes increasingly stressed 'barbarianism', naturalness, strength as part of the German cultural heritage, some members of the old aristocracy remained attached to a courtly ideal of civilization. People like Prince Bülow and Baroness Spitzemberg were critical of behaviours expressing German 'natural strength', which they would rather interpret as 'clumsiness' and 'lack of manners'. Similarly, Herzfeld states that 'cultural intimacy' is built around the binarism between ordinary people and an officially disapproving elite that joins into the external denigration of the supposedly inferior aspects of their national culture (Herzfeld 1997: 14). Nevertheless, with its social rise, the German bourgeoisie slowly came to epitomize the nation. Inexorably, the bourgeois self-image, which included *Kultur* as well as 'natural', i.e., 'uncivilized', manners, became part of German national identity.

Apart from these critical voices, most Germans used 'tradition' and 'modernity' as emic categories, trying to align themselves with both sides simultaneously. At least verbally, middle-class and many aristocratic Germans reacted against the 'West' and celebrated supposedly superior German traditions. At the same time, they were enthusiastic about 'German' technological advances. Thus, the majority of Germans tried to overtake the 'West' on both accounts, being more 'traditional' and 'natural' as well as more 'modern' than the Occident.[6]

Segmentation, encompassment, and orientalism were important structural processes in the period of German nation-building. The inclusion of formerly segmented units occurred on a military and political level. The encompassment of all other units by the most powerful one was a political fact, legitimated by gender imagery in popular culture and political rhetoric. Orientalism operated on a cultural level, with national self-confidence arising from the reformulation of negative stereotypes. The three grammars capture the material and cultural aspects of nation-building, as mirrored in contemporary representations. It would be interesting to see if other nationalisms and nation-building processes could be understood by the same threefold movement: unification and 'liberation' wars, political and cultural precedence of one component of the nation over the rest, and elaboration of a new positive self-image. One might even compare the specificities of the German materials with other chapters in this volume that describe the efforts of (potentially) ruling ethnic groups to encompass others so as to secure their prevalence in the nation-state (cf. Postert [ch.6], Arnaut [ch. 7] and Sprenger [ch. 10]).

Germany, however, has been far more widely known as a breeding ground for the brutal National-Socialist dictatorship in the twentieth century than for its achievement of a nation-state in the nineteenth. So what can the German case teach us about the harmfulness of national grammars?

Genocide

National-Socialist ideology was built upon pre-existing cultural themes. With Hitler (born 1889), a new generation came to power, a generation whose parents had grown up in Imperial Germany and who themselves had lived through the 1914–1918 war. The National-Socialists utilized already well-known images and structures of thought. If the three grammars outlined above contained a certain fluidity and ambiguity – the memory of a segmented and 'female' Germany aspiring to 'Western Civilization' had not been eradicated after 1871 – these structures solidified in National-Socialist ideology. As far as inclusion or segmentation is concerned, the alleged existence of only one German nation, even only one German 'race', was underscored. 'Female' aspects of 'German culture' disappeared altogether – official propaganda stressed maleness and toughness. 'Masculine' virtues such as boldness and aggressiveness were to reinvigorate the country, while women were excluded from any positions of responsibility in the party and the state (Evans 1987: 159–62; Mosse 1986: 176). The complex orientalist/occidentalist positions that were to be found in Imperial Germany lost their multivocal character. Hitler is reported to have said that Germans should accept 'barbarians' as a title of honour, testifying to the 'freshness' of the young German nation in a decaying world (Rauschning 1940: 78).[7] In this way, violent political action appeared to be justified: brutality was thought to impress others and to win over new followers of the movement (Rauschning 1940: 80–81).

If one leaves the level of official discourse and looks at everyday life under the National-Socialist regime, another grammatical instance comes into sight. The barbarity of the regime became possible through the dissolution of a tacit 'encompassment' into a brutal 'orientalism'. Victor Klemperer, then Professor of Latinate Philology at Dresden University and a Protestant Christian with a Jewish family background, described this process in his personal diary, one of the best analyses of Nazi language.

Klemperer notes how, as early as 1933, a distinction between 'Germans' and 'Jews' was introduced. At the end of March 1933, shops with a Jewish owner were declared to be 'Jewish'. If the shop was owned jointly by a 'mixed' couple, the Jewish part was supposed to 'encompass' the other one. On 1 April 1933, Klemperer noticed posters in shop windows saying 'recognised German-Christian company' or 'those who buy from Jews [...] destroy the German economy' (Klemperer 1995a: 17–18). In November 1933, when the winter semester started at his university, Klemperer observed that 'Jewish' students had a yellow student card, while 'German' students had been given a brown one (Klemperer 1995a: 66). The principle is the same: 'German' is taken to exclude 'Jewish' by definition. National-Socialist ideology defined the German *Volk*[8] as an entity threatened by 'enemies' and 'parasites' (Klemperer 1995a: 169). The existence of a Jewish *Volk* was a parallel ideological construction, and Klemperer did not fail or cease to stress its National-Socialist parentage (Klemperer 1946/93: 213–27; Klemperer 1995a: 193, 220; Klemperer 1995b: 178). Klemperer himself belonged to the few people who refused the 'German'/'Jewish' orientalism as mutually exclusive. Sensitive to the effects and meanings of language, he used quotation marks around 'Aryan' and indeed 'German' whenever these words were meant to exclude what he considered to be a part of the nation (at least until 1937; he became less systematic with time).

He opposed the vision of two distinct *Völker* (a 'German' and a 'Jewish' one) with another binarism: Germanness as idea, as culture, and as incorporated by a religiously inclusive nation, *vs.* the National-Socialist regime. The Nazis, and not Germans of Jewish origin, were 'un-German' in his view

(Klemperer 1995a: 210). He disapproved of anybody who accepted the propagandistic division between 'Germans' and 'Jews', including German Jews who said that they could not believe anymore that they were 'German', or those who accepted the concept of a 'Jewish nation' (Klemperer 1995a: 102, 220). However, in the course of time, Klemperer developed the view that National-Socialism was to some extent grounded in German culture, and in Romanticism in particular (Klemperer 1995b: 141, 209), and supported or at least not criticized by the majority of the people around him. In moments of profound doubt he felt 'betrayed' and 'homeless' (Klemperer 1995a: 401; entry on 5 April 1938), realising that Hitler was backed by the people and that he had no possibility to emigrate on account of his lacking foreign language skills, his financial situation, and restrictive laws (Klemperer 1995b: 482; entry on 6 February 1944).

Nonetheless, Klemperer emphasized time and again that he was a *German* when talking to other Germans of Jewish origin. Unlike most of his German-Jewish friends who left Germany one after another, sometimes with the justification of feeling 'Jewish and therefore not German', Klemperer himself stayed on until the end, citing a mixture of lack of alternatives and dissent with being classified as non-German.

What makes cultural or national grammars destructive then? Nazi Germany 'recycled' some grammars that were in use before, and enforced at least one new one; for the transformation of Jewish-German encompassment into an extreme Jewish-German orientalism had not been common sense before 1933. What seems distinctive about those potentially aggressive and genocidal grammars is their rigidity: if the national grammars outlined in the first part of this chapter often swung between two poles (e.g., male/female, one nation/many states, barbarity/civilization), any remaining open-endedness was done away with in Nazi ideology. Eric Wolf suggested that societies under increasing stress, in ecological, social, political and/or psychological crises, such as Germany in the early 1930s, would produce extreme ideological formulations (Wolf 1999: 174). Surely the German political system and economy were in crisis in the late 1920s and early 1930s, but there are too many counter-examples of hard-pressed, yet persistently democratic societies to turn to material factors as the only explanation.

After 1933, the new ideological constellation was bolstered by a new 'ethics': the complete Other could not be tolerated, but had to be eradicated from the 'national body'. National Socialism conceived of the nation as having a body and a soul, and thus being strong or weak, healthy or diseased. The list of national 'diseases' was long: syphilis, tuberculosis, democracy, socialism, and the presence of Jews. Characteristically, National Socialism mentioned 'poisons' like democracy and 'parasites' like German Jews in one breath with actual diseases, thus blurring the metaphorical character of such statements (Hitler 1925–26/92: 224). The genocidal character of this kind of 'orientalism' was achieved through applying metaphors drawn from nature to what was believed to be 'German' or 'un-German', together with an 'ethics' that emphasized the struggle for life according to 'nature'. which was meant to legitimate the destruction of everything 'inferior in society'.

The third observation concerns the power of propaganda and the violence of a dictatorial regime. Obviously, dissenting voices were virtually not allowed to be heard in Nazi Germany so that the solidified and reinterpreted grammars described above reigned supreme in the public sphere. Even in private, as Klemperer noticed, many prime victims of Nazi propaganda accepted its premises, such as German Jews denying their Germanness.

Despite a thorough change of political regime and despite all re-education, the grammatical-orientalist opposition between 'Germans' and 'Jews' persists today. Ignaz Bubis, the highest representative of the Jewish community in Germany from 1992 until his death in 1999, spent a major part of his public activity trying to bring the two terms together again. Tellingly, an authorized biography of his bears the title 'I am German national of Jewish religion'. Nevertheless, countless anonymous threatening letters spelled out that as a Jew, he could not be a German, and even officially elected political representatives would ask him for his opinion about the political situation in what they thought must surely be his home country, Israel.

A conclusion that one might draw from these observations is the necessity to encourage critical consciousness about language and the concepts it conveys, as Klemperer so masterfully did in his time. This critical consciousness must necessarily entail a historical dimension, for without a knowledge of their genealogies, seemingly inexplicable otherings (such as the German/Jewish opposition) will not become visible in their full destructive potential.

Notes

1. In 1890, the psychologically unstable 'culture critic' Julius Langbehn (1851–1907) published *Rembrandt als Erzieher* (Rembrandt as [our National] Educator'), a confused diatribe against rationality, objectivity, liberalism, industrialisation, urbanisation, Jews, and contemporary art and literature. The book hit the increasingly nationalist-conservative, pessimistic nerve of the early 1890s; it went into its forty-second edition in 1893.
2. However, the existence of 'Ethno-Occidentalism' (essentialist renderings of the West by members of alien societies) and 'Occidentalism' (the essentialist rendering of the West by Westerners) has been noted by Carrier 1995.
3. Nietzsche's thought was also characterized by a positive re-evaluation of the 'Barbarian'; cf. fragment no. 900 in *The Will to Power* [1885]: 'I point to something new: certainly for such a democratic type there exists the danger of the barbarian, but one has looked for it only from the depths. There exists also another type of barbarian, who comes from the heights: a species of conquering and ruling natures in search of material to mould. Prometheus was this kind of barbarian' (Nietzsche 1906/68: 478–79).
4. Later, about 500 monuments to Bismarck (built between 1900 and 1910) were inspired by the same building (Mosse 1975: 36).
5. In reality, Theoderic was educated at the Byzantine court; modern historians credit the success of his reign in Italy (493-526 AD) to this cross-cultural experience, which allowed him to unite Romans and Goths in one realm quite effortlessly.
6. Incidentally, a parallel with modern Greece can be drawn here as well: Herzfeld analysed that Greeks have internalised the stereotypes of both Europe and the Orient (Herzfeld 1997: 158).
7. Rauschning's notes of Hitler's dicta are reliable as a historical source as long as they are not taken to be verbatim statements. Rauschning, a high NSDAP official in Danzig until his emi-

gration in 1934, noted down some of Hitler's speeches and private conversations from memory (Schieder 1972).
8. As with the word 'nation' in the English language (Williams 1976: 178), two meanings overlap in the German-language notions of *Nation* and *Volk*. Both are used to designate a 'racial group' and/or a 'politically organised grouping'. At the end of the nineteenth century, the German word *Volk* was used far more frequently than *Nation* (a 'foreign' word of Latin origin); *Volk* tends to connote an organically unified community (Koselleck 1992), possibly with a transcendental 'essence' (Mosse 1966: 4). The connotations of *Volk* are comparable to those of *Kultur*, as opposed to the tendentially more mechanical conceptions of *Zivilisation*, *Gesellschaft* or *Nation*.

References

Banton, M. 1998. *Racial Theories*, second edition. Cambridge: Cambridge University Press.
Berliner Illustrierte. 1892-1945. *Berliner Illustrirte Zeitung*. Berlin : Deutscher Verlag.
Bertaux, P. 1962. *La vie quotidienne en Allemagne au temps de Guillaume II en 1900*. Paris: Hachette.
Bülow, P. von. 1930/31a. *Memoirs: Volume I: 1897–1903*, trans. F.A. Voigt. London: Putnam.
——. 1930/31b. *Memoirs: Volume II: 1903–1909*, trans. F.A.Voigt. London: Putnam.
Carrier, James, ed.1995. *Occidentalism: Images of the West*. Oxford: Clarendon Press.
Cole, J.W. and E. Wolf. 1974. *The Hidden Frontier: Ecology and Ethnicity in an Alpine Valley*. New York: Academic Press.
Dahn, F. 1884. *Ein Kampf um Rom: Historischer Roman,* tenth edition. Leipzig: Breitkopf und Härtel.
Dumont, L. 1980. *Homo Hierarchicus: The Caste System and Its Implications: Complete Revised English Edition*, trans. M. Sainsbury, L. Dumont and B. Gulati. Chicago: Chicago University Press.
Elias, N. 1987 [1939]. *The Civilising Process: The History of Manners*. New York: Urizen Books.
Eulenburg, P. zu. 1923. *Aus 50 Jahren: Erinnerungen, Tagebücher und Briefe aus dem Nachlaß des Fürsten Philipp zu Eulenburg-Hertefeld*. Berlin: Verlag von Gebrüder Paetel.
Evans, R. 1987. *Comrades and Sisters: Feminism, Socialism and Pacifism in Europe, 1870–1945*. Brighton: Wheatsheaf Books.
Firchow, P.E. 1986. *The Death of the German Cousin: Variations on a Literary Stereotype, 1890–1920*. Lewisburg: Bucknell University Press.
Frevert, U. 1996. 'Nation, Krieg und Geschlecht im 19. Jahrhundert' in *Nation und Gesellschaft in Deutschland: Historische Essays*, eds. M. Hettling and P. Nolte. München: C.H.Beck, 151–70.
Freytag, G. 1855/1900. *Soll und Haben: Roman in sechs Büchern*, Fifty-third edition. Leipzig: S. Hirzel.
Gartenlaube. 1853-1937: *Die Gartenlaube: Illustrirtes Familienblatt*. Leipzig: Keil.
Herzfeld, M. 1997. *Cultural Intimacy: Social Poetics in the Nation-State*. New York: Routledge.
Hitler, A. 1992 [1925–26]. *Mein Kampf*, trans. R.Manheim. London: Pimlico.
Jeismann, M. 1992. *Das Vaterland der Feinde: Studien zum nationalen Feindbegriff und Selbstverständnis in Deutschland und Frankreich 1792–1918*. Stuttgart: Klett-Cotta.

Klemperer, V. 1946/93. *LTI: Notizbuch eines Philologen.* Leipzig: Reclam.
——. 1995a. *Ich will Zeugnis ablegen bis zum letzten: Tagebücher 1933–1941.* Darmstadt: Wissenschaftliche Buchgesellschaft.
——. 1995b. *Ich will Zeugnis ablegen bis zum letzten: Tagebücher 1942–1945.* Darmstadt: Wissenschaftliche Buchgesellschaft.
Koselleck, R. 1992. '"Volk", "Nation", "Nationalismus" und "Masse" 1914–1945' in *Geschichtliche Grundbegriffe: Historisches Lexikon zur politisch-sozialen Sprache in Deutschland, Vol.7*, eds. O. Bruner, W. Conze & R. Koselleck. Stuttgart: Klett-Cotta, 389–420.
Langbehn, J. 1890/93. *Rembrandt als Erzieher: Von einem Deutschen,* forty-second edition. Leipzig: C.L. Hirschfeld.
Marlitt, E. 1878. *Goldelse,* ninth edition. Leipzig: Ernst Keil.
McClintock, A. 1995. *Imperial Leather: Race, Gender and Sexuality in the Colonial Contest.* New York: Routledge.
Mosse, G.L. 1966. *The Crisis of German Ideology: Intellectual Origins of the Third Reich.* London: Weidenfeld and Nicolson.
——. 1975. *The Nationalization of the Masses: Political Symbolism and Mass Movements in Germany from the Napoleonic Wars Through the Third Reich.* New York: Howard Fertig.
——. 1980. *Masses and Man: Nationalist and Fascist Perceptions of Reality.* New York: Howard Fertig.
——. 1986. *Nationalism and Sexuality: Respectability and Abnormal Sexuality in Modern Europe.* New York: Howard Fertig.
——. 1996. *The Image of Man: The Creation of Modern Masculinity.* Oxford: Oxford University Press.
Müller, K.A. von, ed. 1931. *Fürst Chlodwig zu Hohenlohe-Schillingsfürst: Denkwürdigkeiten der Reichskanzlerzeit.* Stuttgart: Deutsche Verlags-Anstalt.
Nietzsche, F. 1906/68 [1885]. *The Will to Power,* trans. W. Kaufmann and R.J. Hollingdale. London: Weidenfeld and Nicolson.
Raulet, G. 1992. 'Esprit/Geist' in: *Esprit / Geist: 100 Schlüsselbegriffe für Deutsche und Franzosen,* second edition, ed. J. Leenhardt and R. Picht. München: Piper, 148–59.
Rauschning, H. 1940. *Gespräche mit Hitler.* New York: Europa Verlag.
Reinhardt, V. 1992. 'Der Primat der Innerlichkeit und die Probleme des Reiches: Zum deutschen Nationalgefühl der frühen Neuzeit' in *Deutschland in Europa: Ein historischer Rückblick,* ed. B. Martoin. München: dtv, 88–104.
Schieder, T. 1972. *Hermann Rauschnings 'Gespräche mit Hitler' als Geschichtsquelle.* Opladen: Westdeutscher Verlag.
Stern, F. 1972. *The Failure of Illiberalism.* London: George Allen & Unwin.
Thiesse, A.-M. 1998. *La création des identités nationales: Europe XVIII–XXe siècle.* Paris: Seuil.
Weber, M. 1976 [1926]. *Max Weber: A Biography.* New York: John Wiley & Sons.
Werner, M. 1994. 'La Germanie de Tacite et l'originalité allemande', *Le Débat* 78, 42–61.
Williams, R. 1976. *Keywords: A Vocabulary of Culture and Society.* London: Fontana/Croom Helm.
Wolf, E.R. 1999. *Envisioning Power: Ideologies of Dominance and Crisis.* Berkeley: University of California Press.

Chapter 5

Alterity as Celebration, Alterity as Threat

A Comparison of Grammars between Brazil and Denmark

Inger Sjørslev

This contribution will explore mechanisms of cultural denigration and social exclusion. To this purpose, I shall try out the grammars within two national contexts, those of Brazil and Denmark. The main advantage of the grammars appears to lie in enabling a better understanding of the processes that create exclusion, intolerance, new forms of racism, and ultimately conflict and violence.

My choice of Brazil and Denmark might indicate that I want to compare incomparable units or even units that cannot be clearly defined: after all, who believes in uniform national characters (Neiburg and Goldman 1997)? I propose, however, that it is possible to identify certain cultural models, metaphors and conceptions of collective selfing that characterize dominant ideas in the two countries respectively. I also think it is important to improve our tools for understanding how identity politics and cultural politics work in relation to ideas about rights and citizenship, and what consequences such ideas may have in terms of inclusion or exclusion and unequal treatment. The aim in comparing the two countries is thus to sharpen our analytic tools to understand some of the concrete actions and practices we find in each.

Brazil is my fieldwork area where, in the 1980s and 1990s, I worked on Afro-Brazilian religion, which directed my attention towards the celebration of alterity and also led my interests towards racial politics. Denmark, my home country, is where I read the daily papers and watch television: here, I regard current political developments with deepest concern, particularly the tightening of immigration laws and the popularity of the party that promotes new racism in the disguise of protecting 'Danish culture'. It is in this context that the following is partly based on a recent study performed by ten students who did fieldwork in immigrant organisations and within the Danish Parliament (Schwartz 2002; Nielsen and Sjørslev 2002). For me, the idea of the grammars has inspired quite a new examination of these findings. Together with the comparative glance at Brazilian cultural, racial-political and performative practices, these new insights point towards a dominant Danish folk model of self-understanding: in a nutshell, it can be characterized as one of 'sameness as celebration', as opposed to 'alterity as celebration' which, as I shall argue, characterizes Brazil. The grammars will serve to identify and analyse those structural relations that underlie modes of thinking in the two countries respectively. Through these empirical cases I shall try to show how grammars coexist, intersect and sometimes counterbalance one another. Furthermore, I shall propose that grammars may also work to hide conflicts and to 'lie' about reality, thus preventing substantial changes of that reality – a reality that in both countries implies discrimination and exclusion, albeit in different ways.

Brazil: The Complexity of Grammars

In the case of Brazil, I shall combine an examination of racial politics and cultural politics with a brief glance at alterity/otherness in Afro-Brazilian religion. Brazilian racial politics present what may be called a celebration of mixture. Historically, Brazil is known for its 'happy' inbreeding, 'light' slavery and relatively unproblematic 'mixture of races', as opposed to the hard and conflict-ridden confrontations of North America. I shall not go into the historical validity of these ideas, or rather, into their implausibility. The point is that these views have become an important part of Brazilian national self-understanding, notably through the work of Gilberto Freyre, and that they influence racial politics as they are today. Another historical phenomenon of interest in this context is the (racist) ideology, current in late nineteenth-century Brazil, of 'whitening', *branqueamento* (Skidmore 1974). It indicates that the Brazilian elite accepted the racist theory of white superiority, but at the same time implicitly denied the absoluteness of racial differences. The results were fluid conceptions of 'race' which lived on far into this century and influence popular ideas to this day. The racist theories of the nineteenth century implied that through intermarriage, the blood of the blacks of Brazil, the descendants of the slaves, would over time be 'thinned out' through miscegenation, resulting in a 'race' that was, at the most, light brown: a Luso-tropical meta-race and a truly Brazilian race as it was imagined. The idea of the biological disappearance of the black race by its subsumption into the white race may be regarded as encompassement in a most extreme and literal form, a total subsumption through bodily interaction and through a twisted search for more purity (Gilroy 2002). In contemporary Brazilian practices, we recognize the ideas of intermixture in the celebration of *mulattas*, in the national self-understanding as it is celebrated in carnival, and in the myth of racial democracy. The nation is to see itself as founded upon the harmonious intermixture of races, a happy cultural syncretism, and a 'taking the best of different cultural worlds'. The national symbol and celebration of this project is carnival. I shall return below to the celebration of alterity that carnival implies.

There has been a passionate debate, over recent years, among researchers of racial and cultural politics in Brazil about the consequences of the specific historical ideas with relation to 'race'. It may be briefly summarized as a question: do cultural phenomena like Afro-Brazilian religions, carnival, black music and other practices with strong elements of black culture represent black power in any form? Or are they, on the contrary, confined to the cultural sphere, thus contributing to the pacification of the political potential of blacks in Brazil (Hanchard 1994; Segato 1998). As anthropologist Rita Segato says, in Brazil 'the ethnic paradigm is based on encompassing the other, inclusion is its strong motif, and the myth here is the color-blind myth of an interrelating people' (Segato 1998: 137). The paradigm of inclusion is the tool of the dominant (white) society. Afro-Brazilian religions, on the other hand, are not racialised and can thus not be transformed into racial politics. This is not, as political scientist Michael Hanchard (1994) would understand it, a sign of weakness, but on the contrary, is to be regarded as a strength.The philosophy of these religious codes resists racialisation 'because it perceives itself as bigger than race and aspires to universality. Significantly, it perceives itself as encompassing, embracing the white' (Segato 1998: 143–44). Encompassement thus works from both sides. The white hegemony works through encompassement as expressed in the myth of racial democracy, and the Afro-Brazilian religious orthodoxy on the other hand claims universality of its religion and thus claims that their culture encompasses white culture.

We see here how a grammar of encompassement is prevalent at different levels and within different spheres of Brazilian society. The point is that although there is much truth in Segato's analysis, cultural politics as a whole may present an even more complex picture. The intermingling relations between racial politics, religion, cultural manifestations, the politics of culture and the culture of politics (as formulated by Alvares et al.1998) may be illuminated even further by way of the grammars.

In order to see which kind of grammar works to maintain exclusion mechanisms, we have briefly to move into politics. In spite of the last fifteen years of democratization and five years of leadership by a social democrat, Brazil still suffers from a dominant political culture of authoritarianism, the impact of which is felt in popular conceptions of what democracy can do. As formulated by Caldera, '...the limits of democratisation are deeply embedded in popular conceptions of the body, punishment, and individual rights' (Caldera quoted in Alvares et al. 1998: 13). Brazilian conceptions of civil society are marked by a lack of differentiation between the public and the private in the sense of a differentiation between the loyalty given to one's nearest and the loyalty owed to a larger social unit. Boundaries are blurred, or rather, the public is appropriated into the private sphere, and political relations are perceived as extensions of private relations (Alvares et al. 1998: 13). Favouritism, personalism, clientelism, and paternalism are thus part of regular political practices. In combination with such myths as the purported racial democracy, these practices serve to obscure inequality, they strongly contribute to marginalization, and this marginalization can lead to extreme forms of social exclusion. When in the 1960s and 1970s military regimes emerged throughout much of the Latin American continent, an exacerbated authoritarianism transformed political exclusion into political elimination through state repression and systemic violence (Alvares et al. 1998: 10). This was a period of open repression, and political opponents were imprisoned, tortured, or exiled. In Brazil, these extremes ended with the fall of the military regime in the 1980s, but social exclusion continues in other forms.

In the historical ideas about race, we can identify a grammar of encompassement based upon orientalist thinking. There are the 'them' and the 'us', and the perspective is a white one – that of the Portuguese and other Western colonizers. The 'them' are Black people, slaves, and Indians, and they are 'other' but they are also to be turned into 'us', that is, to be incorporated, as expressed in the ideology of 'whitening', into a Brazilian race and a nation characterized by cultural inclusion and mixture. Considering Brazilian racial politics today, there is no doubt that these ideas have created extreme inequality on the social level, while culturally celebrating alterity as the 'spice' that would create a particularly charming and aesthetically pleasant (racial) 'us'. Socially, Brazil is an extremely polarized country, and the one concept that reveals exclusion mechanisms in quite explicit ways is the conception of 'marginals' (*marginais*). These are very concrete 'others' in Brazilian social life. They are social others, and according to the most extreme current ideas, they should be exorcised to purify Brazil and establish it as an altogether developed and civilized nation. The marginals are street children and petty criminals, though not the big criminals such as the *trafficantes* of drugs, and the inhabitants of the slums as well as the starving immigrants from the poor north. To some, the category includes the Indians, who are considered a hindrance to the economic development of the Amazon Basin and an obstacle to the whole of the country on its path to modernity (Ramos 1998).

In the prevalent idea of *marginais* we encounter a social grammar of the orientalist kind, which locates otherness in the poor and in those who are outside modernity and considered unable to enter it. It is justified by pointing to cultural tolerance in other spheres by way of the encompassing grammar, and it is furthermore supported by the kind of exclusion mechanisms known from political life. Exclusion on the basis of race, however, is an idea conspicuously absent from Brazilian self-understandings. Brazilians do not, in general, see themselves as racists. Racism is confined to South Africa and the United States, which in this respect are the suitable 'others' (Rosa-Ribeiro 2000). Yet there is still a considerable concordance between being poor and being black. Social exclusion in this respect turns into racial discrimination in disguise.

To understand better how these mechanisms of social exclusion actually work, it is useful to examine social relations and certain processes within civil society with an eye upon the relation between the public and the private. It will become apparent that, paradoxically, mechanisms of exclusion also work by way of inclusion or encompassement.

Brazilian anthropologist Roberto Da Matta (1997) has coined the metaphorical terms 'home' and 'street' for the private and the public sphere, respectively. Each of these spheres is reigned by its own ethos. 'Home' is characterized by paternalism, personal relationships, informality, family and friendship relations, and the conception of the person as – precisely – a 'person', rather than an 'individual'. The 'street', on the other hand, is the sphere of contractual relations, of the formal Constitution, the egalitarian code, and the conception of the 'individual' or the 'citizen'. Citizenship indicates treatment on the basis of the law rather than personal relations. Da Matta emphasizes that there is a constant moving back and forth between the two spheres. They exist side by side and complement each other in a manner that creates a fair degree of complexity. The ethos of each of the spheres can be manipulated, and social dramas arise from the two conflicting concepts of the person and the citizen. This can happen, for instance, when a representative of the authorities – within the street sphere - treats a person according to the law and the rules of equality, but the person refers to his or her position within the hierarchical social system in which what you are is who you are related to: family and other relations within the home sphere (DaMatta 1997). There may be good reasons to be sceptical of this rather simplified model of Brazilian social and public life. DaMatta has been criticized for applying a point of view which is biased by a (white) middle class perspective. He does not take into account the point of view from below. Here, however, his argument, heavily influenced by the ideas of Louis Dumont, is a very productive one when seeking a better understanding of how exclusion mechanisms work. Da Matta observes how the 'home' ethos takes precedence over the 'street' ethos, and one may indeed argue that the home sphere in some ways encompasses the sphere of the street.

The concept of the citizen is, in fact, sometimes used pejoratively: *aquele cidadao*, 'this or that citizen', is a term applied to someone in an inferior position. The universalist, distanciated, formal treatment indicated by designating someone as *cidadao* signifies a lack of will to solve whatever business one has with that person in any other than the formal way. It means imposing the rules, the law, and not, as is otherwise the positive cultural rule, to use a *jeitinho* (lit. 'the little skill' – diminutive of *jeito*, the knack or skill of doing something). To use a *jeitinho* means fixing the problem in a friendly manner, as for instance with a policeman thus induced to overlook a traffic offence. It entails establishing a social relation of familiarity and friendship, however temporary, and to find a solution on that basis. To invoke the universal law, on the other hand, is regarded as a negative form of treatment, and the 'citizen' is the one who is subject to the law. The different ethos that characterizes each sphere can thus be consciously manipulated to one's own ends, although some are certainly better equipped to manipulate it than others. One way of achieving this is identified by Alvares et al. (1998) as a strategy shared by elites throughout Latin America, and that is to establish mechanisms for 'a *subordinated form of political inclusion*, in which their own personalised relations with political leaders ensured control and tutelage over a heterogeneous popular participation' (Alvares et al. 1998: 9, my emphasis).

Inclusion must thus be understood both in the general cultural sense as illustrated previously, and in the political sense of manipulating the ethos of the street sphere through that of the home sphere: inclusion cannot be isolated from its opposite, exclusion. Social exclusion, it may be safely stated, is ultimately connected with the ideas and conceptions of what a person, an individual, and a citizen is. In Brazil, individualism is often regarded as something negative, directed against the cultural rules that define and spring from the totality (Da Matta 1997: 76). The community is heterogeneous, complementary and hierarchical, and since its basic units are regarded neither as individuals nor as citizens, but rather as persons rooted in families and groups of relatives and friends, an isolated individual is regarded with suspicion and prone to be understood as a *marginal*.

Speaking in terms of the grammars, this points towards an understanding of exclusion mechanisms by way of an encompassing grammar that subsumes the 'street' ethos under the 'home' ethos. A grammar of encompassment is a forcefull hegemonic tool. In the Brazilian case it can, as we have seen, be detected at different levels of society and within different spheres. In cultural politics, encompassment further illustrates how hegemony works. A good example can be seen in 'the theft of carnival'.

In the poor suburbs, or *favelas*, of Rio de Janeiro, the black communities that have for years been the main actors and the stars of the world-famous Rio carnival, now feel excluded from it. After it was moved to the *Sambódromo*, an architectural construction in the centre of the city, and with the increasing commercialisation and medialisation of the event, it now excludes those who were once the carriers of its vibrant cultural syncretism based on black rhythmic music. Many of them simply cannot afford what it takes to get dressed up and to enter the samba schools. At the same time, white middle-class people are moving in, paying their way into the samba-schools and taking on conspicuous roles in the parades (Sheriff 1999). Thirty years ago, Colin Henfry (1972) showed how hegemony worked to transform the samba groups of Bahia, the *blocos* and *afoxés* ; now it appears that this process has been speeded up and produced concrete exclusion as a result. The performances themselves, carnival, *afoxés*, *blocos* and others related to the Afro-Brazilian religions, represent a grammar of their own, as we shall see. The ways in which the social and economic contexts for the performances have been taken over, however, by the wealthy and the middle-class, and how the cultural substance of the performances was thus incorporated into the dominant system of economic and social relations, betrays a strong hegemonic mechanism based on a grammar of encompassment.

Let me now turn to a movement in a different direction, a counter-hegemonic movement directed towards universalization and citizenship. As I shall argue, it is characterized more strongly by a segmentary grammar.

In a research project on racial and ethnic politics within the black movement, as revealed through the development of an Afro-Brazilian musical group, Brazilian anthropologist Olivia Maria Gomes da Cunha (1998) has shown how the organizing strategies of a black movement shifted from a 'politics of identity' to a kind of political force. The case concerns a group that started out as a local, community-based cultural and musical initiative, organized around the preparations for carnival. Having become involved in the politics surrounding and redefining carnival, the group aimed at transforming itself into an NGO or non-governmental organization. Its objective was to engage in local and regional struggles to improve living conditions in specific neighbourhoods, as well as to develop its own educational business. The steps of this transformation are telling. While in the beginning, the group's music was strictly connected with the drums of the Candomblé, it now introduced reggae. This choice incorporated a vision of what must be called 'modernity', for it opposed the limits of 'tradition' and set against them the musical expressions, urban lifestyles, and political ideas that had been adopted internationally by young blacks (Da Cunha 1998: 235).

The group called itself GCAR, *Grupo Cultural Afro Reggae*, and began to describe itself as an NGO; it detached itself from its strictly local basis, and the community from which it originated was regarded as an emblem rather than a territorial confinement. In the years to follow, other such groups were founded as part of the black movement, and they went further still in distancing themselves from specific local communities and from the prevalent ethos that some of them understood as an essentialist version of black identity. Da Cunha interprets this development as a strategy to legitimate other types of partnerships and engagement with NGOs and institutions (1998: 239). When seen in the light of the grammars, the crucial point in these developments arises from another of her observations. The rationale of these initiatives was recontextualised by way of the notion of citizenship or *cidadania* (Da Cunha 1998: 241). The references to citizenship may, in Da Cunha's interpretation, have to do with an effort to escape the 'logic of identity' and to call attention to other kinds of identity that are defined differently. Speaking in terms of the grammars, an escape from this essentialised 'logic of identity' into the discourse of citizenship signals an even greater departure. It can then be seen as a project to escape from the encompassment by hegemonic definitions of 'identity' into a segmentary grammar of equal and self-defined citizenship.

This case of 'universalizing' the politics of a cultural movement throws a new light on the question how the grammars are operated. Groups that started out with a clear local, cultural and territorial basis and a logic of identity which left them open to cultural encompassment by hegemonic elites developed towards a more universalist code, a code one may call more street-oriented in DaMatta's terms. This can be regarded as a movement away from the (hegemonic) positioning within an encompassing grammar which automatically links (Afro-Brazilian) cultural expressions with certain communities, and ties them up with certain notions of person and cultural identity. The universalization aimed at by the group thus represents a move towards a more explicitly segmentary grammar – with the segmentary grammar being regarded as the closest to democratic ideals and ideas about equality and equal citizenship. Admittedly, citizenship implies a certain degree of loyalty to the state that defines and confers it, and the idea certainly implies disciplinary forces that are sometimes directly employed by state agents. At the same time, however, citizenship implies equality, solidarity, and a shared identification under an 'umbrella' of recognition of equal rights. Beneath this umbrella, there will be a variety of alliances, often temporary and founded on different criteria of solidarity and different cultural identifications. Yet the move from a specific cultural identification, for instance as 'black', to an emphasis on citizenship can be a move out of the confinement of encompassment.

This said, it would be wrong to idealize or idolize the benefits of citizenship in the nation-state and to ignore the romantic and ethnicist heritage of the concept of the nation. It would be just as wrong to parallel a segmentary order as proposed by Evans-Pritchard (1940) for the acephalous polity of the Nuer with the idea of citizenship in modern pluralist societies. Baumann (1999) rightly criticizes the fallacy to view multi-ethnic societies as aggregates of quasi-corporate 'groups', and I must emphasize here that the segmentary grammar should not be understood in this way. Rather, the move of the Afro-Reggae group from the encompassment logic of cultural identification as blacks towards the idea of equal citizenship should be regarded as a move away from any communalist version of culture (Baumann 1999: 97–106). Citizenship entails rights, indeed equal rights, and the concept of rights works best within a segmentary grammar, especially when there are different, shifting, and intersecting cultural and ethnic identifications at work. I shall return to this point when discussing the grammars in the Danish context.

It will be evident from the Brazilian data that the three grammars do not work, and are not operated, in isolation from each other. Grammars are used concurrently, are made to intersect, and are played one against the other at different levels and within different spheres of social and cultural life. Trying them out in the Brazilian case was to throw a new light on the extremely complex problem of cultural inclusion and social (as well as, effectively, racist) exclusion. We may now increase this complexity by addressing the performative dimension which Brazil is so rightly famous for: ranging from the religions of possession to carnival, we shall examine the complexities of performance that throw light on a seemingly paradoxical question: what is it that maintains a system of such obvious and extreme marginalization and injustice, and that at the same time confirms an indisputable kernel of truth in its self-conception as a strong and rich culture that celebrates the alterity represented by the Indian, and in particular the African, elements in the country?

The answer, I propose, is twofold. There is an underlying grammar of orientalism which leads to marginalization and exclusion at the systemic level. At the same time, however, there is a grammar of encompassment which is expressed performatively and may perhaps be related to the ideas about aesthetics voiced by Baumann in this volume. Of these performances, Afro-Brazilian religion is one, music another, and carnival may stand as the epitome of such celebrations of alterity on the basis of ideas that imply a grammar of encompassement: that the 'other' is basically 'us' or enriching a cultural self. The grammar of encompassement as expressed in cultural performance neutralizes the negative aspects of the silent but palpable orientalization of 'others', and in that sense it counterbalances the mechanisms of exclusion. At the same time, and one may almost say, dialectically, it may also work as a legitimization of the hegemonic Brazilian self-understanding as a harmonious non-racist nation and thus reconfirm the hegemonic power structures.

Carnival is a classic performance of encompassement, and it may also be seen as 'ternary' in the classic sense of the term. Carnival in general is the epitome of liminality, or, in complex societies, of the liminoid according to Turner (1986). In Brazil, carnival is a huge encompassing performance. As grammar, it represents othering in the classic sense of role reversals: men dress as women, decent women dress as whores, the clown becomes king, and so on. As a celebration of alterity, carnival is both the celebration of the 'inner' other, as I shall argue ritual possession is in other ways, and the national celebration of the various 'alterities' that combine to the quality of *amor*, the love, joy and pride of the country.

The point about the grammar expressed in performance can be further illustrated by the performance of ritual possession in the Afro-Brazilian religions (Sjørslev 1999). Here we find an even clearer expression of alterity as celebration. Possession is the epitome of this, as we know from Michael Taussig's work *Mimesis and Alterity* (1993) as well as from other works on African religions (Kramer 1987; Boddy 1989). In Afro-Brazilian religion, the possessing spirits are the 'others' *par excellence*, but here, a whole variety of othernesses is expressed, ranging from historical through cultural to social others: African gods, Indian spirits, social marginals like prostitutes, petty thieves and *Nordestinos*, the immigrants from the poor Brazilian north: a miscellaneous group of otherwise non-related social categories but with the common trait of being socially marginal or culturally and historically others. To analyse this in term of the grammars requires all three grammars at once. Orientalism forms the basis; encompassement is the temporary aim, as during possession the self in the most literal sense encompasses the Other; and the segmentary grammar resides in the sort of performative solidarity with those others that in 'real life' one looks down upon as slaves, prostitutes, or blacks.

My idea of including the performance of ritual possession in the comparison is to make one point, namely that the phenomenon of performative celebration of alterity as such, can be seen as a ternary, i.e., as a mediation within a context of differences that would otherwise have an even stronger potential of leading to unequal treatment, suppression, denigration and discrimination. To put it somewhat flippantly, ritual possession – and of course carnival – are good for you! They may not do away with exclusion, discriminatory practices and racism, but they mediate dealing with otherness in ways that prevent an implosion of structures leading to violence. As I shall argue later when comparing the Danish context, performative celebrations of alterity represent an antithesis to the type of encompassment which works on ideas of identity conceived of as a permanent interior state of being 'us'. Ritual possession, by contrast, revolves around the performative dimension, the acting-out of otherness in a celebratory rather than a suppressive way. One may thus approach these ritualized forms of possession in the classical manner of 'pacifying rituals' (Gluckman 1962), although one will certainly need a more elaborate analysis of how they work than is possible within a structural-functionalist paradigm. The analysis of grammars may very well offer a tool for this.

In saying this, I take a somewhat different interpretative route than the one presented by Fernando Rosa-Ribeiro (2000) in his otherwise very convincing description of Brazil as 'the mimetic nation'. He has gone further than Taussig (1993) in showing that in Brazil, national identity is predicated on a powerful mimetic exchange between whites and non-whites. In the movement described by Taussig's 'mimesis and alterity', the white racial identity is predicated upon a mimetic exchange with non-whites, and vice versa. The inclusive character of Brazilian culture is a powerful paradigm when combined with 'the fable of the three races', that is, the myth that Brazil was created as a nation on the basis of a peaceful co-existence (*co-vivencia*) of whites, blacks and Indians. This 'empire of mimesis' creates 'a hegemonic discourse that tries to incorporate and dilute all difference' (Rosa-Ribeiro 2000: 224). The nation is thus built upon a *mythòi*, a sacredness of the nation and its history, and this history is one of mimesis. Rosa-Ribeiro calls his country an anthropologist's paradise, littered as it is with 'rituals, religious forms, imagery feasts and festivals where everybody more or less mimetised everybody else' (Rosa-Ribeiro 2000: 229). Carnival, of course, tops it all as an example of 'mimesis run amok'. Rosa-Ribeiro characterizes it as 'a system that seems open and inclusive, and that shuns radical alterity perhaps as much as it does complete sameness' (2000: 229).

As fine a characterization of 'the mimetic nation' as this may be, we may detect a slightly different picture when viewing it through the lens of the grammars. It seems to me that the delight in playing with alterity revealed in these performative practices is, like the mimetic possession in Afro-Brazilian religion, a way of celebrating alterity which should be understood as a, usually temporary, encompassment placed within an overall segmentary grammar. As I have already hinted at with 'the theft of carnival' above, one needs here to examine the setting, the very 'framework', as Bateson (1972) used the term, to analyse these performances in terms of inclusion and exclusion. Bateson's analysis stressed how it was the frame that determined how that which is framed was to be understood. There is indeed a grammar of encompassment set to work within the frame of carnival. Yet by its very performative quality, its explicit and deliberate demonstration, indeed impersonation of alterity, the mimetic celebration of alterity achieves an inclusivist encompassment, rather than creating exclusive consequences as in other encompassing grammars. To understand what is going on here, we again have to look at the combination of different grammars working at different levels simultaneously.

In the case of Brazil, there are thus different combinations of grammars intersecting within the cultural realm, the social-political realm, and the performative realm. It is their interactions in context which determine the general outcome in terms of inclusion and exclusion. Grammars as enacted within the performative realm represent a positive dealing with alterity, and in the contexts of carnival and possession cults the total combination may be viewed as segmentary: identities and alterities are, in the performative realm, determined according to context. By the same token, the Afro-Reggae musicians' aim of transcending the 'logic of identity' as essentialised 'cultural groups' by appealing to the values of equal citizenship may be regarded as a move towards a segmentary grammar. In the performative realm, there are clear signposts towards an escape from the encompassing grammar that characterizes hegemonic Brazilian ideas of encompassing 'the other'.

The realms of 'cultural' and 'racial' politics, by contrast, revolve around a grammar of hierarchical encompassment. This grammar may be seen as having reached its breaking point. Two grammars are pitched against it. On the one hand, there is the segmentary grammar of equal citizenship. On the other side, there waits the orientalist grammar of exclusion imposed upon the heterogeneous category of 'the marginals'. It is but a short way from this orientalist grammar to the anti-grammar of radical exclusion, as has been demonstrated by some well-documented and organized killings of whole groups of street children. But might it be that the performative realm, in some ways the special gift of this 'mimetic nation', has more to offer to 'cultural' and 'racial' politics than meets the eye? 'Pacifying function' or not, the performative realm has shown a far greater grammatical flexibility towards, and commitment to, 'the other' than was ever predefined in the powerful discourses of 'racial' and 'cultural' politics in Brazil.

Denmark: Hidden Grammars and the Aim of Simplicity

Let me bridge the transatlantic gulf by way of an anecdote. Speaking to a conference organizer (though not an anthropologist) recently, I heard about the 'well-known tactic of 'conference-crashing' by which 'economic refugees' were said to procure visas to rich countries, and my interlocutor flatly stated that people from Ghana and Nigeria were particularly suspect and thus hardly ever let in. She started her explanation by announcing: 'One must not be a racist, but...' Not long ago, she would have said: 'I am not a racist, but...'.

In Denmark, one can indeed observe a sliding effect in what people will allow themselves to say in public. Yet most Danes, like most Brazilians, firmly believe themselves to be a tolerant, non-racist people. This self-conception may very well come from the fact that Denmark has had little occasion to deal with 'racial' differences for most of its history. The self-conception does not, however, conform with Danish reality as we know it today, and this will be clear to anyone who reads human rights reports on the problem of racism in Denmark.[1]

In presenting some Danish versions of the grammars that all have implications for mechanisms of exclusion and inclusion, the first and most widespread is a grammar of encompassment. It is based upon consensus, agreement, unity and equality, but it also relies upon closure in the form of sociality, and its encompassing elements encourage the kind of new racist thinking that is at stake here. It is exemplified by the Danish People's Party (*Dansk Folkeparti*) which has gained much popularity within recent years and received 12 per cent of the votes in the parliamentary elections of November 2001, giving it 22 out of 179 members of the Danish Parliament. As I shall argue, this prevalent grammar of encompassment implies that all forms of alterity which cannot be encompassed are regarded as a threat, and the grammar thus has immediate consequences for the treatment of concrete others such as foreigners and immigrants.

This grammar of encompassment is in action in the most diverse aspects of social life. It was in evidence even when documenting the ideas held by Danish parliamentarians (Nielsen and Sjørslev 2002). These were not necessarily their own ideas, but evidently ideas that they thought their electors held, and thus ideas that they felt they had to take into consideration and deal with. At the same time, the grammar of encompassment can be recognized in the ways in which people run their civil society associations and organizations and in the particular cultural phenomenon best characterized by anthropologist Anne Knudsen (1996). Knudsen singles out a physical metaphor as a model of, or even a model for, Danish conventions about social life, and she calls it the idea of 'sitting down and talking about it'. Sitting down, preferably around a table and thus with faces turned inward, makes it clear who is inside and who is outside, and it relieves us of the unease we feel towards ambiguous identities. It is not easy to enter or even get access to such a group, as the group turns its back on those outside and faces inward towards itself (Knudsen 1996: 14). The norms of equality and seeking consensus lead, here, to inward inclusion and outward exclusion. Karen Salomon and Lisa Goldschmidt (1992), who studied Danish folk models, found a strong emphasis on consensus, agreement, unity and 'sameness' in the way in which people formed associations, clubs, unions, and organizations to manifest political agreement, be it to work for a public cause or just to cultivate a shared private hobby.[2] 'Basically, we all agree', was the headline of these forms of sociality. Such ideas represent the models for participation in Danish culture, and immigrants and foreigners are confronted with them in negative ways. I will sum up this Danish folk model, as we may cautiously call it, as a celebration of sameness. Democratic principles are based not only upon equality in the face of the law, but on the sameness of a certain life style (Koch 1981 [1945]), on common shared values and a strong emphasis on dialogue. We have to be able to sit down and talk about it, and basically we will then find that we all agree.

The epitome of sameness as celebration is the well-known Danish idea of *hygge*, perhaps best translatable as a 'cosy being together'. It implicates an inviting physical environment, comfortable chairs – for like a conversation, *hygge* is best achieved by sitting down - and often a lighted candle or two as the symbol to activate what Edwin Ardener called Danish domesticity (Ardener 1992: 26).[3] Ardener saw this candle as one of the symbols that do not have meaning in itself, but without which something *else* would be rendered without meaning. This something else is what he calls a D-structure: a pattern of accepted behaviour, and of rules invisible to the participants themselves, which nonetheless silently dominate behavioural patterns. These behavioural patterns include the treatment of strangers. They determine what strangers are allowed to do, although they always operate under the common idea that there are no rules at all and that anything is allowed. While Ardener does not mention the idea of *hygge* in this context, it is safe to say that most Danes understand the candle as both epitome and catalyst of *hygge*. The very light that the candle shines upon all alike contributes to an encompassing grammar of 'sameness' and the dominant structures behind it. It seems, as Ardener says, to 'merge into a consistent inner world view' which equals Danishness with domesticity. At the same time, it makes it difficult for Danes to formulate their own identity. The passionate debates, in recent years, about Danishness and the way in which these were related to the necessity to keep foreigners out, seem to have proven Ardener's *impromptu* observation. The salient point here is that *hygge* implies an absence of conflict: it does not go well with quarrels, disagreements or even passionate discussions. Rather, *hygge* spells silent complicity with each other's points of view, or at least a shared suppression of potential disagreements. This agreement to suppress disagreements often comes as a puzzle to foreigners and immigrants, not least when they try to participate in political life (Schwartz 1985; 2002).

In a recent study on young immigrants' participation in political associations, some of the informants expressed this vividly. One of them, asked why so many had difficulties in participating in political discussions, answered: 'There are certain frames, broad frames that are pre-determined' (Iversen in Schwartz 2002). She might have added: frames and frameworks (Bateson 1972) that are implicit, not spoken about, and taken for granted in silence. These frames and conventions on how to negotiate, how to talk, and how to reach agreement seem to impede immigrants' participation in Danish politics as well as society. On the whole, the findings of this research project point to the fact that the overall Danish paradigm is one of an encompassing integration: immigrants must become like 'us', like the Danish majority who are already 'inside'. This vision of 'Danishness' builds upon a Western doctrine of truth, that is closely related to Protestant Pietistic values. True feelings lie in the *inner self*, and in an inner core of sincerity and authenticity. Schiffauer et al. (2003) have presented a similar interpretation in the case of German 'civil culture', and there may even be a connection here. Hal Koch's (1981 [1945]) seminal book *What is Democracy?* dates from the year of Denmark's liberation from Nazi occupation. Koch, an eminent Lutheran theologian, educator, and public debater at the time, remains an authoritative influence on Danish ideas about democracy to this day. The universalist thinking he advocated in his book is based on a folk model of consensus, but it also emphasizes the quality of sameness. Democracy, so he argues, cannot be reduced to a political system or enclosed in a juridical form, but is to be understood as a form of life which is to be developed through four achievements: awaking (*vækkelse*), enlightenment (*folkeoplysning*), education and upbringing (*opdragelse*). Conversing without conflict, *samtalen*, (lit. 'to speak with each other') is the key norm here, and this, together with mutual respect and understanding, is regarded as the true basis of democracy.

While, no wonder, this way of thinking had great impact in the years just after the Nazi occupation of Denmark, it is still dominant in an implicit and taken-for-granted way today. This has immediate consequences not only for the Danes and 'their' immigrants, but also for an examination of the grammars here discussed. These consequences appear the more clearly when Koch goes on to say that the new Danish Constitution is to be understood as 'the sum of human experience', and that people have thus to be 'democratised, formed, shaped and educated' (an anthropologist might have said: socialized anew.)

We may conclude that this kind of political thinking, influenced by Hal Koch's ideas about democracy, sees it as something ingrained in people's personality. One of the researchers on the project on immigrant political participation saw how this had remarkable consequences for the young immigrants' possibilities of participating in political life. She heard one immigrant say, 'now we live in Denmark. Denmark is the land of conversation (*samtale*). The thing to do here then, is to sit down and talk about it.' Danish ideas of democracy have to be incorporated, and there is a dimension of power in this, which reveals itself in the interaction between Danish and immigrant political activists (Kehlet in Schwartz 2002). In this – as we may call it – celebration of sameness, we find an encompassing grammar, which, in opposition to the Brazilian emphasis on performance, plays upon *essence*. Incorporation is not temporary but expected to be permanent, and there is no celebration of alterity. Rather, it is the opposite, namely, that interaction across any kind of difference is considered almost impossible. People have to be brought up to a certain life style from the start, in order for *samtale*, conversation and dialogue to take place.

It is not difficult to agree in a general way with Koch's ideas, or to feel sympathetic to the concept of *hygge*. But the point here is that the inclusive mechanisms implied in the overall folk model have consequences in terms of exclusion. The much-praised dialogue implies that you talk with people who are like yourself, and with whom you basically agree. But what do you do when you do not agree? These 'soft' ideas, positively valued and attractive in many ways, clearly have negative effects leading to exclusion.

The overall grammar behind this, then, is a grammar of encompassment, and the irony is that it is built upon a self-conception of democracy, tolerance and understanding, i.e., ideas that normatively would imply that differences among people are legitimate and should be valued.

If we take a closer look at the mechanisms of inclusion and exclusion within this overall paradigm, we find, however, that there are also other grammars at stake. The grammar represented by the Danish People's Party (*Dansk Folkeparti*), which has recently surged in popularity, may at first sight seem to be a classic orientalist one. 'We' are here, and 'they' are there, and never the twain shall meet. It is acceptable to 'have different cultures', it says, but fundamentally we are so different that the best we can do for the others, and for Muslims in particular, is to keep them at a distance; let them stay 'where they belong'. This implies the legitimization of the extreme anti-immigration policy for which Denmark has become sadly famous over the past few years.

The neo-nationalism of the Danish Peoples' Party is revealed in its exclusion of foreigners and immigrants, by fencing them in within 'their' culture, a culture that is also seen as backward. The grammar is a highly hierarchical form of orientalism, making it easier for people not to define themselves as racists. The argument is culturalist, and its emphasis is upon the incompatibility of cultures. It exemplifies what Verena Stolcke has called 'cultural fundamentalism', a strategy that segregates cultures spatially and wishes to put each culture in its place (Stolcke 1995: 8).

The combination of an encompassment grammar pretending to be inclusive and an orientalist grammar aimed at exclusion places immigrants and foreigners in a deeply ambiguous position, and they are easily turned into victims of symbolic violence. They either have to become Danes or disappear. There are diverging ideas about their possibilities of becoming Danes. The Danish People's Party all but says they never can, and Muslims certainly cannot, and therefore they should not be here at all.

There are exorcist mechanisms built into the dominant paradigms of integration to which the ethnic minorities are subject, among other things because their very presence has accentuated the need for the dominant group to know what 'Danishness' is. The new racism often operates by relativizing the differences between reified cultures. In comparison with 'classic' racist thinking, the new racism, or what Stolcke (1995) has called 'cultural fundamentalism', places cultures within a hierarchy of civilization. It maintains that it will be possible for those lower down the ladder to absorb the dominant culture, to learn the necessary skills to be able to climb up in the hierarchy and ultimately to reach the top. In the Danish People's Party way of thinking this means becoming 'real' Danes. The criteria for what this means, however, are determined by the dominant group, and they are shifted strategically. Whenever the excluded have fulfilled a criteria, such as speaking very good Danish, new demands are presented, and a no-win situation is often the result (Røgilds 2002).

A different way of thinking about immigrants, multiculturalism, Danishness and citizenship is presented by those who have recently come to be known under the ironic label of *Halal-hippies* (Khader 2000). This, I would argue, is also orientalist at its core, but its implications are so different that ultimately, it may be interpreted as a segmentary grammar. It is based on cultural relativist thinking, – a fact which has made some intellectuals criticize cultural relativist thinking as such – and it states that the cultures of the 'others' are so 'other' that we should be extremely careful in dealing with them. We should respect that arranged marriages, strong ideas about honour (leading sometimes to violence), keeping women in the house, clitoridectomy, in short, cultural practises that would be condemned according to basic Danish values, are an integral part of 'their' culture, and that therefore they must be treated with respect. 'We must respect the culture of the others' (*Vi må have respekt for de andres kultur*) is its refrain.

Although orientalist at root, the elaboration of the argument reveals a tendency towards a segmentary grammar. This becomes clear when it comes to the question of solidarity and the implications that 'respecting the culture of the others' should have in terms of policy and rights. 'Culture' does not here have a direct implication for rights, as in the orientalist grammar represented by the Danish People's Party. Cultural differences should create equal rights, often phrased as cultural rights or collective rights within the human rights discourse. Halal hippies recognize that identity and alterity are relative terms, and they emphasize that there are internal differences among, for instance, the Muslim immigrants, just as Danes, too, differ by class, region, and other factors. In this regard, it would therefore be better described as a segmentary grammar, and its consequences are very much different from those of orientalization. It argues that, 'We Danes are different from each other, and they have locally different cultures, too'. On this basis, it advocates state support for schools to teach mother-tongue languages such as Turkish and Somalian, and it views common citizenship on the basis of cultural differences as the just and rightful goal.

The label *Halal hippies* was not meant to be flattering by its inventor, a successful second-generation Dane, Naser Khader, who has become a well-known and popular speaker and politician. Some of those to whom it is meant to apply, and who see themselves as just multiculturalist democrats, regard it as an insult both to *halal* and to hippies. To understand better the cultural and political thinking of those who have been so labelled, one may turn again to Stolcke's arguments about cultural fundamentalism. Neither the *Halal hippies* nor those who would prefer to describe themselves as multiculturalists are cultural fundamentalists, but they are, nonetheless, culturalists. The important thing, and this is where the grammars are of help, is that their thinking tends towards the segmentary grammar. It thus leaves behind both the orientalist grammar with its absolute distinction between 'them' and 'us' and the grammar of encompassment with its demand to 'become like us or get out of here!'

The use of the segmentary grammar far removes them from the cultural fundamentalists exemplified by the Danish People's Party who, in Stolcke's terms, see nationality and citizenship as rooted in a shared cultural heritage. There is no doubt that they are cultural fundamentalists in the sense that they 'have as the core of their ideology of collective exclusion the idea of the "other" as a foreigner, a stranger, and the assumption that formal political equality presupposes cultural identity and hence cultural sameness is the essential prerequisite for access to citizenship' (Stolcke 1995: 8). This is precisely not the thinking of the multiculturalists. While the conclusion may be evident, the differentiation of the three grammars may well be of help to see how the difference actually operates.

While Stolcke gives a very pertinent description of cultural fundamentalist thinking, she does not consider the fact that there is a kind of thinking which is also culturalist, but draws different consequences from its version of culturalism. The difference, I would contend, lies in the ideas about citizenship. One may well think here of the Brazilian move away from the encompassment grammar and towards universalization and an emphasis on equal citizenship. The multiculturalists will support the granting of citizenship to people with different cultures on the basis of universalist thinking and an egalitarian attitude. Their grammar is therefore segmentary. They recognize differences, and not only cultural but also local and regional ones within nation-states, and recognize differences within the immigrant communities as well. Solidarity is thus based on a form of segmentary alliances with political rather than cultural agreements, attitudes, themes, and elements as the basis, and the state as a body of citizens equal before the law as the apex. This vision, although culturalist, could thus be seen as a move away from the requirement that you have to be 'same' to be equal (Baumann 1999: 97) – an essential idea in the hegemonic Danish folk model.

As we saw in Da Cunha's (1998) case of the cultural groups turned NGOs in Brazil, the rationale of this move was recontextualised by the notion of citizenship and it aimed at a more contemporary universalist approach. This emphasis on citizenship might well entail an effort to escape a certain logic of identity imposed by others, and to call attention to other kinds of identity that were differently defined.

As general Western social thinking goes, extreme positions – whether of a religious fundamentalist or more extreme political kind like fascism – are to be combated by a strong democratic society, a human rights ideology and practice, good governance, reflexive attitudes, and general tolerance towards cultural differences and other human beings. To detect different intersecting grammars set to work in this project helps to reveal the complexities that lie behind such positive ideas. The grammars may thus further our understanding of the difficulties entailed in reaching such goals.

Conclusion

As a tentative conclusion on the basis of the cases presented here, one may perhaps say that complex grammars, and different grammars that work simultaneously and concurrently, have advantages in terms of dialogue, flexibility and space for action. But the grammars can also be used to deceive others or indeed to deceive oneself and to hide real conflicts. What Denmark and Brazil have in common is that both countries reveal national self-understandings of non-racism and tolerance which are in different ways contradicted by reality. In Brazil, one celebrates alterity through numerous performative practices. In Denmark, alterity is seen as a threat. The difference does not, however, hide the fact that there are strong mechanisms of exclusion at work in both countries.

We need theoretical tools that enable us to investigate agency on the basis of structure in a comparative manner. The grammars are an excellent tool better to understand the mechanisms of inclusion and exclusion that lead to new racism, cultural fundamentalism, and ultimately extremes like genocide and ethnocide. Moreover, the grammars may also help us better to understand the kind of action and practices that aim to move away from the 'traps' that certain types of grammar put people in, for instance by way of a certain logic of identity. It may seem that in my analysis I have viewed the grammars of orientalization and encompassement in a negative light and have celebrated the grammar of segmentation as the best option. There is some truth in this, but clearly, the matter cannot be simplified in this way. Rather, as long as we have a variety of grammars to be identified and there are intersecting grammars at play, then on the whole, this highly complex picture lessens the dangers of totalitarianism, fascism and extreme exclusion. Yet they remain under the surface, and close scrutiny of how the different grammars are set to work may help us to identify the points of danger.

Baumann (this volume) proposes that the breakdown of language is a critical step in turning from grammatical otherings to the non- or anti-grammar of systematic violence. This may indeed be the crucial element of the theory. In the cases presented here, there are grammars at work in complicated intersecting ways, with the common consequence of creating a contradiction between collective self-understanding and hard reality. There is a lot of 'language' at work, and thus, the cases may serve to illustrate how grammars are made to keep each other in balance, keep each other in check, or enter into conflict. I would propose that examining the ways in which different grammars intersect and are made to work together or played out against each other in contradictory and complementary ways may also lead us to a better understanding of how extremes come about in the form of systematic violence.

In the cases of Brazil and Denmark, an analysis by way of the grammars helps to reveal how seemingly positive values and norms can hide conflicts and produce negative consequences, just as much as the other way round: how negative, conflict-seeking or exclusionist elements within a social field may be counterbalanced by the use of certain grammars. We thus cannot easily identify some grammars as 'better' than others. The social and cultural outcome is to be detected through the complex interplay of different grammars in their mutual historical constellations.

Notes

1. Report on Racism and Xenophobia, April 2001; see also articles from *The Guardian* by Stephen Smith, 5 June 2002, 'Copenhagen flirts with fascism', and Andrews Osborn, 29 June 2002, 'Danes justify harshest asylum laws in Europe. The United Nations is questioning the legality of Denmark's immigration rules to be passed on Monday'.
2. 'Sameness' could be translated into *ligner* (alikeness; similarity) in Danish. *Ligner* derives from the same word as *lighed* (lit. likeness) which also means equality. There is thus a close etymological link in Danish between 'similar', 'same' and 'equal'.
3. Ardener's ideas were presented orally at a conference in Cracow in 1986. They were reconstructed by Kirsten Hastrup, Malcolm Chapman and Shirley Ardener and published in the Danish anthropological periodical *Tidsskriftet Antropologi* 25 (1992).

References

Alvares, Sonia E., Evelina Dagnino and Arturo Escobar. 1998. 'Introduction: The Cultural and the Political in Latin American Social Movements', in *Cultures of Politics, Politics of Cultures. Re-visioning Latin American Social Movements*, eds. Sonia E.Alavares, Evelina Dagnino and Arturo Escobar. Boulder: Westview Press, 1–29.
Ardener, Edwin. 1992. 'Ritual og socialt rum', *Tidsskriftet antropologi* 25: 23–29.
Bateson, Gregory. 1972. 'A Theory of Play and Phantasy', in: *Steps to an Ecology of Mind,* ed. Gregory Bateson. New York: Ballentine Books, 177–193.
Baumann, Gerd. 1999. *The Multicultural Riddle. Rethinking National, Ethnic, and Religious Identities.* New York: Routledge.
Boddy, Janice. 1989. *Wombs and Alien Spirits.* Madison: University off Wisconsin Press.
Da Cunha, Olivia Maria Gomes. 1998. 'Black Movements and the "Politics of Identity" in Brazil', in *Cultures of Politics, Politics of Cultures. Re-visioning Latin American Social Movements,* eds. Sonia E. Alvares, Evelina Dagnino and Arturo Escobar. Boulder: Westview Press, 220–52.
DaMatta, Robert. 1997. *A Casa & A Rua. Espaco, cidadania, mulher e morte no Brasil.* Rio de Janeiro: Rocco.
Freyre, Gilberto. 1946. *The Masters and the Slaves: A Study in the Development of Brazilian Civilization.* New York: Alfred A. Knopf.
Gilroy, Paul. 2002. Interview by Flemming Røgilds, *Social Kritik* 84: 44–64.
Gluckmann, Max, ed. 1962. *Essays in the Rituals of Social Relations.* Manchester: Manchester University Press.
Hanchard, Michael. 1994. *Orpheus and Power. The Movimento Negro of Rio de Janeiro and Sao Paulo, Brazil, 1945-1988.* Princeton: Princeton University Press.
Henfry, Colin. 1972. 'The Hungry Imagination. Social Formation, Popular Culture and Ideology in Bahia', in *The Logic of Poverty,* ed. Simon Mitchell. London: Routledge, 133–83.
Khader, Naser and Jacob Kvist. 2000. *'khader.dk', sammenførte erindringer.* København: Nyt Dansk Litteraturselskab.
Knudsen, Anne. 1996. *Her går det godt, send flere penge.* København: Gyldendal.
Koch, Hal. 1981 [1945]. *Hvad er demokrati?* København: Gyldendals Uglebøger.
Kramer, Fritz. 1987. *Der rote Fes. Über Besessenheit und Kunst in Afrika.* Frankfurt am Main: Athenäum.

Neiburg, Frederico and Marcio Goldman. 1997. 'Anthropology and Politics in Studies of National Character', *Cultural Anthropology* 13 (1): 56–81.
Nielsen, Finn Sivert and Inger Sjørslev, eds. 2002. *Folkets repræsentanter. Et antropologisk blik på Folketinget.* Århus: Århus Universitetsforlag.
Ramos, Alcida. 1998. *Indigenism: Ethnic Politics in Brazil.* Madison: University of Wisconsin Press.
Rosa-Ribeiro, Fernando. 2000. 'Racism, Mimesis and Anthropology in Brazil', *Critique of Anthropology* 20 (3): 220–41.
Røgilds, Flemming. 2002. 'Den nye racisme. Aktører. Forhistorie. Modstrategier', *Dansk Sociologi* 13 (3): 101–111.
Salamon, Karen and Lisa Goldschmidt. 1992. 'I grunden er vi enige. En ekskurs i skandinavisk foreningsliv', *Tidsskriftet Antropologi* 25: 105–116.
Schiffauer, Werner, Gerd Baumann, Riva Kastoryano and Steven Vertovec, eds. 2003. *Civil Enculturation. Nation-State, Schools and Ethnic Difference in Four European Countries.* Oxford: Berghahn.
Schwartz, Jonathan. 1985. *Reluctant Hosts: Denmark's Reception of Guest Workers.* Copenhagen: Akademisk Forlag.
———. 2002. *Medborgerskabets mange stemmer.* Århus: Århus Universitsforlag.
Segato, Rita Laura. 1998. 'The Color-Blind Subject of Myth: Or, Where To Find Africa in the Nation', *Annual Review of Anthropology* 27: 129–51.
Sjørslev, Inger. 1999. *Glaube und Bessessenheit. Ein Bericht über die Candomblé Religion in Brasilien.* Gifkendorf: Merlin Verlag.
Sheriff, Robin. 1999. 'The Theft of Carnival. National Spectacle and Racial Politics in Rio de Janeiro', *Cultural Anthropology* 14: 3–28.
Skidmore, Thomas. 1974. *Black into White.* New York: Oxford University Press.
Stolcke, Verena. 1995. 'Talking Culture. New Boundaries, New Rhetorics of Exclusion in Europe', *Current Anthropology* 36 (1): 1–13.
Taussig, Michael. 1993. *Mimesis and Alterity. A Particular History of the Senses.* New York: Routledge.
Turner, Victor. 1986. 'Images and Reflections: Ritual, Drama, Carnival, Film, and Spectacle in Cultural Performane' in *The Anthropology of Performance*, ed. Victor Turner. New York: PAJ Publications, 21–33.

Step III

From Power to Violence – when Grammars Implode

Chapter 6 Completing or Competing? Contexts of Hmong Selfing/Othering in Laos
Christian Postert

Chapter 7 'Out of the Race': The Poiesis of Genocide in Mass Media Discourses in Côte d'Ivoire
Karel Arnaut

Chapter 8 Dehumanization as a Double-Edged Sword: From Boot Camp Animals to Killing Machines
Jojada Verrips

Chapter 6

Completing or Competing?

Contexts of Hmong Selfing/
Othering in Laos

Christian Postert

In contemporary highland Laos, Hmong identity is a contested topic. Various observers attest to the presence of a marked consciousness of a Hmong self being different from all other ethnic groups. The idea is that the Hmong denial of foreign rule, their uncompromising desire for liberty, and a certain martial spirit drove and still drive them time and again into violent conflicts with the hegemonic powers in their respective regions of settlement. Such instances occurred between 1855 and 1872 in China, in 1911 in colonial French-Indochina, again between 1918 and 1921 in China and colonial French-Indochina, and in 1960 and 1967/68 in Northern Thailand (Tapp 1989: 18, 35–37, 78, 98, 140). In Laos, Hmong identity construction is still deeply affected by the aftermath of the Vietnam War. The majority of the Laotian Hmong fought for the American side, and only a minority fought for the Socialist *Pathet Lao*. This placed all of them in the limelight of suspicion by the later Socialist government. Although today most Hmong villagers tend to comply with the demands of the Laotian nation-state, guerrilla activities carried out in present-day Laos are still perceived to be mainly Hmong-backed. In a situation of great power differentials, all Hmong villagers experience a heightened pressure of integration into a transethnic national polity. What does this mean for the feasibility of discourses about Hmong identity in Laos?

Apparently, there are diverse strategies of context-relative self representation that are adopted by Hmong villagers. Some of these could be observed during my fieldwork from 2000 to 2001 in a Hmong highland village in Luang Prabang Province, Laos. Hmong villagers tend to use different constructions of identity/alterity according to different interactive settings. Three contexts involving different models of constructing identity/alterity will be discerned in the framework of this essay: firstly, Hmong village officials interacting with supralocal Laotian officials; then, Hmong village officials interacting formally with Hmong villagers; and lastly, Hmong villagers interacting informally among themselves. These contexts will be analysed by a heuristic use of the framework of orientalist, segmentary and encompassment grammars as specified in this volume. Special consideration will be given to the seeming paradox of a rather flexible switching between what appear at first sight as rather inflexible images of self and other. Especially revealing for the question of the negative instances when the grammars cease to work (see Baumann, this volume) are the frequent millenarian uprisings of the Hmong, when all grammars giving legitimacy to the existence of the other seem to implode. As a historical case, I shall discuss a Hmong rebellion shaking colonial French Indochina between 1918 and 1921. A few concluding remarks address issues concerning applicability, terminology and agency in the framework of the grammars as proposed.

The Grammar of Encompassment

In official contexts of socialist administrative affairs, conversations between local Hmong village officials and government officials, who are mainly of ethnic Lao, T'ai or Khmou origin, took place both in the village and in the respective offices of the district and provincial capital, Luang Prabang. All interlocutors usually preferred Lao language for these conversations, the only officially recognized language and lingua franca in Laos. Even when it was a Hmong who was working on behalf of the district or provincial administration, the villagers rather spoke Lao with him, so as not to affront Lao or Khmou officials who might be suspicious if unable to follow their exchanges. In this context, Hmong village officials typically adopted the classic encompassing grammar of the Laotian nationalist ideology that had been elaborated in the 1940s by the leaders of the first independence movement *Lao Issara* (Kossikov 2000: 231–32). This way of constructing, or rather deconstructing, cultural differences has remained the relevant model to deal with ethnic diversity in the Laotian provinces. It was first inspired by the need of an ideological basis that would legitimize the encompassment of the tremendous variety of ethnic groups in Laos in one national polity. Later, Laotian socialism perceived cultural diversity as an obstacle to development and a legacy that had to be overcome. Thus, although there are sixty-eight different ethnic groups whose existence is officially acknowledged by Laotian authorities, referring to one's identity in cultural terms is something to be avoided in the Laotian version of universalist socialism. The construction of a unifying national category in Laos consequently tends to neglect culture as a marker of difference.

Analytically, three different steps can be discerned in the process of constructing this encompassing national identity in Laotian official discourse. In the first step, culture as a marker of difference is substituted by differences that appear less suspicious from an official point of view, that is, differences according to geomorphological criteria. Affiliation to different ethnic identities is conceived to be less important than affiliation to a preferred area of settlement, for instance the valleys, the mountain slopes or the mountain tops of Laos. Thus, a huge variety of differences in terms of culture is conceptually broken down into a small number of differences in terms of geomorphological living conditions. In the second step, these differences in terms of geomorphological living conditions are used to construct transethnic group identities. The result is a trinomial model that knows only three meta-ethnic groups (see figure 6.1): all inhabitants of Laos whose principal area of settlement is presumed to be the lowlands are classified as *Lao Loum* or '*Lao* of the Valleys', corresponding more or less to the groups of the T'ai-Kadai language family. Laotians who are perceived to live in lower altitudes of the mountains are subsumed under the category of *Lao Theung* or '*Lao* of the Mountain Slopes', corresponding more or less to the Mon-Khmer language family. Finally, all inhabitants of higher altitudes are collectively classified as *Lao Soung* or '*Lao* of the Mountain Tops', corresponding more or less to the Miao-Yao language family.

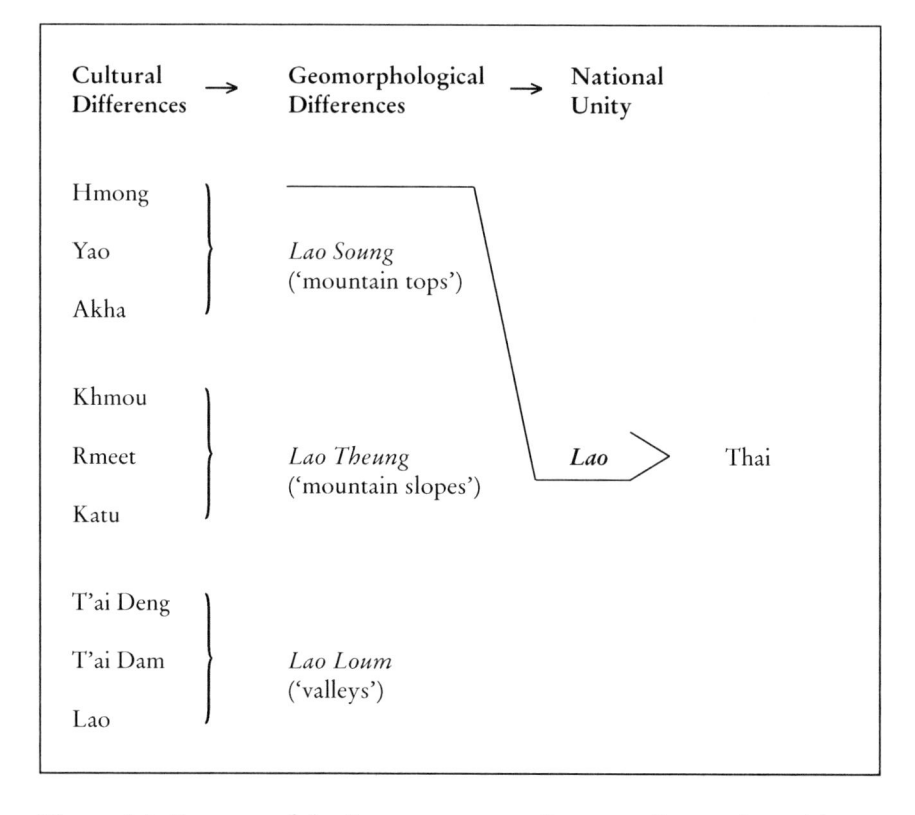

Cultural Differences →	Geomorphological Differences →	National Unity
Hmong, Yao, Akha	*Lao Soung* ('mountain tops')	
Khmou, Rmeet, Katu	*Lao Theung* ('mountain slopes')	***Lao*** > Thai
T'ai Deng, T'ai Dam, Lao	*Lao Loum* ('valleys')	

Figure 6.1 Contexts of the Encompassment Grammar: Interaction with Supralocal Officials

It is worth noting that the basic common term chosen in all of these neologisms is '*Lao*'. *Lao* refers to the ethnonym of the dominant ethnic group in Laos, the Lao, and it is evidently used here conceptually to encompass all inhabitants of Laos, although less than half of the country's population would consider themselves to be ethnic Lao. Nevertheless, this usage of the term is conceived to refer to a common national identity, the broader transethnic category of *Lao* in the sense of Laotians-as-citizens-of-Lao-PDR. In the framework of this essay, I will use the term 'Laotian' to refer to the national polity constituted by the Lao PDR, the term 'Lao' to refer to the dominant ethnic group in Laos, and the cursive form '*Lao*' to refer to an official usage of the term which takes the ethnonym as representing the national polity.

In the trinomial model, the basic underlying unity of the term *Lao* is only differentiated in a secondary manner, by contingent attributes referring to geomorphological criteria: *Loum*, *Theung* or *Soung*. Thus, ethnic groups who would not consider themselves as belonging to the same category of people are nevertheless classified as such, for instance the Hmong and the Yao. These two different ethnic groups are both categorically presumed to be *Lao Soung*, which is due to their preferred areas of settlement high in the mountains. It is not surprising to see that this Lao term has no correspondence in Hmong language.

The subsequent third step follows the logic of the preceding steps and can be observed in today's official rhetoric (see figure 6.1): the sole *raison d'être* for the introduction of geomorphological differences was the replacement of cultural differences in official discourse. Once members of ethnic minorities learn to represent themselves in terms of the trinomial classification, as can be observed in the context of official interaction in present-day Laos, representatives of the Laotian nation-state proceed with the project of merging differences into the one and unified national category. Thus, the relevance of geomorphological differences that have just been introduced to substitute ethnic differences is played down again. Tellingly, on the occasion of a Hmong New Year ritual, a Lao representative of the provincial administration delivered a speech to the Hmong village population in which he stressed: 'There are no *Lao Loum*, there are no *Lao Theung*, there are no *Lao Soung*: there are only Lao!' Thus, in the process of an ongoing categorical merging, geomorphological differences apparently become obsolete and are subsequently played down in favour of a uniform national category of the Lao, which hierarchically encompasses all differences imaginable in the nation-state. The geomorphological differences of the trinomial model are neglected in favour of a unity that is expressed in terms of the same model: exclusive emphasis is put on the Lao, not on the *Lao Loum*, *Theung* or *Soung*. The obvious aim is the construction of a shared Laotian identity based on the conception that the identity of a person is primarily defined by his or her status of being a citizen of a specific nation-state. A basic and resulting value statement is that first and foremost, every citizen of the Lao PDR should be *Lao*. This national identity is implicitly valued higher than the contrasting category of the Thai who, though historically and linguistically closely related, are perceived to be morally corrupted through Western influence.

Thus, in official contexts, Hmong village officials and Laotian officials tend to represent Hmong villagers as hierarchically encompassed by the broader transethnic category of the Lao in the sense of Laotians-as-citizens-of-Lao-PDR.

The Grammar of Segmentation

Hmong village officials interacting within the village act in a different context: they have to give credibility to their official duties and responsibilities and to engage villagers into cooperation with the supralocal institutions. Thus, within the village they often refer to a segmentary grammar that constructs the polity as a federal one (see figure 6.2). In this grammar, Lao and Hmong are described as equal partners united by the former common fight against the ternary category of the foreign intruder, the U.S.A. in the times of the Vietnam War. This of course ignores the fact that the majority of the Hmong were fighting for the American side. When searching credibility for this grammar, Hmong officials usually refer to Mr Kaysone, the deceased former President of the Lao PDR who was then made out to be a *huab tais*, a term best translated as 'great ruler, emperor, legendary Hmong king, king' (Heimbach 1979: 56). Proof of his authority as messianic leader *huab tais* is the fact that he was fighting from the mountainous areas of Northern Laos against an enemy situated in the southern plains, thus topographically fitting into patterns of traditional legitimization of Hmong messianic rulership (Savina 1924: 259; Alleton 1981: 31–35, 37; Tapp 1989: 78). Although he is of Lao-Vietnamese origin, his superabundant love for all the different segmentary units in Laos allegedly enabled him to unite them against the exterior enemy. Contextually ascribing to Kaysone both the status of a *huab tais* and of the unifying leader of this Hmong–Lao segment, aims at legitimizing the grammar of segmentation as a plausible option.

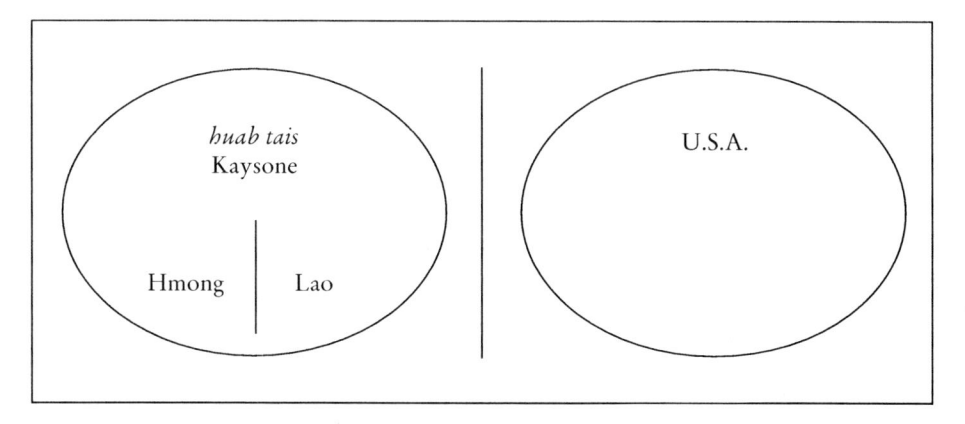

Figure 6.2 Contexts of the Segmentary Grammar: Formal Hmong–Hmong Interaction

This kind of segmentary grammar is restricted to Hmong officials engaged in formalized communication and the execution of official duties within the village.

The Grammar of Orientalization

Informal interactions within the village are characterized by a more recognizably orientalist grammar (see figure 6.3). On the one hand, Hmong stereotypes depict the Lao to be clever and indolent, whereas the Hmong self is characterized by attributes such as hot-headedness and stubbornness. Thus from a Hmong point of view, Lao people are described as being efficient and profit-seeking traders, qualities that are not primarily attributed to the Hmong self. In this context, the difference between Hmong self and Lao other is believed to contribute to the complementarity between Hmong farmers growing vegetables and the Lao merchants in the valleys to whom these are sold, thus stabilizing their relations in that regard. On the other hand, Hmong people are described as being industrious and honest, Lao people as lazy and treacherous. In that aspect, their relations are endowed with contingency and aggressive competition.

Hmong self **Lao other**

industrious clever
honest indulgent

competing completing

hot-headed lazy
stubborn treacherous

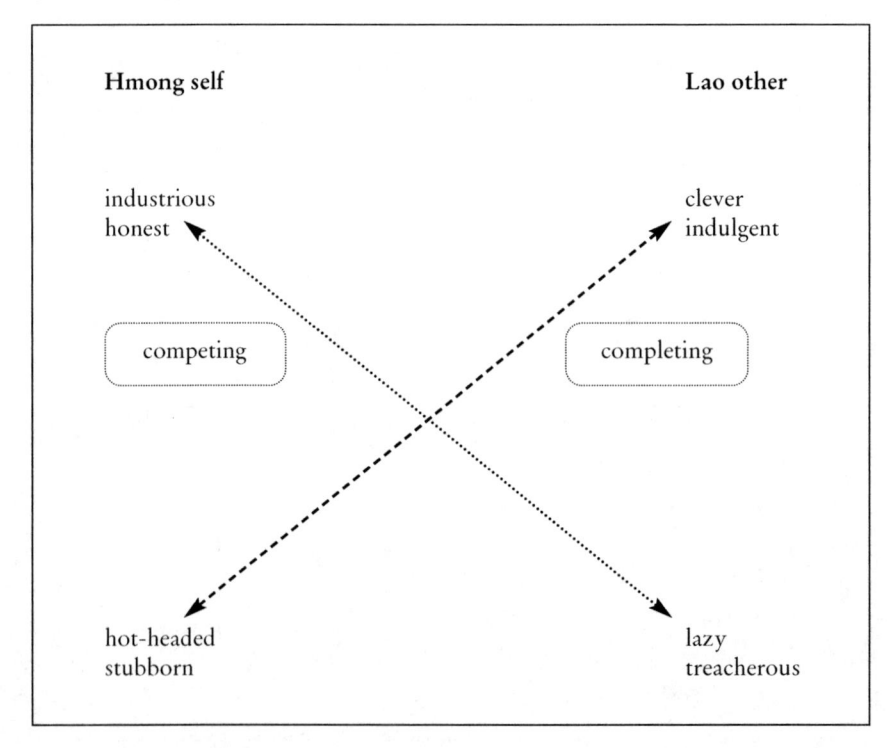

Figure 6.3 Contexts of the Orientalizing Grammar: Informal Hmong–Hmong Interaction

Crucial in this tension is the expectation that, since the Hmong are far more proficient in the manipulation of the geomantic system, there will be a time in the future when the present situation will be reversed and will lead to a millenarian utopia. This utopia is modelled upon a mythical past and foresees a future when no complementary other is needed because of a superabundance of material and non-material goods that abolish the necessity of exchange with the other. Lao Buddhist monks in this context seem to fit into a ternary category: in contrast to ordinary Lao people, they are considered to be generally benevolent and in addition, they are not traders. They might be consulted by Hmong in curing rituals, although they very rarely are, and they know how to manipulate the geomantic system. This skill is evidenced by the fact that they tend to build their monasteries on auspicious geomantic sites. Nevertheless, Lao Buddhist monks are not thought as liable as the Hmong to make effective use of this knowledge, since they burn their dead instead of burying them, with burial considered a prerequisite substantially to profit from geomantic places.

Status of Identity Statements

It has to be stressed here that in general, keeping harmony with an interlocutor is highly appreciated in Hmong culture. Even if consensus does not exist, conformity is very often expressed because the utterance of opposing views is felt to be embarrassing for both interlocutors, especially when they do not know each other very well. To assess the status of statements about identity/alterity, one observation might be of key interest here. Within each of the contexts outlined, the actors themselves quite often tend to describe the respectively constructed identities and alterities as context-stable and enduring entities irrespective of time and space. Thus, one may be tempted to characterize interactions within a given context as a kind of 'essentialising' type of discourse about identity/alterity. However, a few moments later and in a different interactive context, informants might easily switch to other conceptions of identity/alterity, but then again, often with the same 'essentialist' claims. As this way of identity construction allows for a certain practical flexibility in spite of its ideological claims, and as the term 'essentialist' is perhaps best reserved for typifying certain types of Western academic discourse, I will in the following call it 'contextual-absolute' instead of 'essentialist'. One might then characterize Hmong identity discourse in Laos by two general statements. One, statements about identity/alterity gain their validity only on the basis of a specific interactive context and cannot be separated from these. Secondly, however, ideological relativity seems not to be foreseen within any of these respective contexts. Rather, it is social action, in particular the changing of interactive contexts, that introduces relativity in that it allows the step from one 'contextual-absolute' construction of identity/alterity to another. If and when the context was seen to change, the same actors could thus switch from one grammar to another with the greatest ease and without revealing obvious signs of cognitive dissonance.

A 'Mad War'? A Hmong Messianic Rebellion in French Indochina (1918–1921)

To address now the 'n+1' question raised by Baumann (in this volume), the question of when the grammars might cease to operate, I turn to a historical case study. In the best-documented example of a Hmong messianic rebellion, excessive taxation by Lao authorities working for the French colonial regime led to the biggest uprising in French Indochina. In colonial reports, it was documented as the *Guerre du Fou* (Savina 1924: 235–39; Ngaosyvathan 2000: 247–49). The rebellion started in China where the excessive taxes imposed by mandarins on Hmong opium production threatened to drive the producers into poverty. Under the leadership of a messianic leader and *huab tais* called Paj Caj, Hmong villagers started to revolt against the Chinese authorities and destroyed the market places, until then the most obvious locations demonstrating aspects of a complementary coexistence of these groups. The rebellion soon spread across to colonial French Indochina, where the French had given rise to similar distress by installing a local and corrupt elite of Lao and Vietnamese officials who collected comparably excessive taxes for the colonial regime (Alleton 1981: 31, 35, 37–41). In this historical case, it is of course difficult to reconstruct in retrospect which different kinds of grammars were at work in local Hmong discourses of identity. As will be shown, however, the discussion of the historical data suggests that the different types of grammar previously discussed might have been at least partially active in diverse contexts of constructing self and other.

In situations of external oppression, individuals who would be considered deviant in ordinary contexts, reportedly being offspring from a wild boar and thus without clearly definable social bonds in human society, could, in Hmong society, be considered to be reincarnations of the mythic ruler *huab tais* (Tapp 1989: 98). It is in this historical case that Paj Caj emerges, a Hmong who might be regarded as antistructural to any society in so far as he is an orphan and cannot be attributed a fixed position in the webs of kinship ties. Being placed outside most social relations, he acquires identity primarily in relations to the celestial realm. In his role as *huab tais*, he can overcome the column that separates earth and sky and can get in touch directly with the highest celestial deities whom he regularly meets by climbing up a tree into the sky (Savina 1924: 237; Mottin 1980: 83). The celestial authorities reciprocally protect those they have chosen and convey objects to them that in the mythical past were in Hmong possession. Especially important in this respect is the script of the Hmong language that according to origin myths has been lost in ancient times in a fierce competition with the Chinese (Mottin 1980: 163; Tapp 1989: 75, 122). A recurring feature of messianic leadership is this recovery of the script in dreams or by letters sent from the sky *ntuj*, the ultimate and highest creator deity in Hmong cosmology, to the *huab tais* (Alleton 1981: 35; Tapp 1989b: 81). Paj Caj accordingly distributed pieces of white cloth among his adherents, on which he had written characters supposed to be those of the mythical Hmong script. As these were considered to make the bearer invulnerable to bullets, Hmong insurgents exposed themselves to French rifles without seeking shelter, one of the many reasons why the ignorant colonial authorities called this a 'mad' war (Alleton 1981: 42–43; Tapp 1989: 128). Paj Caj's messianic rulership is further legitimized by his origin high up in the North, a frequent prerequisite to being recognized as a messianic ruler (Savina 1930: 259; Alleton 1981: 31–35, 37; Tapp 1989: 78). The messianic vision of society, certainly as documented for the rebellion of the 1960s, seems to entail the end of society as it was known before: all people would be equal, all socially differentiating distinctions annihilated. Rice and silver would be freely available to all Hmong without the necessity of exchange with the, hence obsolete, other (Tapp 1989: 78).

In analysing such recurrent messianic rebellions in the light of the grammars, one can see how the complementary aspect of the orientalist grammar, with its assumption of reciprocal exchange, would lose its legitimacy for the Hmong in a situation of obvious exploitation. Thus, the credibility of an orientalist grammar conceiving of the other as a meaningful complement of the self gave way to an emphasis on contingency and competition instead. The segmentary grammar was broken up by a process of fission, opposing the segments of different Hmong subgroups against the exterior Lao/French enemy, with the latter then switched from a segmentary other to ternary outsider. The encompassing grammar did not yield encompassment any longer as the Hmong overtly rejected belonging to a transethnic polity of whatever kind, be it Lao or French, with the latter again reduced to a ternary outsider. The Lao/French other thus became nothing more than a hindrance in attaining an ultimate status of self that no longer needed others to define itself.

Hmong who witnessed Paj Caj's millenarian uprising in Laos stress the unprecedented violence exerted by the Hmong in the pursuit of their rebellion. According to a report on the later phases of the turmoils, some of the rebels physically annihilated the obsolete other, killing male Lao civilians and raping and slitting up Lao women to examine the functioning of their organs of reproduction (Mottin 1980: 92–95). Although these Hmong reports do not have the status of historical documents, their view reflects very well what might have happened on an ideological plane. Apparently, the other as a human category ceased to exist and attained the status of an object that can be dissected out of sheer curiosity. Extinguishing the other in this way means extinguishing the former social self as well: with the categorical and physical annihilation of the other, differences between 'self' and 'other' that were constitutive of the social self are collapsed. Behind this, one can assume the longing for a finality of existence that societies usually reserve for a mythical past or a mythical future, the longing for a mode of existence in which social exchange is not necessary, in which the realm of the human is not yet or no longer socially fragmented into 'selves' and 'others' by historical processes (Platenkamp 1997: 7).

Speaking from analytical distance, one must ask, of course, whether a self without others could ever be experienced by social human beings: the ultimate, eternal self that does not need others would be socially dead insofar as it negates all differences that are constitutive of social structures. It would put an end to society as living human beings know it. There might then be a hidden necessity why these non-grammatical outbursts of violence tend to be neutralized by a re-asserted grammar in a retrospective Hmong explanation: the sky *ntuj* as the ultimate authority of the whole universe (one might say, the highest level of encompassment imaginable) was angered by this limitless violence and made Hmong warriors vulnerable again (Mottin 1980: 93–97). It was thus that the Hmong insurgents were defeated and Paj Caj was betrayed and executed. The remaining Hmong rebels were forced to subordinate themselves to French rule: Paj Caj's first lieutenant Phya Chan, like most Hmong very probably an adherent of the ancestor cult, was compelled to submit to the Lao king and to French rule by praying in a Lao Buddhist pagoda (Gunn 1986: 116). The underlying symbolism seems obvious: this gesture of subjugation was conceived to restore his and his followers' submission to the encompassment grammar that legitimated the Lao/French colonial polity.

Conclusion

The hypothesis of the three grammars has proved to be a very useful heuristic device in the analysis of different contexts of Hmong selfing/othering. Nonetheless, I would suggest a certain caution. Firstly, I would opt for a rather pragmatic use of these models, that is, to use them as a pair of glasses through which to examine one's data. Either one detects interesting and recurring or alternating patterns of social categorisation, or else one recognizes nothing. In that case, one should leave them aside and try another pair of glasses. Glasses, or analytical models if you prefer, are after all an inevitable prerequisite for the interpretation of data, and even the so-called 'Western common sense', credited by some with being 'less theoretical' and 'closer to reality', is nothing more than a pair of glasses.

Baumann, too, stresses that his delineation of the respective grammars is adapted, rather than adopted from Dumont, Evans-Pritchard and Said. Thus a term like 'encompassment grammar' refers only metaphorically to the concept of 'encompassment' as Dumont has coined it (see also Sprenger in this volume). In spite of Baumann's clarification, there will nevertheless be predictable criticisms that will question the legitimacy of the terminological parallels: should one really call a grammar 'orientalist' if Said had something different in mind? It might be preferable, and useful in preventing fruitless terminological debates, to opt for different terms without reducing the analytic value of the grammars hypothesis.

What appears to be particularly interesting in pursuing the grammars hypothesis is to focus on the actual actors in their processes of switching from one grammar in one context to another grammar in another context. Is this a case of the maximising individual freely disposing of different grammars, switching them on and off at will and as strategic tools for the benefit of his or her own interests? My own data do not confirm this, and the notion seems uncomfortably close to discourses of modern Western individualism constructing the single person as an independent entrepreneur of his or her identity, thereby neglecting the social conditioning of individuals in their very basic interests and in their uses of discourses of identity/alterity. Is the actor, alternatively, a group of people with common interests, a group that consolidates itself in the pursuit of collectively defined goals? This second approach tends to conceal that it takes for granted what should be explained by analysis: the process of constituting a collective self. How does it come about that several persons recognize a mutual sameness in terms of interests as a constitutive element in the construction of a collective 'we'? Or perhaps, as a third alternative, are the 'real' actors to be found in specific patterns of alternating interactive or ideological contexts in which different dominant discourses arise and constitute context-relative 'selves' and 'others'? Such a view tends to cover the strategic uses that individual actors may actually make of different grammars according to changing social settings and different interests. With this last criticism, the wheel comes full circle as we are led back to the shortcomings of the first approach. Thus on the one hand, none of these approaches appears to do justice to complex social phenomena if they are applied in isolation. On the other hand, an eclectic combination of these different approaches gives rise to a certain analytic unease as the procedure is not only intellectually less stringent, but combines explanatory models and underlying conceptions of social action that diverge so widely that they sometimes seem to exclude each other. Yet in the attempt to grapple with complex social realities, unease is perhaps not a bad omen.

References

Alleton, Isabelle. 1981. 'Les Hmong aux confins de la Chine et du Vietnam. La révolte du "Fou" (1918–1922)', in *Histoire de l'Asie du Sud-Est. Révoltes, réformes, révolutions*. Edited by P. Brocheux. Lille : Presses universitaires de Lille, 31–46.

Gunn, Geoffrey C. 1986. 'Shamans and Rebels. The Batchai (Meo) Rebellion of Northern Laos and North-West Vietnam (1918–1921)', *Journal of the Siam Society* 74: 107–21.

Heimbach, Ernest E. 1979. *White Hmong-English Dictionary*. New York: Cornell Southeast Asia Program.

Kossikov, Igor. 2000. 'Nationalities Policy in Modern Laos', in *Civility and Savagery: Social Identity in Tai States*, edited by A. Turton. Richmond: Curzon Press, 227–44.

Mottin, Jean. 1980. *Contes et légendes Hmong Blanc*. n.p.: Don Bosco Press.

Ngaosyvathan, Mayoury. 2000. 'Tribal Politics in Laos', in *Civility and Savagery: Social Identity in Tai States*, edited by A. Turton. Richmond: Curzon Press, 245–62.

Platenkamp, Josephus D.M. 1997. 'Half Persons, Complete Societies', *MINPAKU Anthropology Newsletter* 5: 7–8.

Savina, F.M. 1924. *Histoire des Miao*. Hong Kong: Missions Étrangères de Paris.

Tapp, Nicholas. 1989. *Sovereignty and Rebellion. The White Hmong of Northern Thailand*. Oxford: Oxford University Press.

———. 1989b. 'The Impact of Missionary Christianity upon Marginalized Ethnic Minorities: the Case of the Hmong', *Journal of Southeast Asian Studies* XX (1): 70–95.

Chapter 7

'Out of the Race'

The Poiesis of Genocide in Mass Media Discourses in Côte d'Ivoire

Karel Arnaut

On 26 October 2000, Laurent Gbagbo, leader of the Socialist Party FPI claimed victory over General Robert Guëï in the Ivorian presidential elections.[1] One day later, some fifty-seven corpses, mostly of young men, were discovered in a mass-grave in the suburb Yopougon of the capital Abidjan. Many hundreds of civilians, protesters, militants of different political parties, and security forces were killed in street violence over the following days. It was, however, the mass-grave that caught international attention. The United Nations established a Commission of Enquiry that identified the perpetrators as members of the security forces and their henchmen as civilians, some of them militants of the victorious Socialist Party FPI (United Nations 2001: 17). Most prominent among the executioners, the report said, were state policemen (*gendarmes*) who wanted to take vengeance for the killing of one of their commanding officers. The policemen had attributed this murder, as well as other aggressions in Abidjan, to militant members of the Republican Party RDR (*Rassemblement des Républicains*) who had been massively contesting the presidential elections because their leader, Alassane Ouattara, had been excluded from standing as a candidate.

The relatives of the mass-grave victims found support from the Belgian NGO *Prévention génocides* which provided assistance in filing a case of 'crimes against humanity' in a Belgian court, a procedure still possible at the time. The accused were four political leaders, among them President Gbagbo himself and the former Head of State Robert Guëï. In addition, *Prévention Génocides* set up a media campaign spearheaded by the video film *Côte d'Ivoire, poudrière identitaire*, or 'powderkeg of identities'. The film claimed to present a scientific analysis of identity politics and violence in Côte d'Ivoire over the past decade. Since the death of the 'Father of the Nation', President Houphouët-Boigny in 1993, the film explained, one group of people had been the target of discrimination and inferiorisation by subsequent governments: this referred to an ethnic group labelled 'Jula' and comprising Muslims, RDR militants, people from the northern part of Côte d'Ivoire, and migrants from other West African countries. The film observed how 'the Jula' had been increasingly diabolized in government-sponsored mass media, and it concluded that the Yopougon murders were part of a genocidal build-up in which 'the Jula' were being threatened with annihilation.

The resignification of the Yopougon mass-grave as evidence of a genocidal action against an identifiable group of people sparked off a series of reactions which revealed, contested, and at times completely reversed the identities of the victims and the perpetrators.

Reversing Identities

The Gbagbo government rejected both the UN's and the NGO's enquiries. Their findings were invalidated, subverted, and even reversed in different ways. The UN report was 'scientifically' re-appropriated and its conclusion turned on its head in a government publication distributed free of charge across the country (Côte d'Ivoire 2001). The volume featured a presidential statement in which the UN Commission was accused of merely defending the cause of the RDR opposition party against the Gbagbo government. Moreover, it contained a report of a government-sponsored medical committee which concluded that: 'the mystery of the origin (*constitution*) of this "mass-grave" remains intact' (155, emphasis original). The stress on 'the constitution', and the scare quotes around 'mass-grave' conveyed the government's view that the Yopougon mass-grave was a fabrication: a number of dead bodies had been brought together by RDR militants and 'shot' with police guns in order to frame policemen and accuse the government. The president of the Parliament, Mamadou Koulibaly, spelled out the desired conclusion in public: 'National and international opinion is now aware that it [the mass-grave of Yopougon] is but a *montage*' (Koulibaly 2001). This 'conclusion' implies more than meets the eye, for the word *montage* entails a *double entendre*: *monter* may not simply mean editing, assembling or mounting, but also setting up, framing, and trapping. While most of the victims were indeed never identified officially, the implication is that they may well have been followers of the governing FPI, some of whom were certainly killed during the street violence that accompanied the presidential elections. In combining the 'scientific' conclusion that the mass-grave remained an enigma and the political assertion that it was an act of 'framing' by post-mortem impersonation of the other party, the issues of police and political violence were evacuated into a space of make-believe and morbid manipulation. A similar strategy was also used in discrediting the spectacular, mass-mediated re-appropriation of the film *Côte d'Ivoire, poudrière identitaire*.

Even before its official release, the 'Powderkeg of Identities' film was shown and debated widely in Côte d'Ivoire. As early as 14 August 2001, the government organized its broadcasting on national television, followed by a seven-hour debate among a panel of experts. The debate opened with a question about the 'real' intentions of the filmmaker, Benoît Scheuer. This question cleared the ground for all sorts of speculations. One of them, put forward by Deputy Mamadou Ben Soumahoro and widely accepted among government supporters, was that Scheuer was a paid agent of Alassane Ouattara, the leader of the opposition party RDR who had been excluded from standing as presidential candidate. The RDR, after all, was notorious for operating and instrumentalising the international mass media, as Deputy Soumahoro could imply. Once a member of the RDR, Soumahoro had changed his political alliances twice in the previous two years, now to end up as a Gbagbo activist and a virulent opponent of Ouattara.

Like the mass-grave before, the Powderkeg film was characterized in the debate as 'a *montage*', a deceptive mixture of fake testimonies and unrelated images of violence. Soumahoro, now introduced as a media expert, exposed the fictional character of the film. He pointed out, for instance, that the film did not have credit titles at the end and thus obscured its sources and 'actors'. Anyone who had seen the film broadcast just before the debate had seen its credit titles; but no-one contradicted Soumahoro's 'expert' observation. Instead, the next day's newspapers stressed how so many viewers had found Soumahoro's explanations pertinent and even enlightening. The film, it was argued, falsely represented one group of people, which it called 'the Jula', as the victims of discrimination, political exclusion, and state violence. One participant in the debate demonstrated in the most tangible way how identities were deceitful and manipulable, and he did so by performing a remarkable act of impersonation. This was the former student-leader, now turned Gbagbo enthusiast, Charles Blé Goudé. He was remembered, by those Ivorian youth who fell within the category of RDR members, such as 'northerners' and Muslims, for having spread hate speech and violence against them on the university campuses of Abidjan during the summer of 2000, just preceding the elections. In the television debate, they saw the Christian Blé Goudé dressed in a *grand boubou*, the festive dress of Muslims. The victims saw their hangman wearing their clothes.

Both the film of the NGO and the report of the UN aimed at confronting people with the naked facts: demonstrating how the Ivorian State dealt with an identified group of political enemies and reconstrued the Yopougon mass murder as a violent explosion of identity politics. In pro-government Côte d'Ivoire, however, this international expertise was turned on its head by a whole succession of nationally staged 'games' of mistaken identities. Members of the UN Commission of Enquiry were 'identified' as militants of the opposition party RDR; corpses of RDR victims were re-'identified' as corpses of FPI members; the film director Scheuer was 'identified' as an aid agent of the RDR's excluded presidential candidate Ouattara. At the same time, the mass grave was neutralised as a 'mystery' and discredited as a '*mon-*

tage' 'without actors' credits by the most grotesque denials of reality. To top it all, blatant mock impostures and disguises had billed Deputy Soumahoro as a media expert and the Christian radical Blé Goudé as a Muslim in festive garb. There is good reason, thus, to situate these phenomena in a dynamics of 'grammatical implosion', as Baumann (this volume) has called it.

Disentangling Implosions

Baumann's chapter situates 'implosion' right at the moment when all dynamic selfings/otherings are stopped by being made to collapse into the deadly game of 'us good, you bad; us alive, you dead': the 'ungrammatical binarism' of ethnic cleansing or genocide. Such implosions, one may add, are accompanied by a triple silence: victims or witnesses find it impossible to narrate their experience (Agamben 1999); the executioners find it redundant to engage in any dialogue at all (Jackson 2002: 190); and the researchers find themselves almost tongue-tied as they face, in Appadurai's words, 'not only the limits of social science but of language itself' (1996: 154). Such deadly silences, however, are often preceded by the opposite: loud hate speech, racist propaganda, and mobilizing orations. As Chrétien (1995: 307) has shown in the case of the Rwandan genocide, 'violence is in the words before it is in the acts'. This confirms Baumann's hunch, as well as the analyses by both Müller and Verrips (chapters 4 and 8 in this volume), that one can discern a pronounced 'brutalization of language' even before a regime turns to massive violence against its stereotyped others. Yet how, one must ask now, can things go so far: what is the basis of the self-confidence, the noisy hybris, the sheer brutality of the propagandists' dehumanizing discourse?

Baumann postulates a gradual inscription of racism, 'first [in] *parole* and soon afterwards [in] *langue*'. The issue of inscription is also raised by Appadurai (1996) and Tambiah (1996) in trying to account for the massive and profound support enjoyed by movements aiming at radical political violence. Both these authors use Raymond Williams' concept of 'structures of feeling' to investigate how 'ethnic claims and sentiments and ethnic stereotypes [...] are imprinted simultaneously in our minds and bodies as patterns of ideas and sentiments'(Tambiah 1996: 140). They thus sharpen their attention on what happens in everyday life. This may comprise an 'unmarked daily domestic life', but also 'marked' festivals and rituals (140); it may also reach further, going from 'casual conversations' through a 'low-key editorialising' to 'collective reading' (Appadurai 1996: 153). All three authors, however, put forward a further suggestion for investigation, and it is this that I want to pursue in order to come to grips with the dynamics of implosion.

In tracing these dynamics, I no longer seek to locate mass-mediated political manoeuvres in the kind of dramatic contexts illustrated above. Instead, and *pace* Appadurai (1996) and Tambiah (1996), I shall turn to the manufacture of genocide by analysing the manufacture of language. I shall do so, not by homing in on cheap targets such as openly genocidal rhetorics, but rather by focussing on three apparently 'serious', sometimes seemingly 'scientific' newspaper articles that were published in the months preceding the Yopougon mass grave. The three articles here examined can be seen to expose the main characteristics of an 'implosion of grammars' in the making: they spell out a radical resignification of the 'other' into a non-entity, and they do so both in a global setting of official identities and in the intimate sphere of private relationships.

In tracing genocidal politics to the manufacture or poiesis of texts, I follow Tambiah's call to give detailed attention to the 'performative devices' that are deployed in 'mass participatory politics' (1996: 141) in order to mobilize people in a dynamic of ethnic polarisation. Broadly speaking, Tambiah uses the phrase to point to the political uses of genres of performance 'taken from public culture and popular religion'. Other scholars, such as Achille Mbembe (1992) and Andrew Apter (1999), have provided a wealth of material to analyse the 'stagings' by which both politicians and 'civil society' operate profound resignifications and revaluations of reality. Mbembe describes this strategy as the very condition of the postcolony: 'its unusual and grotesque art of representation [and] its taste for the theatrical' (Mbembe 1992: 14). Apter (1999) has successfully applied Mbembe's idea of a 'simulacral regime' to the 'politics of illusion' of a former Nigerian president. These analyses show how resignifications, such as the identification and characterization of 'us' and 'them', privilege those formats and genres of communication which enjoy a high degree of what Gramsci would call 'plausibility': they may be grounded in popular culture or religious ceremonial, or they may employ established media-formats such as discussion programmes led by experts or, in one case here discussed, a newspaper column authored by a university professor.[2]

The three newspaper articles that I will analyse in detail exemplify three different formats: the report, the editorial, and the column. Each of them exhibits its own way of resigifying 'the other': the report constructs the Republican Party RDR as one among various 'political others'; the editorial turns it into an 'ethnic enemy' embodied in the life-style of its leader Alassane Ouattara; and the column turns this ethnicised adversary into a racialised other – 'the Jula' who have all the attributes of 'a people', comprising a typical character, a historical tradition and a common destiny. I have chosen the term 'poiesis' for three reasons: to stress the performative character of this overall 'low-key' editorialising, to trace how the techniques of 'staging' allow for increasingly radical modes of resignification, and to document how the authors imaginatively exploit these techniques to other the other ever more blatantly. 'Poiesis' is meant to express the semantic re-engineering that takes place in the subjunctive spaces of mass-mediated (popular, religious, political) ritual and writing, and it indicates one way of comprehending the process of 'implosion'.

The term 'implosion' is perhaps best explained by Appadurai (1996) who proposes to examine brutal ethnic conflicts less as 'explosions' than as 'implosions' since they reveal how public political identities are made to 'fold into [… the] local imagination and become dominant voice-overs in the traffic of ordinary life' (1996: 154). Appadurai thus calls up the spectre of how, in the global-local articulation of conflicts, friends and neighbours become redefined, or rather 'uncovered', as, for instance, 'foreign invaders', 'labour migrants', 'allochthones', 'Muslim fanatics', or even potential 'international terrorists'. Such 'glocal' articulations are 'implosive' due to their encompassing, that is, world-wide and indeed 'cosmological' dimension and by a transfer of this dimension into the intimacy of the private sphere. Here, too, one could refer back to Mbembe's suggestions that the political leaders of the 'postcolony' offer their nations a comprehensive 'cosmology', as well as to Apter's observation that Nigerian presidents succeed in creating a simulacrum of their autocratic regime as a proper democracy. Appadurai goes one step further, however, and invites us to look well beyond national mythologies and observe how they collide with transnational ones. This is where Appadurai locates the experience of ethnic or other conflicts as reckoning with 'deep categorical treachery'.

In the case of Côte d'Ivoire, it is crucial to stress that political identities, such as 'the Jula', have been defined, at least since the period of colonization, not only in a local space of ethnic differentiation but also in a regional space of migration and allochthony, as well as in a global space of 'racial' hierarchies and, more recently, international inequalities of financial or media power. The three newspaper articles demonstrate precisely this gradual 'unmasking' of members of the RDR party as 'the Jula people'. This 'unmasking' is of a double encompassing nature. On the one hand the image of 'the Jula' conjures up the global system of cultural and religious differences and socio-economic inequalities, on the other hand it inserts these into the private sphere of mixed families and town quarters and of 'cross-ethnic' civil society (see Bazin 1999). One could go so far as to say that the newspaper articles' gradual unmasking of the RDR as a 'Jula' party was later thematised in the government-sponsored debate on the Yopougon mass–grave, in the frantic search to reveal the 'real' identities of the UN commissioners, of the 'powderkeg' filmmaker, of the 'victims' and the 'executioners'. 'The revelation of hated and hateful official identities behind the bodily masks of real (and known) persons seems crucial to the perpetration of the worst forms of mutilation and damage', writes Appadurai (1996: 155) as he tries, in the words of Jackson (2002: 126), to 'existentialise' the phenomena of modern ethnic cleansing and genocide.

Combining Tambiah and Appadurai will help, I propose, to specify Baumann's idea of an 'implosion of grammars' as a gradual process and as a choice of techniques in transforming selfings and otherings. The poiesis of genocide exemplified by the three newspaper articles can be situated, structurally if not historically, *before* the actual (or final) implosion takes place. At the same time, it is this poiesis of language and techniques, of manipulating genres and formats, that spells out the process of implosion in the making. The moment of poiesis is thus situated in the 'revealing' moments of the construction of radical (global/local; public/private) identities in the subjunctive spaces of creative ritual and inventive writing. Examining implosion as a process, this chapter will use the three grammars to examine when and precisely how they are made to implode into the anti-grammar of genocide. My approach to testing the three grammars is thus to see how far they may characterize the different stages in the genesis of a genocidal discourse. To analyse three newspaper articles, I shall arrange them according to a genocidal crescendo. The first article, imperious in its tone, works with a segmentary construction in which the journalist reports on a quarrel between two parties. The second article, antagonistic in tone, constructs an orientalist grammar in which the journalist takes sides against the victim. The third article presents a final encompassing moment and is the only one that can be called explicitly 'genocidal'. This genocidal quality resides in the fact that it effects a dehumanization of the 'other' from without (the global, the official, and the scientific) as well as from within (the local, the 'known', and the 'humane'). This dehumanization not only constructs a radical difference from without between 'us' humans and 'them', the less than humans, but it shows a moment of identification which allows the advocate of genocide to situate himself right inside the victim.

This reconstruction adds a new dimension, I think, to Appadurai's *problematique* of 'violence in relation to treachery, intimacy, and identity' (1996: 155). It asks how the public deals with revelations of identity in its private sphere, and it enquires how such 'intimacy' is actively created by the authors of revelatory ritual and writing. In reconstructing the process of implosion, I concentrate on one specific technique of code-switching which is particularly effective in integrating the other into the discourse of the self: the technique and performance of code-crossing (Rampton 1995) or double-voicing (Bakhtin 1984 [1929]). The genocidal crescendo effected by the three newspaper articles is due to an increasingly sophisticated and complex use of code-crossing. This technique allows one to see the sophistication employed in discursive projects of a genocidal nature. Genocides may not rely so much on the single-minded butcher as on the cultured professor, and they may not dwell so much in bloodthirsty hate speech as in the well-crafted, reflective, and even seemingly compassionate text. Before hate speech and butchery aim at 'getting rid of the other', the poiesis of genocide uses its skill and sophistication to get 'right into the other', and it does so by the technique of code-crossing.

The term 'code-crossing' or 'crossing' was coined by Ben Rampton (1995) and designates 'the use of a language which isn't generally thought to "belong" to the speaker ... [and] involves a sense of movement across quite sharply felt social or ethnic boundaries' (Rampton 1998: 291). Rampton explains code-crossing with reference to Bakhtin's (1984 [1929]) concept of 'double voicing' in which 'speakers use someone else's discourse (or language) for their own purposes' by inserting a new semantic intention into another discourse. Thus, 'in one discourse, [there appear] two semantic intentions, two voices' (Rampton 1998: 304). In some cases, this semantic intention may correspond to the original one; in other uses, such as ironic or inimical ones, the speaker 'introduces into the original discourse a semantic intention directly opposed to the original one' (Rampton 1998: 305, quoting Bakhtin 1984 [1929]). Parallel to manipulating the meaning of the original discourse, code-crossing allows for transforming the identity of the original speaker. The issue of speakerhood in code-crossing performances is raised by Jane

Hill (1999, 2001). She observes how the use of a particular quote or token-expression within another code (e.g., the Spanish 'cojones' in an English statement) can project certain characteristics (e.g., vulgarity) on to the original speakers of the quoted code ('the' Spanish speakers as against 'the' English speakers) or on to individual speakers associated with the quote, be it explicitly or implicitly.

Let me then use these theoretical insights to analyse how the code-crossing use of the phrase *bori bana* acts as a discursive instrument in the poiesis of genocide. In order to ease the reader's way through the complexities of the case, I shall distinguish between Jula as a language and 'Jula' as an ethnonym or quasi-ethnonym, be it self-ascribed or ascribed by others.

Bori bana: A Token of Jula Language and of 'Jula' History

Between January and May 2000, the important newspaper *Notre Voie* published three articles which carried the expression *bori bana* in their titles.[3] The phrase is Manding for: 'the running is finished', with *bori* signifying running or racing.[4] In each case, the phrase *bori bana* is attributed to a different target person or group, but all of them are (political) opponents associated with the Republican Party RDR. Like all other major newspapers in Côte d'Ivoire, *Notre Voie* is allied to a political formation, in this case the Socialist Party FPI of Laurent Gbagbo.[5] As stated by OLPED, the media watchdog for Côte d'Ivoire, such an allegiance means that most newspapers act rather 'like tools for political struggles and the conquest of government power' (OLPED 2001: 9–10).

The use of Manding, or for that matter any other regional African language is rare in the predominantly Francophone mass media of Côte d'Ivoire. The use of the expression *bori bana* is thus an instance of marked code switching: unexpected and thereby especially significant.[6] Moreover, the expression indexes a linguistic group and represents a historical feat associated with a political 'other'. In printing the phrase *bori bana*, *Notre Voie* not only transgresses a linguistic boundary, but it also appropriates an expression attributed to a historical culture that it sees as radically distinct. This, too, identifies the use of *bori bana* as an instance of code-crossing.

In order to analyse *bori bana* as a code-crossing performance, this section will briefly reconstruct the 'original' meaning of the phrase as a personal quote and as a token of the history of Manding speakers, often designated as 'Jula'. The latter term designates an emerging ethnic identity produced and transformed throughout the history of colonial and postcolonial Côte d'Ivoire. I will show how, in the articulation of an ethno-nationalist ideology called *ivoirité*, this 'Jula' ethnicity crops up as a composition of several aspects of 'foreignness' developed across the *longue durée* of Ivorian history.[7] This deconstruction of *bori bana* and 'Jula' attempts to identify the resources which the three authors use to take their readers on a code-crossing trip into the discourse of their (political) opponents. Who, then, 'are' these Manding-speaking 'Jula'?

Manding languages are spoken in large parts of West Africa, and thus in many countries to the west and north of Côte d'Ivoire: Gambia and Senegal (Mandinka), Guinea (Maninka), Mali (Bamana), and Burkina Faso (Jula) (Derive 1976). Within the territory of precolonial Côte d'Ivoire, Manding was spoken by two groups of largely Islamized peoples: the so-called Malinke of the north-western region, and the Jula speakers of the merchant cities of Kong and Bondoukou further to the east. After many generations of labour migration and the penetration of Jula-speaking merchants from the Manding areas into southern Côte d'Ivoire, several millions of Manding speakers now reside in the southern zones of Côte d'Ivoire: in the urban centres such as Abidjan, Bouaké and Daloa, and in the coffee and cocoa plantation areas in-between. In this southern and diasporic area, the Manding language is often named Jula; it is a *lingua franca* of the informal sector, of long-distance commerce, of the town or village marketplace, and of religious (Muslim) communication, used by first-language speakers of Manding as well as many others (Derive 1976, 1990).[8] The expression *bori bana* is readily intelligible to any of them. Explained in this way, one could conclude that the code-switching performance of *bori bana* is merely a straightforward language shift between two *linguae francae*, the formal French and the informal Jula, written by authors and read by an audience who are at least bilingual. The phrase *bori bana*, however, is also easily recognised as an emblem or token of a 'Jula' historical era, with 'Jula' construed as an ethnonym or quasi-ethnonym.

The composite 'Boribana' is the name given by the late 19th-century warlord Samori Touré to a fortress he built in present-day northern Côte d'Ivoire in order to resist attacks from the French and British colonial armies. Built in 1897, the purportedly unconquerable fortress called 'The Fleeing is Finished' embodied Samori's military and personal defiance, but it also foreshadowed the end of his reign less than a year later and his death in exile in 1900. The story of Samori and Boribana has been well-publicised ever since colonial times. The colonial literature praised Samori's bravery, his military strength and tactical shrewdness, the better to allow its French authors to glorify their own colonial heroes who outmanoeuvred him (Person 1968–75, I). In the post-independence era, Samori was re-styled into an anti-colonial resistance hero and a state-builder (Ki-Zerbo 1978). Crucial to this postcolonial re-invention of Samori is the work of Yves Person (1968–1975) and his three-volume book entitled: 'Samori: A Jula Revolution'. By the latter term he meant a military revival movement led by the Muslim Manding Samori and blocked by the European colonial forces.[9]

Bori bana is thus not only an expression in Jula language, but also a token of a 'Jula' history. To appreciate it as such, one can rely on at least two textual traditions: the colonial one that is cunningly complimentary, and the postcolonial one that is forthrightly empowering. Instances of the latter can be found in the more recent work of two prominent Ivorian artists who themselves grew up in a Manding environment: the song *Bori Samory* (1984) of reggae star Alpha Blondy (born Seydou Koné) and the novel *Monnè outrages défis* (1990) of the prize-winning novelist Ahmadou Kourouma.[10] Yet however strongly these popular lyrics/texts imposed the image of a defiant Manding ancestor, they did not herald the demise of the 'colonial' Samori. In the three *bori bana* articles in *Notre Voie*, the authors progressively unearth a fortress Boribana that is a mere delusion of haughtiness. Moreover, they reactivate the colonial texts about Samori in an attempt to situate the expression *bori bana* in the immediate context of Samori's capture and deportation, and they thus relocate Samori's statement in the voice of the person who captured and expelled the 'Jula' trouble maker. Such an astonishing re-reinvention and inimical appropriation (or recolonization) of the 'Jula' token *bori bana* amounts to a historic *tour de force*, which takes place in a context of shifting political power balances between the 'Jula' and their antagonists. Before delving deeper into how three *Notre Voie* contributors in the first months of 2000 undermine 'Jula' audacity and transform its defiance into failure, we must situate such shifts in a longer history of socio-economic, political, religious and cultural differentiation and emergent inequalities.

'The Jula' as Triple Strangers

Early ethnography and colonial ethnic policy constructed a 'Jula' tribe of Muslims active in long-distance trade and spread all over the northern parts of Côte d'Ivoire.[11] Such a proliferation was deemed synonymous with rootlessness, as exemplied by Delafosse (1901: 3) who contended that 'nowhere does [this population] represent the autochthonous element'.[12] Even if colonial ethnographers such as Nebout (1904) granted certain Jula communities the status of an 'indigenous population', they retained the distinct aspect of an itinerant, quasi nomadic people.[13] Currently, many authors agree that 'Jula' as an ethnic identity in Côte d'Ivoire is characterized by a combination of at least three elements: 'northern people' associated with 'commercial activity' and 'Muslim' (Launay & Miran 2000, Boone 1993, Lewis 1973). A related element concerns the 'Jula' penetration of certain 'geosocial spaces' (LeBlanc 2000a: 89). These may be regional, establishing ties with other countries such as Mali and Burkina Faso, or global links with the world-wide Muslim community (Launay and Miran 2000: 71). Related to such positionings, then, emerges the factor of nationality, by which the 'Jula' are seen as either partly foreigners (Marguerat 1981-82: 321; LeBlanc 2000b: 447) or at least, in Bayart's term, comparatively 'extravert' (Bayart 1999).

Like any ethnic identity, however, that of the 'Jula' in Ivorian society cannot be recounted in a unilinear narrative of invention, reproduction and transformation. Rather, one needs to embrace the many changing collateral relationships that incessantly reconstitute this shifting 'identity'.[14] Instead of opting for a complex, and probably inconclusive, historical reconstruction, and with an eye to relating these shifting 'Jula' 'identities' to the antagonisms of the most recent past, it is sensible here to turn to some theoretical guidance provided by Mamdani (1998, 2001). In relating colonial legacies to the creation of political identities in Africa, Mamdani suggests three dimensions in the constitution of subjects in situations of governance. His model of colonial and postcolonial 'subjection' distinguishes three aspects in the creation of political selves and others: the socio-economic, the civic, and, perhaps less obviously, the so-called 'racial'.

In the domain of race relations, African colonies witnessed, in the terminology of Mamdani, not only the imposition of a 'dominant race' of white Europeans over the different groups of 'subject[ed] natives', but also the invention of a 'subject race' situated on a racial scale in between the colonized natives and the white colonizers. 'Subject races' were deemed to share with the dominant race a certain proclivity toward 'civilization' and later 'modernisation' and were therefore openly instrumentalised as agents of progress (Mamdani 2001: ch. 1). During the first decades of the colonization of Côte d'Ivoire, the role of 'subject race' was ascribed to the 'Jula' Muslim merchants who, as translocal busybodies, disseminated French produce and were seen as bringing 'natives' into contact with 'civilization' (Triaud 1974: 554). By the same token, the Jula language became a direct instrument of colonial rule. Jula language was seen as a *lingua franca* transcending the linguistic fragmentation of the colony and enabling communication across French West Africa at large: it became the language of commerce and of the African section of the army (*tirailleurs sénégalais*). Only French was ranked above it as the language of official communication in administration and education. Although 'the Jula' probably played no larger role in the official administration than the other, 'native' peoples, Jula-speaking Muslims did achieve some feeble participation in the French secular and missionary educational systems.

Other ethnic groups, however, such as the southern Baule people, showed a far keener interest in French education, and in the process formed an educated elite who gathered the kind of symbolic capital that turned out to be a strategic asset in their repositioning as a newly emerging alternative 'subject race'. The two other assets that were critical in the rise of the Baule were the economic wealth they accumulated through active participation in the expanding plantation economy, and the capital of governmentality which they acquired by reinventing themselves as the nation-builders *par excellence*. The repositioning of the 'the Jula' in late colonial and postcolonial times needs thus to be related to the Baule's rise to socio-economic and political prominence. In postcolonial times, the competition between the 'Jula' and the Baule and other Akan-speaking elites retained a softly racialised dimension. This was palpable in the ways in which both categories claimed a special relationships with the hegemonic powers now increasingly situated outside the national sphere: France, the United States, the *'umma* of the Muslim world, and the world of international finance and politics (Bazin 1998, 1999).

Economically, the Baule were well equipped for this replacement of a former 'subject race' identified as 'Jula'. Populating the central part of southern Côte d'Ivoire, they participated fully in the coffee and cocoa economy by providing labour for the French and 'indigenous' plantations, as well as establishing their own plantations not only in the Baule region but also far beyond. They migrated and expanded first into Agni lands to the east and later into

Bété lands to the west. The Baule thus situated themselves at the heart of the economic success of Côte d'Ivoire, a feat that also attracted millions of other labour migrants from the hinterland of northern Côte d'Ivoire and the neighbouring colonies and countries. Although they deeply permeated the southern societies, these northern migrants largely assimilated the culture considered to be 'northern' or 'Jula'. With the northern migrants, the Jula language was disseminated exponentially and Islam became the most important religion in Côte d'Ivoire. With this simultaneous influx of both southern (Baule) and northern migrants, the plantation belt gave rise to an emerging identity of the autochthone or native, as opposed to the allochthone or immigrant settler (Chauveau 2000). In this polarisation however, the position of the Baule underwent a gradual shift throughout the postcolonial period. It turned from ethnic allochthones (which they had been, for instance, in Agni and Bété country) to national autochthones, that is, people who, unlike 'the Jula', were credited with having ethnic roots at least somewhere within the nation-state boundaries. The classification of the 'northern' settlers, and more importantly here, 'the Jula', by contrast, was increasingly highlighted as 'allochthonous'. Both the Ivorian and the non-Ivorian northerners came to be perceived as having no ancestral roots within Côte d'Ivoire, and for the purportedly footloose and extravert 'Jula', this spelled out the demotion from colonial 'subject race' to postcolonial 'allochthones.' This development of 'national allochthony' went hand in hand with a specific articulation of Ivorian nationalism in the 1990s, the governmentally enforced ethno-national programme called *ivoirité*.

To address the 'civic component of subjection', Mamdani (2001) poses the question how, and how far, the political and civil rights of nationals are granted to natives as opposed to settlers, autochthones as opposed to allochthones. From the 1930s on, the cosmopolitan southern region of Côte d'Ivoire had witnessed the emergence of a distinct Ivorian national awareness, voiced at the level of civil society (Chauveau and Dozon 1985). With decolonization, the central issue was increasingly voiced in ethnic terms: who could best voice this nationalist concern ? It happened to be the Baule – joined in time by the Agni and the Lagune peoples to form the Akan people – who were credited with possessing a distinctive '*sens de l'Etat*' (Memel-Fotê 1999: 24). Through an ingenious reinvention of tradition, the precolonial 'Baule State' was ascribed 'the value of a model of governance [and] of [the] political management of an ensemble of local diversity' (Memel-Fotê and Chauveau, 1989: 38). In managing this 'diversity', the first president of independent Côte d'Ivoire and a Baule 'chief', Houphouët-Boigny (1960-1993) can be seen to have deployed a double strategy. Political opposition from southern 'autochthones' (first the Agni and later the Bété) was delegitimized as being 'ethnic' and therefore antinational (Gbagbo 1983). At the same time, the foundation president tried to disempower the northern 'Jula' elites by eliminating their leaders (Diarra 1997), then to take control of their trade networks by means of a nationalist programme of 'ivoirianisation' (Boone 1993). In the long run, however, these strategies were only partly successful. What emerged against them were two major political parties, one predominantly southern, the other predominantly northern, who both traced their origin to their respective suppression of the southern and northern 'resistance'. The effectively southern Socialist Party FPI seeks its origins in Houphouët's clampdown on the Bété insurgencies of the 1960s and 1970s, while the effectively northern Republican Party RDR is said to find its origin in the so-called 'Northern Charter' – a document edited in the early 1990s and expressing the frustrations of the 'northerners' whose aspirations had been neglected for decades by Houphouët-Boigny.

This translation of emerging political, socio-economic and ethnic identities into ideological projects and political parties was a complex process which, in 2000, resulted in three major formations (Dozon 2000). The former unitarist PDCI-RDA of President Houphouët's successor, Henri Konan Bédié, abandoned its self-ascribed 'national' vocation and was increasingly seen as a southernist 'Akan' Party to defend the interests of the plantation elite, the autochthonous populations and, increasingly, the nationals as against the large groups of residents whom it labelled 'dubious' Ivorians and foreigners. The Socialist Party FPI of Laurent Gbagbo shared this proclivity for 'national autochthones' with the PDCI-RDA and linked its consideration for the economically and educationally underprivileged with its ethnic profile as a party representing the Bété, the historical underdogs in Ivorian society. Finally, the Republican Party RDR of Alassane Ouattara, a 1994 break-away from the PDCI, was readily seen as representing the interests of 'the Jula' as triple strangers: 'internationals', 'national allochthones' or even non-nationals by their 'civic' status; mainly Muslim; and economically associated with formal and informal international trade, commerce and finance.

The presidential candidate of the RDR, Alassane Ouattara, however, had been prevented from standing at each election preceding our three articles, and the RDR had thus never participated in any presidential or parliamentary elections before. At the same time, the three-party configuration as just described was the result of almost a decade of multipartyism and a concommittant ethnicisation of politics. This ethnicisation gained all the more ground when Houphouët-Boigny's successor as president, Henri Konan Bédié (1993–99), proclaimed an ideology of national unity and 'multiculturality' called *ivoirité*. A series of presidential statements and academic documents inscribed the precolonial inhabitants of southern Côte d'Ivoire as 'national autochthones' and thus awarded them a privileged role in creating the melting-pot of a future Ivorian society (Touré 1996; Bédié s.d.). Complementing inclusion by exclusion, *ivoirité* nominally disqualified 'the Jula' from being 'national autochthones' and thus full Ivorian citizens, and instead 'invited' allochthones, settlers, and non-nationals to adapt themselves to the national-culture-in-the-making (Niangoran-Bouah 1996).

The end of Bédié's presidency in 1999 hastened increasing international isolation and deepening intranational divisions. The latter seemed suddenly to be halted when a military mutiny turned into a *coup d'etat* and Bédié was thrown out of office in December 1999. The new military head of state, General Robert Guéï, announced the end of all exclusions and in January 2000 set up a government that combined the two former opposition parties, the northern Socialist FPI of Laurent Gbagbo and the southern Liberal RDR of Ouattara to leave out the previous government party, the PCDI. In the course of the next four months, however, this unity collapsed when Guëï reintroduced *ivoirité* with the support of the FPI and against the RDR. General Guëï launched a campaign to delegitimise the RDR as a proper political formation and now supported a rewriting of the Constitution again to marginalize 'national allochthones'. Events took a decisive turn in May 2000. The three articles here discussed were published within the period between General Guëï's coup d'état of December 1999 and his sudden and vigorous revival of a renewed new policy of *ivoirité* in May 2000.

Three *bori bana* Articles: A Genocidal Crescendo

The three *bori bana* articles published in *Notre Voie* comment on topical issues in Ivoiran politics and voice the opinion of the Socialist Party FPI. To do so most effectively, they instrumentalise words from a linguistic group (Jula) and a historical personage (Samori) in the form of an established expression with strong cultural overtones. In other words, the acts of code-crossing function in a discourse that culturalises or ethnicises political events and adversaries. To this end it engages complex and entangled processes of political and ethnic selfing/othering. My analysis of the newspaper articles will identify which political and ethnic 'others' are evoked and how this is achieved by activating certain voices and particular meanings by way of the token *bori bana*.

Following their chronological order, the three articles combine to a crescendo on several levels. On the level of selfing/othering, one can perceive a widening of the 'other' group from political opponent via ethnic antagonist to racialised other. In terms of the three grammars introduced by Baumann, this hardening and broadening of selfings/otherings is achieved by operating, successively, the segmentary, the orientalist, and the encompassing grammar. On the level of code-crossing, this crescendo is matched by an ever-deepening implication of the author into the broadening category of the 'other' which almost leads to the authors identifying with the 'other'. This combination of a hardening othering and a deepening incursion reaches its climax in the third article when the author radically transforms the voice and the meaning of *bori bana* in order to let the racialised other express his exclusion not only from the political arena or as an ethnic stranger, but from humankind in general. That is the 'moment' when I will dare to speak of a genocidal encompassment of the other through radical discursive penetration. Let me thus reconstruct the gradual build-up in the ways in which *Notre Voie* contributors construct their political adversaries by crossing into their language.

The first article, hereafter called 'the Bédié article', dates from six days after the *coup d'état* of December 1999 and is entitled: 'That's it, *bori bana* for Bédié' ('*Ça y est, bori-bana pour Bédié*'). In the short piece journalist Maurice

Lohourignon (2000) reports on the whereabouts of President Bédié who had been chased from Côte d'Ivoire just a few days ago. He begins by saying that 'Bédié has fallen', has been ousted, and has left the country: first to Nigeria, then to Togo, and finally to Mali. But his travels and travails are to no avail: no-one is willing to support him. The article ends with: 'In Bamako [Mali], Bédié bursts out in tears. His long and foolish race is over. Bori-bana! Pity for N'Zuéba'. The last sentence repeats the *bori-bana* of the title to summarize the ousted president's fruitless search for international support, but it also adds in another ethnic marker: '*N'Zuéba.*'

This second instance of code-switching utilizes a Baule expression to point to the ousted Bédié while the Jula language expression *bori bana* indexes their main opponents: Alassane Ouattara and the Republican Party RDR. Until the *coup d'état* of December 1999, the Socialist Party FPI of Gbagbo had indeed considered *ivoirité* as a battle-ground engaging two political elites: the Baule or Akan planters of the PDCI-RDA versus the commercial and financial elites represented by the RDR. The first *bori bana* article reflects this constellation and reports on the antagonism between the two camps. Its last sentence indicates both camps by a code-switching mannoeuvre: the Baule expression '*N'Zueba*' points to Bédié and the PDCI-RDA, while the Jula expression *bori bana* indexes their main opponents: Ouattara and the RDR. *N'Zuéba* is the self-attributed nickname of Bédié and means 'small river' in Baule, the mother tongue of the ousted president.[15] Now, the article makes it clear, the small river of Bédié has ceased to flow. In order to signal this end, the journalist uses the Jula expression *bori bana*. In the absence of any explicit reference to Samori's unconquerable fortress, the expression is associated with his *fin de carrière* – a desperate end that, according to the official FPI view, was directly provoked by the RDR, initially suspected of organising the December *coup d'état*.

In the juxtaposition of *N'Zueba* and *bori bana*, the topical political reality is reported and explained quite literally in ethnic terms within a textual construction that is clearly 'segmentary'. In terms of code, the French-speaking journalist distances himself from both the Jula-speaking RDR and the Baule-speaking PDCI-RDA. Making use of the language ideology in which French outrivals the national vernaculars, he places himself above both parties whose quarrel is presented as an ethnic one. In terms of political ideology, the journalist plays on the idea launched by Houphouët-Boigny and repeated by Bédié that 'ethnic' opposition (*tribalisme*) is politically illegitimate and detrimental for the nation as a whole. Thus, in the segmentary construction at hand, the journalist reserves for himself, his newspaper and the Socialist Party FPI the position of state-builder. This attitude would soon be translated into political action: a few days after the article was published, the FPI decided to join the RDR in the government of coup leader General Guéï, and it announced that it would help to rebuild the nation after the disaster of the Bédié administration. In this project, which later came to be known as the 'refoundation' (*la refondation*) of Côte d'Ivoire, the FPI faced one main competitor: the RDR led by Alassane Ouattara. This political 'other' would be dealt with a few months later in the second of the *bori bana* articles.

This second article was published in May 2000. During that month, a split had occurred within the transition government whereby the Head of State General Guëï took sides with the FPI-members in his cabinet and started to work towards excluding the RDR from the political arena. On Friday 12th, Guëï publicly announced his volte-face by openly accusing the RDR of planning a *coup d'état* and by stating that the constitution would exclude presidential candidates if one of their parents were not Ivorian by birth. This was widely read as a frontal attack against the RDR-leader Alassane Ouattara whose Ivorian nationality had been cast into doubt ever since he had first entered into competition with Bédié for the highest office in 1995.

Now, in May 2000, *Notre Voie*'s top journalist and senior editor, Freedom Neruda, published an article under the title 'Dramane Ouattara: bori bana' (Neruda 2000), hereafter called 'the Ouattara article'. In this long piece, Neruda rereads the history of Côte d'Ivoire from the moment when Ouattara first appeared on the political scene as a prime minister under President Houphouët-Boigny in 1990. The author holds Ouattara responsible for destabilising the country ever since, and he links this with the personal history of Ouattara who is presented as a person constantly travelling in and out of the country and changing his nationality as he sees fit. In the final paragraph of the article, the author asserts how General Guëï's recent announcements will put an end to Ouattara's political aspirations. The article ends: 'Dramane Ouattara is now completely out of the race. The man can retire to [....the village] Sindou, because BORI BANA.'

Like the Bédié article, the Ouattara article seems simply to report on the end of a major politician's career, and thus merely to re-activate the general sense of *bori bana* as a *fin de carrière*. The obvious difference is that, while the first article focuses on Bédié's final career moves, the second article narrates in broad lines the story of Ouattara's entire political curriculum and life-style. Its narrative features all the stereotypes of the typical 'Jula' which had been inscribed by Bédié's version of *ivoirité*: the RDR leader is portrayed as a 'national allochthone' who, apart from economic profit, also seeks full political citizenship and power, and therefore lies about his real roots outside the country. This 'lie' is evoked by 'Sindou' which is presumed by Ouattara's political opponents to be his place of birth in Burkina Faso – something which Ouattara himself denies. The ethnic profile that emerges from the meticulous description of Ouattara's life is that of the 'national allochthone': born abroad and leading a life of migration and fortune-seeking (*bori*, 'running') while changing loyalties and identities in the process. The article concludes with a verdict that calls an end (*bana*) to this wandering existence and shows people of the Ouattara type that they have no place as full citizens of, or even in, Côte d'Ivoire and had better seek their rights in the countries where their roots are. This narrative of Ouattara's life draws a 'phantom portrait' that offers a wide scope for further applications. To the extent that '*bori*' stands for the endless mobility of a typical 'Jula' life, the *bana* calls for an end to it and asks them to go back to wherever they came from.

By contrast to the first article, the one about Bédié, the second one, which I have called the Ouattara article, implicitly broadens its target from the individual politician's fate to a whole ethnic group's future. In the Bédié article, the author placed himself at the seemingly neutral apex of a segmentary order, where one of the branches had lost the battle. In the Ouattara article, the author clearly situates himself as one of the parties and uses a grammar of the orientalizing kind. Here, the senior editor uses the editorial column to merge observation and opinion in order to express the repositioning of the FPI in the changing political landscape. Politically, the author-editor engages the FPI in a cross-party alliance that at the time is beginning to be known as 'TSO' (*Tout sauf Ouattara* – 'Anything but Ouattara'). In the ethnic register, the author-editor fully re-activates the discourse of *ivoirité*. Sketching a paradigmatically non-Ivorian way of life, he insinuates a consensus about an Ivorian way of life. The latter is directly imported from the discourse of *ivoirité* which now re-appears not as the Akanist project of the isolated President Bédié, but as part of a general programme to rebuild the nation (Dozon 2000).

To summarize, the code-crossing use of *bori bana* shows a crescendo from the neutral, if perhaps ironic tone of the first article to the partisan and sarcastic tone of the second. This change of tone signifies a change in the political position of the FPI. Having been a relative outsider to the main developments (*ivoirité* and the *coup d'état*), it proceeded actively to take part in a programme to 'refound the nation'. In pursuing this programme, it meets the same major opponent as Bédié had met in his own time: Ouattara and his Republican Party RDR. At this stage, it tries to exclude the RDR, not by furthering an ethnic quarrel within the nation, but by constructing a new national narrative in which there is no space for the itinerant, border-crossing, 'running'(*bori*) 'Jula'.[16]

The third article will go even further in widening the code-crossing scope of the word *bori*. Here, as I will show, all movement by 'the Jula' is interpreted as treason, and all 'breathing space' is to be made impossible. In order to persuade his readers to such a conclusion, the author will further manipulate the meaning and voice of the original *bori bana*. If the two previous articles vaguely situated *bori bana* in a *fin-de-carrière* context similar to the one of Samori, the third text blatantly relocates the phrase in a context of capture, deportation, and exclusion from the human race. Remarkably, its author uses the *gestus* and *ductus* of 'scientific' language to do so. While the Ouattara article had 'only' sought to expatriate Alassane Ouattara and 'the Jula' from the confines of the nation, the third article seeks to exclude 'the Jula' from humanity.

'"Out of the Race": Autopsy of an Expression' or, Vivisection of a Code-Crossing Performance

Dramane Koné, University Professor of Literature at the University of Abidjan and currently also Minister of Culture, runs a weekly column in *Notre Voie*. His Saturday column entitled *Dire bien* ('Well-spoken'), often presents highly technical linguistic analyses of topical political discourse. On 21 May 2000, Koné published his column under the title: '"Bori bana", Autopsy of an Expression'. This article, hereafter called the Koné article, sets out to analyse the use of the expression *bori bana* in the Ouattara article of the journalist Neruda, published four days before. The text consists of two parts. In the first part Koné reveals the historical origin of the expression *bori bana* while the second part is reserved for linguistic considerations and personal reflections on what *bori bana* might or should mean at the time of writing. In searching for the historical origin of the expression *bori bana*, Koné's text negotiates between the Ouattara article written by his colleague Freedom Neruda and the established historiography of Samori. Neruda, like his colleague who wrote the Bédié article, firmly placed the phrase *bori bana* in the context of a political *fin de carrière*. In the first part of his article, Koné lends this position a 'scientific' endorsement by situating the historical *bori bana* in the story of Samori's final flight. In the second part, however, Koné exploits this image to broaden its target and meaning in an astonishing text about 'final stages'.

The origin of the expression *bori bana*, so Koné states, is the capture of Samori Touré by the French in 1898. More precisely, he points out that *bori bana* is part of a quote from a Malinke lieutenant who was pursuing the fleeing Samori and who exclaimed in Jula, the colonial army language that he shared with Samori: '*i lo Samori, i lo Samori, bori banna!*' – 'Hey you stop, Samori, hey stop, Samori, the fleeing is finished!'. This remarkable rendition of the story entirely dissociates *bori bana* from the unconquerable fortress Boribana and removes the words from Samori in order to relocate them in the voice of Samori's captor. With this reversal, Koné turns the motto of a defiant hero into a symbol for his final humiliation. In a couple of sentences, the entire postcolonial, empowering text tradition about Samori is turned on its head.

Does this mean that Koné reverts to the French colonial tradition that only used Samori as an excuse to demonstrate the strength and wit of those who captured him? In some ways it does; but Koné obscures this congruence by playing two classic tricks of his trade: first, he provides a seemingly objective bibliographic reference to a book by an African historian; secondly, he calls the expression 'an utterance sadly renowned' (*un énoncé tristement célèbre*), thus inferring that his re-attribution represents common knowledge and simply recuperates local historical lore.

Tracing the bibliographic reference indeed leads us to the right author, but to the wrong book. Koné cites a biography of Sékou Touré in which the author, the Guinean historian Ibrahima Baba Kaké (1987), mentions Samori Touré as the presumed forefather of the postindependence leader Sékou Touré. In this book, however, there is no mention of the '*i lo*' anecdote which, so far as I can trace it, only occurs in another publication by Kaké (1989). The latter is an anthology of short articles written during the colonial period and published previously in French colonial periodicals. This collection contains a short essay on the capture of Samori, based on a report written by the French colonel Lartigue in 1898/1899. Lartigue narrates how the French army took Samori by surprise in his village and how he fled while African soldiers (*tirailleurs*) went after him. Then, 'the soldiers who were ahead shouted: 'Ilo Samori; ilo Samori! Stop Samori!' (*les tirailleurs de tête crient: 'Ilo Samory; ilo Samory! Halte Samori!*) (Baba Kaké 1989: 83). In the hands of Professor Koné, this colonial report is turned into: 'a Malinke lieutenant, Al Kamissa, pursues Samori and exclaims, while gasping for air: "i lo Samori, i lo, bori banna"'. In other words, Koné replaces the French *Halte Samory* by the Jula expression *bori bana*. Koné's palimpsest not only hides the French colonial source of the story, but also replaces the French rendition by a superimposed translation into Jula: *bori banna!*

What the article thus insinuates as common historical lore and African historiography, is therefore a piece of French colonial propaganda with the 'French' writer removed and the French language translated into Jula. The place of the French is not simply taken by Africans, but more specifically by a Malinke sergeant, that is, by a speaker of Manding or specifically Jula. The story that it was a Malinke sergeant who captured the Malinke warlord Samori is indeed told by the Malinke historian Baba Kaké, born and raised in Kankan, the 'Jula' capital of Guinea. Exploiting this Manding version of rewriting French colonial history, Profesor Koné can now pursue his code-crossing journey into the present situation of 'the Jula', and not only those far away in the north, but also those nearby in the capital Abidjan. This second manoeuvre takes place in the second part of the text which it is worth quoting at length.

> In Jula, the verb 'bori' has the peculiar characteristic of allowing for two postpositions, namely nya and kô, which correspond to the French prepositions 'ahead' and 'behind'. [...]
> In the second case, where you are after something in order to catch it, if you get it, *boli banna*, but if the thing that appears unattainable escapes you, *bori banna*. Such as power. So good judgement advises this: 'what you pursue, if you can't get it, stop and let go'. It is without doubt the latter representation that one finds among the inhabitants of the town quarter bori bana of Bamako (Mali) and the town quarter 'Boribana' of Attécoubé (commune of Abidjan), a town quarter surrounded by the lagoon, inaccessible on foot. 'We call this quarter "Boribana" because we have searched everywhere, we haven't found a place to stay, we have enough of it, we stay here where we are, because we have not reached the goal we were after,' thus confided in me, sombrely, an Ivorian resident in one of the streets called street of broken dreams. A street that is of one piece with the particular situation of its inhabitants. Those are, half-lost like the militants of a political party (which I don't need to name because you know it) in a complex network of streets and gutters, awaiting an event that hovers over their heads like a thunderstorm of deception and gestation. They don't even know that the negative that is presented to them risks to turn into parody, into humiliation. The summit of the satanic, really, for all the vanquished who refuse bori bana. To be taken into consideration, without respite before the crumbling of dreams…and the running of tears (Nyadji).

This second part of the article highlights the present-day dimension. It is introduced by a linguistic analysis that connects the Ouattara article with Koné's subsequent political and socio-economic considerations. Koné points out that one can either run ahead of something or behind it. Running ahead of something means that one is fleeing or being chased. In this case, *bori bana* means that one is caught. This is obviously the case in the Ouattara article where Alassane Ouattara is caught by the two interventions of Guëï announced during the previous week. Koné, however, says he chooses to focus on the second case, when somebody is running behind something, more specifically something 'unattainable', as he specifies wryly, 'like power'. Subsequently he identifies the two (interrelated) groups who are pursuing unachievable 'power': first, the Republican Party RDR who, if the Ouattara article is correct in its verdict, has lost its leader Alassane Ouattara, and secondly, the people who share the same itinerant (*bori*) ethnic profile with the RDR but who, instead of being prosperous and successful, inhabit a quarter of the capital that '*we* call [...] "Boribana"' (emphasis mine). Koné makes it clear that he is referring to non-national migrants and settlers when he specifies that *Boribana* quarters can be found both in Abidjan and in Bamako (Mali), and he characterizes the socio-economic situation of the settlers by referring to their habitat: impoverished and hopeless. Again, as in the historical part, Koné appears merely to register what his sources tell him: it was the people themselves who called their own town quarter *Boribana,* and it was they who told him about the significance of the term.

Koné uses *bori bana* to associate the two groups and construct them into one constituency of political and socio-economic desperados. The first group, the RDR, is a political formation with an ethnic profile which, already in the Ouattara article, was built around the idea of itinerancy and border-crossing (*bori*). The second group consists of non-national settlers (Malians) and 'national allochthones' (with Malian or 'northern' roots), both equally impoverished. Together, they form a kind of political 'people' who share Jula as a common language and who, by virtue of the phrase *bori bana*, share a common history and a common fate. Like Samori who is their historical model, the 'Jula' have a tradition of fanatically pursuing unattainable goals. Like Ouattara who is their contemporary model, 'the Jula' are coming to a point where they have to let go, unless, Koné cogitates, they want this pursuit to turn 'into a humiliation' and into 'the summit of the satanic': 'the shattering of dreams and the running of tears (Nyadji)'. This last word of the article, the Jula language word for 'tears', is a cunningly implicit way of indexing, again through code-switching, that the tears will be shed by 'the Jula'. At that point, the title of the article begins to make sense: Koné performs an 'autopsy' of an expression, but the pre-empted death of the expression prefigures the death of the people whose fate is sealed by it.

In the crescendo of the three *bori bana* articles, the column by Koné represents the apex of selfing through othering in that it combines a most complex code-crossing performance with a selfing/othering grammar of radical exclusion by radical encompassment.

To contrast the stages of this crescendo, the first, the Bédié article had presented a rather simple case of code-crossing whereby an author lends a quote from one party to address it to a third party. In this segmentary structure the

French-speaking journalist stands above the Jula-speaking accuser (RDR, *bori bana*) who targets the Baule-speaking victim (Bédié, *N'Zueba*). In the second, the Ouattara article, the voice of the journalist collapses into, or merges with, the voice of the opponents of Ouattara. Only two positions remain: Ouattara versus the TSO, the 'Anything but Ouattara' movement. This second discursive strategy of dealing with the 'Jula' code word *bori bana* may lend itself to a comparison with the English adage of 'making the other eat his words'. By force of this merger into an orientalist scheme, *bori bana* is turned into a bi-local statement that originates in the Ouattara ('Jula') constituency, is then appropriated by the TSO movement against Ouattara, and is finally fed back to Ouattara for him to mull over when he retires to his ancestral village. To remain in this, admittedly somewhat gargantuan metaphor of ingestion, the journalist swallows the Jula expression only to spit it out again in the form of a venomous judgement.

The Koné article, finally, adds different layers of speakers (the Mande soldier), authors (the historian Kaké), sources (Samori) and targets (RDR voters and migrants/settlers) to the *bori bana* affair. This inextricable maze of voices, however, collapses, as we have seen, into one 'Jula' voice and the *bori bana* expression. Above this manoeuvre, there presides the author. First, the Jula voice is appropriated by Koné the historian who hands it over to Koné the linguist, who in turn surrenders it to Koné the Everyman. Immediately after explaining the syntax of *bori*, Koné engineers a change of character introduced by: 'Therefore, good judgement advises this'. From then onwards, Koné leaves the ivory tower of historiography and linguistics and takes his place among 'the people' when he reports what an inhabitant of the Boribana slums 'confided' in him 'somberly' (*'me confia, l'air navré'*). Here at last it becomes clear that 'Jula' is now also the language that links Koné to the subjects of his enquiry. The linguist Koné not only has a certain expertise in the Jula language (Koné 1988), but he is also, most probably, a first-language speaker of Jula. Born in Bouaké and carrying the patronym Koné makes him readily recognisable as 'a Jula'. Thus, once Koné mixes among 'the Jula', he can do so simultaneously as 'a Jula' and as their fiercest antagonist. These different positions correspond to different targets. Koné the historian evokes the historical 'Jula', Koné the linguist is facing the (perpetual/traditional) 'Jula speaker', while Koné the Everyman or Koné 'the Jula' confronts the 'RDR/Jula' people in their general condition as human beings.

The crescendo of successive 'generalisations' reaches its climax when Koné formulates his conclusions about the foreseeable end of 'the Jula'. One might call this the moment of ultimate encompassment: all the multiple voices are captured by one personage: the sensible, humane voice who represents humanity and who finds around him 'the Jula' who 'do not even know that the negative that is presented to them risks to turn into parody, into humiliation'. The parody is that 'the Jula' themselves are a parody of what it means to be a human being: they do not listen to good advice, they do not know their past, their language and their nature, and they are thus incapable of facing their future which holds nothing short of an ill-fated end. Such encompassment is sustained by a triple movement of insinuation. As a scientist, a historian and a linguist, Koné penetrates 'Jula' tradition and language from above. As a visitor credited with confidences in 'Jula' language, he meets them as an empathetic observer. As a purportedly neutral Everyman ('Jula' or anti-'Jula') he prophesizes the imminent 'tears' that 'the Jula' will shed.

Bori bana, Civil War, and Three Dynamics of Implosion

At the time of writing this chapter, a civil war is tearing apart Côte d'Ivoire. Since 19 September 2002, one group of rebel soldiers has occupied most of the northern half of the country, while two other small groups have taken possession of smaller parts of western Côte d'Ivoire. The political wing of the rebels, called the MPCI (*Mouvement patriotique de Côte d'Ivoire*), is presently negotiating a peace agreement with the Ivorian government. The issues on which the negotiations have made no progress whatsoever are two political problems labelled 'nationality' and 'identification' (*Projet d'accord,* 2002). Who is Ivorian, and how can someone identify him- or herself as such? These questions linger at the heart of the ongoing conflict, and they are being discussed against the background of continuing suspicions and 'revelations' about the 'real' identities of the rebels, and the 'real' intentions of the different parties in the conflict: the Gbagbo government, the French peace-keeping troops, the rebels, the neighbouring countries, etc.).

Soon after the conflict broke out, the government launched the idea that the rebels are in fact 'international terrorists'. It chose the Washington National Press Club to let its Economy Minister announce: 'I do not exclude the hypothesis that they [the rebels] enjoy the support of terrorist groups and you [Americans] know these groups. After all, the attack against our democracy took place in September; maybe there is a link' (in *L'Inter*, 5 November 2002). On 30 September, the original day of this government announcement, the American Section of the Ivorian Republican Party RDR organised a demonstration in Washington to protest against the way in which the government was handling the rebellion. The protesters stressed that in government-held territory, non-national migrants were the object of persecution and abuse. Thereupon, the Ivorian Embassy in Washington issued a statement on the internet, saying that the RDR-U.S. 'organised a manifestation in support of the terrorists' (Ambassade de Côte d'Ivoire à Washington, 2002).

Following the revelations that the rebels were terrorists and the RDR militants their supporters, the government announced that it would start to smoke out the insurgents who remained in the government-held southern part of the country. One measure taken in that respect was the systematic destruction of all 'problematic quarters' (*quartiers précaires*) of the capital Abidjan, because they could conceal weapons and hide terrorists from neighbouring countries, such as Burkina Faso, Mali and Guinea. Soon afterwards, an article appeared in the pro-government newspaper *Le National*, welcoming the government's measures but asking for the immediate and total destruction of the Boribana quarter of Abidjan. Boribana, so *Le National* wrote, needed to be 'razed immediately' and 'without worries' (*sans état d'âme*). After all, given its strategic position near the lagoon and the presidential palace and because its allegedly large stock of arms, it was to be considered a 'powderkeg' (*poudrière*) (P.L. 2002).

The 'powderkeg' word made its re-appearance in a series of articles published on the pro-government website *Ivoire Forum* and dealing with a new mass-grave of about 120 corpses that was discovered in early December 2002 along the frontline in central-west Côte d'Ivoire. One article 'revealed' that this mass grave was a *'montage'* set up by the rebels. The explanation was that the rebels swear by their own immortality and are convinced of their immunity against bullets. After many of its troops had been killed in a battle with government soldiers, the author explained, the rebel leaders had tried to hide the corpses in a mass-grave in order to 'mask the trickery of the immortality of their troops' (Bakary 2002). If the corpses succeeded in fooling the rebels, another article argued, then they would also mislead Benoît Scheuer, maker of the film *Côte d'Ivoire, poudrière identitaire*. Scheuer, the author said, was absolutely right when in his film he predicted a future genocide. Only, the recent mass-grave proved, according to the author, that the filmmaker mistook victims for executioners: it should be obvious to the international community that the north was now implementing its long-planned genocidal project against the south (Ebrokié 2002). The rebels for their part are equally making use of Scheuer's prediction of genocide when on their website they publish articles such as 'Gbagbo legalises the genocidal machine' and 'Gbagbo, Goebbels, Goudé' (MPCI 2002). The former article likens the FPI youngsters to the Rwandan *'Interahamwe'* while the latter text compares the ex-student leader Blé Goudé with the Nazi minister of information because, it states, both are responsible for encouraging the people in expressing their xenophobic hatred. These observations make clear how the discourse of the ongoing Ivorian conflict over 'nationality' and 'identity' is expanding both in time and in space. Speaking of time, one observes how the conflict accommodates chunks of national and global, recent and ancient history.

In this chapter, I have focussed on the phrase *bori bana* in order to elicit the re-working of history in terms of the ongoing conflict. In passing, I also mentioned that *ivoirité* unearthed precolonial history in order to identify the 'national autochthones' of Côte d'Ivoire, or, that the history of recent genocides (Nazi Germany, Rwanda) and global conflicts ('September 11th') is being inscribed into the arguments of the conflicting parties. Perhaps more obvious is the geographic expansion of the conflict's discourse in the way it implicates Côte d'Ivoire's neighbouring countries (Mali, Burkina Faso, Guinea), the international community (UN, *Prévention Génocides*), and global politics ('the war against terrorism'). Here, too, *bori bana* in its guise as the capital's quarter Boribana, provides an instructive case. In the Koné article, Boribana housed historically 'hopeless' people who found themselves literally and metaphorically in a dead-end street. In the recent conflict the overcrowded Boribana is said to hide weapons and international terrorists in a site that becomes redefined as a strategically positioned base camp for attacking the president and the entire population of Abidjan.

The case presented in this chapter exemplifies the way in which the ongoing conflict in Côte d'Ivoire expands globally while it gets articulated in the local idiom of *bori bana*. Therefore, I think, this case productively illustrates the process of implosion in the three senses pointed out in the introductory parts of this chapter.

First, *bori bana* is the site where, in the terminology of Appadurai (1996), nationally constructed identities collide with transnational ones and the latter are 'discovered' to be the disguise of the former. In the *bori bana* token, the journalist uncovers his former President Bédié as a political pariah both in his own country and in the West African region. In the same Jula expression, the senior editor unmasks his former prime minister Ouattara as a migrant and a foreigner with no political future in his host country. In merging the phrase *bori bana* and the capital's quarter Boribana, the university professor discovers that a destitute urban population in the heart of Abidjan are national allochthones and non-nationals who have a history of self-isolation and thus a future of self-annihilation. In sum, *bori bana* represents the discursive site where Ivorians reckon with 'deep categorical treachery' and insecurity in the immediacy and intimacy of their own historical and contemporary society.

Second, *bori bana* is turned into an object of resignification in the subjunctive spaces of the printed, mass, and electronic media. The long history of the renarration of *bori bana* features a broad range of media that obviously illustrate rival interests. In colonial diaries and magazines, the fortress Boribana recounts the history of Samori's overconfidence and French superior strength and wit. In the heavy volumes of Person's post-independence historiography, the colonial story is discredited as ideological, and Samori is given back the kind of historical importance which is later broadcast in the early postcolonial genres of spoken and musical theatre, followed by the internationally acclaimed African literature of Kourouma and the reggae music of Alpha Blondy. From the 1990s, *bori bana*, now firmly established as a token of Jula language and turned into a token of an ethnicized 'Jula' history and identity, is reworked in a newspaper, the favoured medium of the multiparty Republic of Côte d'Ivoire. These newspapers offer a wide variety of genres, ranging from the standard report through the editorial piece to the weekly column of a university professor. The latter's *bori bana* article permits him to insert into the chief medium of party-political propaganda such conventions and strategies as bibliographic references and sociological generalizations from his domain of 'science'. The result is a mobilising analysis that lends its plausibility from his ostensible familiarity with African historiography, Jula language, and the 'Jula' predicament. Finally, we observe how, in the most recent phase of the Ivorian conflict, the worldwide web gains prominence. Were it not for the internet, how could a rather minor journal like *Le National*, as biased a source as the Ivorian Embassy in Washington or a needy organisation like the MPCI, ever hope to reach transnational audiences?

In sum, the uses, appropriations and reappropriations of the phrase *bori bana* may well serve to illustrate the apparent explosion in reach, but also the fragmentation by bias, of the mass media. More interestingly perhaps, it also demonstrates how increasing links of intertextuality (clustered around concepts such as 'migrants', 'terrorists', 'Muslims', etc.) interact with an increasing intensity of generic amalgamations (ranging from the popular to the 'scientific'). Combining these two factors, both local and global meanings are transformed, resignified and revoiced in a continuous exchange, and the resulting mixture can indeed be made to implode into local and national articulations of violence.

Focusing on the third dynamic of implosion, the crescendo of the three *bori bana* articles shows how the former two dynamics are paralleled by the kind of implosion in selfing/othering that Baumann identifies as an essential precondition of genocide. Among the three grammars that Baumann proposes, encompassment is probably the most ambiguous scheme of selfing/othering. In this grammar, inclusion and exclusion seem to be inextricably bound together. The study of code-crossing or double-voicing may perhaps offer a productive way of tracing genocidal phenomena to implicitly genocidal rhetorics: the poiesis of genocide. This poiesis seems to require discursive techniques of 'getting *into*' the other, while at the same time it must engineer a major distancing operation (see Baumann, Müller, and Verrips in this volume). To express this in terms of discursive strategies, this double operation is paralleled by, first, a radical appropriation of the other and secondly, a resignification of the appropriated other as a non-partner in any possible dialogue. Here, too, the linguistic processes leading from civic exclusion to genocidal annihilation bear a chilling resemblance to Benveniste's distinction (raised by Baumann in this volume) between binary grammars of possible dialogue and ternary grammars of total exclusion.

The introductory and concluding parts of this chapter have illustrated how the resignifications of the three articles were put to new uses and staged in mass-mediated performances. These new uses purported to 'unmask' events and identities and to 'explain' them in broader, global 'cosmologies' of interests and antagonisms. This shows how, in their search for plausibility and legitimacy, the authors of what Mbembe would call 'simulacral' universes activate the globally dominant mythologies of their times. During the Cold War, Houphouët-Boigny imprisoned and eliminated political opponents on accusations of being communist revolutionaries. In the post-Berlin Wall era, Bédié and his professors built *ivoirité* around the concepts of international migration, autochthony and multiculturality. In present-day Côte d'Ivoire, the migrants, allochthones and cultural 'others' are being investigated and persecuted for being potential 'international terrorists'. These subsequent dominant identities circulate globally and are inscribed in the encompassing projects of selfing/othering and the implosions that they feed into. 'Genocide' therefore lends its local implosive strength from the plausibility and the legitimacy of the identities that are manufactured in the hegemonic centres of the globe. It may be easy to identify the producers of the 'poiesis of genocide' in Côte d'Ivoire, but their sources and providers are found far beyond the confines of this nation that seems to be thoroughly captivated by the global open economy of 'good' and 'bad' identities.

Notes

1. This chapter is based on research conducted in Côte d'Ivoire, France and Belgium, and is funded by the Department of African Languages and Cultures (Ghent University, Belgium). A first draft of this paper was presented at the workshop Grammars of Identity/Alterity of the EASA Biennial Conference 2002 at Copenhagen. I wish to thank all the participants at the workshop and above all Gerd Baumann and Andre Gingrich for their comments and encouragement in the laborious project of turning the initial paper into a chapter. I also want to thank all the people who helped research this paper, and in particular: Soualiho Ouattara, Ibrahima Ouattara, Jan Blommaert, Sarah Verhees, Ahmed Kouadio, and Ali Ouattara. I should point out, perhaps, that the name Ouattara is one of the most popular Muslim patronyms in the region and that it does not indicate any ties of kinship between my interlocutors and the politician of the same name who figured prominently in the events to be analysed here.
2. 'Plausibility' is one of the three conditions that Gramsci sees in the formation of counter-hegemonic movements. The other two are equally useful for understanding mass-mediated resignifications: the presence of organic intellectuals and the relative isolation in which the resistance is organized (Billings 1990). My understanding of the potential of resignification in the 'subjunctive' spaces of mass media is largely based on Bayart's Foucaultian reworking of Gramsci, more particularly, on his use of 'discursive genres' and 'espaces-temps' (1985) and the Comaroffs' critique of civil society resistance (1999).
3. *Notre Voie*, together with *Le Patriote*, *Fraternité-Matin*, and *Ivoir' Soir* are the most popular daily newspapers in Côte d'Ivoire (HPCI & Panos 2001).
4. Following Derive (1990) and Boone et al. (1999) I use 'Manding' to refer to the Mandekan languages (Bamana, Maninka, Jula) spoken from Gambia to Burkina Faso and from Mali to Côte d'Ivoire. In Côte d'Ivoire, Mandekan is most often labelled 'Malinké' as distinct from Southern Mande languages such as Guro and Dan.
5. Since its creation in 1991 and until it changed its name in 1998, *Notre Voie* was called *La Voie*. On the website of the Socialist Party FPI, it is listed under 'The Journals of the FPI' (*Les journaux du FPI*) (http://www.fpi.ci/publications.html; 02/12/2002).
6. Code-switching is the alternative use of two or more languages within the course of one speech event (Hinnenkamp 1987: 138). It 'may convey certain meanings about the speaker' as well as function to redefine the relationship between interlocutors. Code switching is 'marked' when it 'does not conform to expected patterns' (Mesthrie et al. 2000: 169).
7. There is a long-standing discussion whether 'ivoirité' is a strategically vague concept employed to exclude ethnic/political opponents, or, as its proponents argue, a model for peaceful coexistence in a multicultural Côte d'Ivoire. Together with Dozon (2000), I choose to characterise 'ivoirité' as an ethno-nationalist ideology which can be put to diverse political uses (see below).
8. The linguistic situation in the urban and rural migration areas is a complex one. In 'urban Jula' Partman (1975) further distinguishes between 'Dioula véhiculaire' which Manding speakers use to communicate with each other and 'tagbusikan', a slightly pidginised Jula used by non-Manding and despised by Manding speakers.
9. In the wake of Person's publications (see also 1969 and 1977), Samori became 'the symbol of the new African nationalisms' (Mandingue, s.d.). Sekou Touré, the first president of Guinea, claimed to be Samori's successor (Baba Kaké, 1987) and Samori featured prominently in the popular music theatre piece *Regards sur le passé* performed by Sekou Touré's national orchestra, Bembeya Jazz National (1969). In Côte d'Ivoire, Samori was the subject of the much-acclaimed play, *Les Sofas*, by former Minister of Culture Bernard Zadi Zaourou (1969).
10. In the song *Bori Samory*, Alpha Blondy (1984) associates Samori with other victims of colonial or racial violence, such as Patrice Lumumba, Kwame N'krumah, and Malcolm X. 'Bori' here is in the imperative form; the singer exhorts Samori to run fast (*'bori'*), because the 'white man' (*'nazarew'*, *'tubabu'*) is out to kill him. In his second novel *Monnè outrages défis*

(1990) Ahmadou Kourouma recounts the story of Samori's Boribana fortress and contrasts Samori's resolve with the weakness of his successors under French colonial rule.
11. According to Person (1968–75) and Lewis (1973), this is an amalgamation. In northwestern Côte d'Ivoire (and beyond, in Guinea and Mali) the term 'Jula' referred to a category of Islamicised merchants, while in the northeastern part of the country (Kong, Bondoukou) 'Jula' referred to an ethnic group.
12. Unless stated otherwise, all translations from the French are mine.
13. In the east of Côte d'Ivoire (Kong and Bondoukou), Delafosse hinted at the existence of a few Jula 'of pure race', an observation to which the French colonial agent in Bondoukou, Nebout, subscribed by lending these Jula communities the status of an 'indigenous population'. Nonetheless, he stressed the aspect of itinerancy when he stated that, 'with the exception of the Jula [of Bondoukou,] all the natives are sedentary' (1901: 181).
14. Excellent examples of such complex reconstructions of ethnic identities can be found in Bazin (1985) and Amselle (1998). In his reconstruction of 'Fulani, Bambara, Malinke' identity in West Africa, Amselle perceives how this 'trinity' forms a 'system of transformations with a logic of its own' (1998: 56). Although I find the term 'system' debatable, Amselle takes an important step, I believe, towards unpicking the interrelations between local identities, without neglecting the regional and global layers of identity formation.
15. Bédié (1999) claims that he was given this name when on the day of his birth it started to rain and the water formed a small river in the village. Not only was this a sign of benediction, but also, according to Bédié himself, an indication of his future career as a leader and president.
16. In the period following the *bori bana* newspaper articles, the chat section of Côte d'Ivoire's major website, Abidjan.net, featured one intervention that spoke of the RDR militants as *boribaga* ('those whose profession/nature it is to run/flee'), and one which resigified the acronym of the Republican Party RDR (*Rassemblement des Républicains*) as: '*Rassemblement des Réfugiés*' ('Party of the Refugees').

References

Agamben, Giorgio. 1999. *Remnants of Auschwitz: The witness and the Archive*, trans. D. Heller-Roazen. New York: Zone Books.
Alpha, Blondy. 1984. *Bori Samory* (album: Cocody Rock).
Ambassade de Côte d'Ivoire à Washington. 2002. 'Le RDR organise une manifestation en faveur des terroristes à Washington' (30 September 2002) [http://www.abidjan.net/actualites/article/index.asp?n=31351], accessed 2 December 2002.
Amselle, Jean-Loup. 1998. 'Fulani, Bambara, Malinke: A System of Transformations', in *Mestizo Logics: Anthropology and Identity in Africa and Elsewhere*, ed. J.-L. Amselle. Stanford: Stanford University Press, 43–57.
Appadurai, Arjun. 1996. *Modernity at Large: Cultural Dimensions of Globalization.* Minneapolis: University of Minnesota Press.
Apter, Andrew. 1999. 'IBB = 419: Nigerian Democracy and the Politics of Illusion', in *Civil Society and the Political Imagination in Africa: Critical Perspectives,* eds. J. Comaroff and J. Comaroff. Chicago: University of Chicago Press, 267–307.
Baba Kaké, Ibrahima. 1987. *Sékou Touré, le héros et le tyran*. Paris: Jeune Afrique Livres.
——. 1989. *Journal de L'Afrique, Tome 3 (1885–1949)*. Abidjan: Edition Ami.
Bakary, Koné. 2002. 'Le charnier de Monoko-Zohi un montage du MPCI?' *Ivoire Forum: La voix de la diaspora,* 8 [http://www.ivoireforum.com/develop], accessed 20 Decermber 2002.
Bakhtin, M.M. [1929] 1984. *Problems of Dostoyevsky's Poetics*. Minneapolis, University of Minnesota Press.

Bayart, Jean-François. 1985. 'L'énonciation du politique', *Revue française de science politique*, 35/3: 343–63.
——. 1999. 'L'Afrique dans le monde: une histoire d'extraversion', *Critique Internationale* 5, 97–120.
Bazin, Jean. 1985. 'A chacun son Bambara', in *Au coeur de l'éthnie: ethnie, tribalisme et Etat en Afrique*, eds. J.-L. Amselle and E. M'Boloko. Paris: La Découverte, 87–128.
Bazin, Laurent. 1998. *Entreprise, politique, parenté: une perspective anthropologique sur la Côte d'voire dans le monde actuel.* Paris: L'Harmattan.
——. 1999. 'Domination extérieure et dénonciations ethniques en Côte-d'Ivoire', *Autrepart* 10, 77–90.
Bédié, Henri Konan. 1999. *Les chemins de ma vie.* Paris: Plon.
——. s.d. *Ecrits et propos du Président Henri Konan Bédié sur les véritables principes de l'Ivoirité* [http://www.cotedivoire-libertes.org/hkb_livreblanc.htm], accessed 2 August 2002.
Bembeya Jazz National. 1969. *Regard sur le passé* (album: Bolibana Collection).
Billings, Dwight. 1990 'Religion as Opposition: A Gramscian Analysis', *American Journal of Sociology* 96 (1): 1–31.
Boone, Catherine. 1993. 'Commerce in Côte d'Ivoire: Ivoirianisation without Ivoirian Traders', *The Journal of Modern African Studies,* 21 (1): 67–92.
Boone, Douglas and Catherine Boone. 1999. 'Enquête sur les dialectes Mande Nord de Côte d'Ivoire', *Mandekan* 35: 17–71.
Chauveau, Jean-Pierre. 2000. 'Question foncière et construction nationale en Côte d'Ivoire', *Politique africaine* 78: 94–125.
Chauveau, Jean-Pierre and Jean-Pierre Dozon. 1985. 'Colonisation, économie de plantation et société civile en Côte d'Ivoire', *Cahiers O.R.S.T.O.M., Série Sciences Humaines* 21 (1): 63–80.
Chrétien, Jean-Pierre. ed.1995. *Rwanda: les médias du génocide.* Paris: Karthala.
Comaroff, John & Jean. 1999. 'Introduction', in *Civil Society and the Political Imagination in Africa: Critical Perspectives,* eds. J. and J. Comaroff. eds. Chicago: University of Chicago Press, 1–43.
Côte d'Ivoire, République de. 2001. *Rapports sur les événements d'octobre et décembre 2000 en Côte d'Ivoire.* Abidjan: CEDA.
Delafosse, Maurice. 1901. *Essai de manuel pratique de la langue mandé ou mandingue.* Paris: Ernest Leroux.
Derive, Marie-Jo. 1976. 'Dioula véhiculaire, dioula de Kong et dioula d'Odienne', *Annales de l'Université d'Abidjan, Série H. Linguistique* 9/1: 55–83.
——. 1990. *Etude dialectologique de l'aire Manding de Côte d'Ivoire.* Paris: Peeters.
Diarra, Samba. 1997 *Les faux complots d'Houphouët-Boigny: fracture dans le destin d'une nation.* Paris: Karthala.
Dozon, Jean-Pierre. 2000. 'La Côte d'Ivoire entre démocratie, nationalisme et ethnonationalisme', *Politique africaine* 78, 45–62.
Ebrokié, César. 2002. 'Enfin, le génocide de Benoît Scheuer', *Notre Voie* 9 December 2002.
Gbagbo, Laurent. 1983. *Côte d'Ivoire: pour une alternative démocratique.* Paris: L'Harmattan.
Hill, Jane H. 1999. 'Styling Locally, Styling Globally: What Does it Mean?', *Journal of Sociolinguistics* 3/4: 542–56.
——. 2001. 'Language, Race, and White Public Space' in *Linguistic Anthropology*, ed. A. Duranti. Oxford: Blackwell, 450–64.

Hinnenkamp V. 1987. 'Foreigner Talk, Code-Switching and the Concept of Trouble' in *Analysing Intercultural Communication*, ed. K Knapp et al. Amsterdam: Mouton de Gruyter, 137–80.
Jackson, Michael. 2002. *The Politics of Storytelling: Violence, Transgression, and Intersubjectivity.* Copenhagen: Museum Tusculanum Press.
Ki-Zerbo, Joseph. 1978. *Histoire de L'Afrique Noire.* Paris: Hatier.
Koné, Dramane. 1988. 'Pour une caractérisation syntaxico-sémantique de la notion de verbo-nominal, dans le Jula de Côte d'Ivoire', *Journal of West African Languages* 18 (2): 70–82.
——. 2000. 'Bori bana', autopsie d'une expression', *Notre Voie* (21 May 2000).
Koulibaly, Mamadou. 2001. 'Ni révision constitutionnelle ni reprise des élections: la construction de la nation doit continuer', speech held at the Forum for National Reconciliation (Abidjan, 30 October 2001) [http://www.woyaa.com/frn-ci/forum/30102001/assemblee.html], accessed 5 December 2002.
Kourouma, Ahmadou. 1990. *Monnè outrages et défis.* Paris: Seuil.
Launay, Robert and Marie Miran. 2000. 'Beyond Mande *mory*: Islam and Ethnicity in Côte d'Ivoire', *Paideuma* 46, 63–84.
LeBlanc, Marie Nathalie. 2000a. 'From *Sya* to Islam: Social Change and Identity among Muslim Youth in Bouaké, Côte d'Ivoire', *Paideum* 46: 85–109.
——. 2000b. 'Versioning Womanhood and Muslimhood: "Fashion" and the Life Course in Contemporary Bouaké, Côte d'Ivoire', *Africa* 70 (3): 442–81.
Lewis, Barbara. 1973. 'The Dioula in the Ivory Coast' in *Papers on the Manding*, ed. C. T. Hodge. Bloomington: Indiana University Press, 273–307.
Lohourignon, Maurice. 1999–2000. 'Ça y est, bori-bana pour Bédié!!!', *Notre Voie*, 31 December 1999 to 1–2 January 2000.
Loucou, Jean-Noël. 1996. 'L'ivoirité ou l'esprit du nouveau contrat social du Président Henri Konan Bédié' in *De l'ivoirité*', ed. S. Touré. Abidjan: Presses universitaires de Côte d'Ivoire, 19–24.
Mamdani, Mahmood. 1998. When Does a Settler become a Native? Reflections on the Colonial Roots of Citizenship in Equatorial and South Africa. Inaugural Lecture held at University of Cape Town, South Africa, 13 May 1998.
——. 2001. *When Victims become Killers: Colonialism, Nativism, and the Genocide in Rwanda.* Princeton: Princeton University Press.
Mandingue. n.d. *L'épopée Mandingue.* [http://mandingue.levillage.org/histoire.php], accessed 12 August 2002.
Marguerat, Yves. 1981–1982. 'Des ethnies et des villes: analyse des migrations vers les villes de Côte d'Ivoire', *Cahiers O.R.S.T.O.M., Série Sciences Humaines* 18 (3): 303–40.
Mbembe, Achille. 1992. 'The Banality of Power and the Aesthetics of Vulgarity in the Postcolony', *Public Culture*, 4 (2): 1–30.
Memel-Fotê, Harris. 1999. 'Un mythe politique des Akans en Côte d'Ivoire: le sens de l'Etat', in *Mondes akan: identité et pouvoir en Afrique occidentale*, eds. P. Valsecchi and F. Viti. Paris: L'Harmattan, 21–42.
—— and Jean-Pierre Chauveau. 1989. 'L'identité politique baule (Côte d'Ivoire)', *Revue de la Bibliothèque Nationale* 34: 33–40.
Mesthrie, Rajend et al. 2000. *Introducing Sociolinguistics.* Edinburgh: Edinburgh University Press.
MPCI 2002. *Support MPCI.* [http://www.supportmpci.org/], accessed 19 December 2002.

Nebout, A. [1904] 1906. 'Le Cercle de Bondoukou: renseignements historiques et économiques', in *Dix ans à la Côte d'Ivoire*, ed. F.-J. Clozel. Paris: Challamel, 169–84.
Neruda, Freedom. 2000. 'Dramane Ouattara: bori bana', *Notre Voie*, 15 May 2000.
Niangoran-Bouah, Georges. 1996. 'Les fondements socio-culturels de l'ivoirité' in *L'ivoirité ou l'esprit du nouveau contrat social du Président Henri Konan Bédié*, ed. S. Touré. Abidjan: Presses universitaires de Côte d'Ivoire, 45–52.
Olped [Observatoire de la liberté de la presse, de l'éthique et de la déontologie de Côte d'Ivoire]. 2001. *OLPED, a Pioneer in Media Self-Regulation in Africa*. Brussels: International Federation of Journalists.
Partman, Gayle. 1975. 'Quelques remarques sur le Dioula véhiculaire en Côte d'Ivoire', *Annales de l'Université d'Abidjan, Série H, Linguistique* 8 (1): 241–59.
Person, Yves. 1968–75. *Samori: une révolution dyula*, Mémoires de l'Institut Fondamental d'Afrique Noire, 80. Dakar. IFAN.
——. (avec la collaboration de Françoise Ligier). 1969. *Samori: la renaissance de l'empire mandingue*. Paris: Editions ABC.
——. 1977. *Samori, construction et chute d'un empire*. Paris: Jeune Afrique.
P.L. 2002. 'Avis. Situé à quelques metres de la présidence et de la base nasale: Bori-Bana est une poudrière', *Le National* 26 October 2002.
Prévention Génocides. 2001. *Côte d'Ivoire, poudrière identitaire* [video]. Brussels.
Projet d'accord. 2002. *Intégralité du projet d'accord soumis à l'appréciation du gouvernement ivoirien et du MPCI*. [http://www.abidjan.net/actualites/article/index], accessed 15 December 2002.
Rampton, Ben. 1995. *Crossings: Language and Ethnicity among Adolescents*. London: Longman.
——. 1998. 'Language Crossing and the Redefinition of Reality' in *Code-switching in Conversation: language, Interaction and Identity*, ed. P. Auer. London: Routledge: 290-320.
Tambiah, Stanley J. 1996. 'The Nation-State in Crisis and the Rise of Ethnonationalism', in *The Politics of Difference: Ethnic Premises in a World of Power*, ed. E. Wilmsen. Chicago: University of Chicago Press, 124–43.
Touré, Sekou, ed. 1996. *L'ivoirité ou l'esprit du nouveau contrat social du Président Henri Konan Bédié*. Abidjan: Presses universitaires de Côte d'Ivoire.
Triaud; J.-L. 1974. 'La question musulmane en Côte d'Ivoire (1983–1939)', *Revue Française d'Histoire d'Outre-Mer* 61 (225): 542–71.
United Nations. 2001. *Côte d'Ivoire: Rapport de la Commission d'enquête internationale pour la Côte d'Ivoire*. New York: United Nations.
Zadi Zaourou, Bernard. 1969. *Les Sofas*. Abidjan: NEA.

Chapter 8

Dehumanization as a Double-Edged Sword

From Boot-Camp Animals to Killing Machines

Jojada Verrips

> If you ladies leave my island, if you survive recruit training, you will be a weapon, you will be a minister of death, praying for war. And proud. Until that day you are pukes, you are scumbags, you are the lowest term of life on earth. You are not even human. You people are nothing but a lot of little pieces of amphibian shit. (Senior Drill Instructor Gunnery Sgt. Hartman in *Full Metal Jacket*)

In introducing the grammars of identity/alterity based on orientalization, segmentation and encompassment, Baumann has raised the question of which circumstances would have to arise for the three grammars to cease to work. He proposed this would happen if they were made to 'implode' by 'a corruption of language' which would 'reduce the complexity of each grammar to the blatancy of an unmitigated binarism: "us good, they bad"'. 'It is when language makes the grammars implode,' so he argues, 'that unmitigated binarism helps violence explode'. I want to expand on this argument by showing that such an implosion might be accompanied at the same time by at least a temporary humiliation and dehumanization – for instance, through the use of a similar kind of invective language – of exactly those men or women who are to fight or destroy the others represented as 'bad', 'disgusting' and therefore 'destroyable'. In other words, I want to make clear that negative ways of classifying and labelling people may not only lead to radical exclusion, elimination or extermination, but may also lead to radical inclusion in particular social groups. Invective and dehumanizing language seems to be a double-edged sword. Dehumanization not only leads to the most violent exclusion of the other, but it is also a means toward the most violent inclusion of selves into an overpowering 'us'.

Dehumanizing Language and the Crucial Role of Fantasy

The example of the nazification of everyday language in Germany (see Baumann and Müller in this volume) is a powerful and convincing one, for it was already in an early phase of Nazism that particular groups and categories, such as Jews, Gypsies, and homosexuals, were designated as parasites and vermin (*Parasiten* and *Schädlinge*) spoiling the body social. Yet the idea that certain categories of people represented a kind of malevolent microbes threatening the sound development of society is older than Nazism. It was already in circulation at the end of the nineteenth century before it gradually spread in Germany among politicians, physicians, and laymen. After the Nazis came to power, the medicalization of social issues gained momentum and, fully in line with this, lead to the radical extermination of thousands and thousands of unwanted citizens. In a sense, the Nazis saw themselves as performing a big surgical operation on their own society, which they perceived to be polluted by, and suffering under, the attack of several very dangerous creatures that had succeeded in penetrating it. Their language, as Klemperer (1999) has shown, was of a very particular nature and played an important role in putting aside or letting implode whichever of the grammars of alterity had previously been in use for the Jews, Gypsies and other persecuted groups and categories.[1] Due to this *L(ingua) T(ertii) I(mperii)*, as Klemperer called the language of the Nazis, the road was paved for the Holocaust and the radical extinction of people called 'sub-humans' (*Untermenschen*) and worse. It is worth stressing here the direct link between dehumanizing language or images and the systematic execution of a genocide virtually unhindered by a public infested – if one may reverse the obnoxious metaphor – by corruptive language.

> Nazism crept into the flesh and blood of the masses by means of single words, turns of phrase and stock expressions which, imposed upon the people a million-times over in continuous reiteration, were mechanically and unconsciously absorbed by them. The presentation of the Jews as corroding and poisonous parasites, as vermin, as bacteria and bacilli, everyone infesting and striving to destroy the body of the German people as a whole and each individual German with a demonic power – this presentation paralyzed to a large extent any internal resistance on the part of the masses. Lagarde's phrase, still used as a metaphor, of the bacilli not to be negotiated with but to be exterminated could, in the atmosphere of Bio-Mythology, become a horrible reality. (Alex Bein cited in Koenigsberg 1995: 84)

Yet it was not only the Nazis who, by means of a particular language use with regard to specific others, first marginalised them and later embarked on their more or less systematic extermination. One can probably trace or reconstruct the route from the introduction of dehumanizing language via the implosion of grammatical otherings to the legitimation of large-scale bloodshed in many more cases of war and genocide. The paradox in these cases is that this type of language which implies the dehumanization, depersonalisation, animalisation and/or objectification of fellow human beings is used in order to reach a state of social purity and orderliness and with it, a pure and orderly state (cf. Moore jr., 2000; Labrie 2001). The implicit and explicit degradation and devaluation of people via specific words, especially negative adjectives and metaphors, almost always seems to be the first step on a road which may ultimately lead towards a more or less radical elimination.[2] A classic and widespread denigration of others whom one wanted to fence in and/or wall out (or worse) has been and still is that of 'dog' (cf. White 1991). Even here and now, such political leaders as Muammar Gadafy and Saddam Hussein are frequently spoken of as '(mad) dogs' (Fowler 1991: 110 ff.). Hardly less widespread is the comparison of disliked and hated others with rats, pigs and other animals. Currently, President Bush jr. produces fascinating data for any social scientist with an interest in how language plays a crucial role in preparing the waging of a war against particular governments seen as representatives of 'evil' on earth. Though his predecessors also knew how to use pejorative qualifications for political opponents whom they wanted to get rid of, eventually in a violent way – *vide* Reagan and Bush sr. – Bush jr. seems to surpass them all where it concerns debunking language. Since others in this volume treat this topic, I will refrain here from further statements on this aspect of the subject.

Instead, I will pursue another question in this connection, namely *why* people start developing this kind of language and *why* they want to depict others in this way. If corrupted language facilitates an implosion of the grammars of alterity, what is the cause of the process of this language corruption? As I have indicated, the wish to keep or return one's social environment, or indeed 'the world', to a state of 'purity' and 'order' seems to play an enormous role. But that is not enough. Perhaps the Lacanian philosopher Slavoj Žižek, who in the last decade has written much about outbursts of concrete violence, can help us better to understand the source of this pernicious language use by his attention to fantasies, their origins and their sometimes disastrous influence on human behavior.

Like Lacan, Žižek makes use of the notion of the 'Real,' a 'something' that pushes people forward but is too big for words and therefore horrible. In order to hide from this horrible 'something' as well as somehow to get a grip on it, people use their capacity for fantasy. With the help of this faculty they produce fantas(ma)tic fictions that they then mistake for reality, but which conjure up exactly what they prefer to hide, that is, the horrific of the 'Real'. As Žižek remarks: 'The relationship between fantasy and the horror of the Real that it conceals is much more ambiguous than it may seem: fantasy conceals this horror, yet at the same time it creates what it purports to conceal, its "repressed" point of reference' (1996: 79). Yet Žižek considers these fictions or fantasies not simply as the results of particular desires, but as important for their formation. Seen from this perspective, one can say that specific fantas(ma)tic representations, for instance seemingly irrational political dreams with a millennial flavour, have a manifold meaning. They are hiding places, means to both express and understand, and shapers of desire. As shapers of desire, such products of the imagination can, in my view, channel this desire in at least two directions: a socially positive and a socially negative one.[3] In the first case, they teach us by showing up extreme positions and allow us to see how these extremes are in the end untenable and therefore better avoided (cf. Lévi Strauss 1967: 30; see also Verrips 2001). In the second case, we do not observe avoidance but rather face the ways in which desire is realised in a more or less sadistic and inhumane way, be it on a large or a small scale. I am interested in both variants, but in this context especially in the socially negative one, and here I think that Žižek's ideas are particularly helpful for a better understanding of a-social variants, such as the new forms of racism and extreme nationalism. Very sensitising is, for example, his idea that we are completely unable to put into words what race and a nation(-state) stand for and what they really mean. Žižek argues that for most of us, they are just 'Things' to which we relate through fantasies. And that is what it is all about when we talk about a 'threat to our way of living' by 'the Other'. What is at issue in the case of racial and ethnic tensions is always that national 'Thing'. We imagine or fantasize that the Other wants excessively to enjoy himself at the expense of our enjoyment, that the Other wants to steal our pleasures by ruining our way of life and that the Other has access to a kind of enjoyment which we do not know of.[4] It is exactly these kinds of fantasies which can function as a frame for the formation and concretisation of aggressive feelings in such a way that seemingly decent citizens can turn into wild men and women who end up killing.[5] It is these fantasies that trigger the corruption of language with regard to others and form the source of the implosion of the grammars of alterity and the explosion of violence. Of course, in order to understand more of (racist and national) violence we will have to pay close attention to such important factors as (global) economic and political contexts. There is no lack of studies which deal with these phenomena. However, what we urgently need now are (anthropological) studies in which an interest in these contexts is coupled with an interest in fantasies – those often horrible products of the imagination we find not only among others but also in ourselves – and their sinister role in generating corrupted, and therefore corrupting, language.

Dehumanizing Language in Boot Camps

Having briefly sketched how I think Baumann's route to an explosion of violence can be expanded by including the role of fantasies, I want now to concentrate on a particular category of people often charged with carrying out the elimination of the 'mad dogs', the 'vermin,' or 'human things' obstructing progress or civilization, that is, the soldiers. What I am particularly interested in, here, is the ways in which they are drilled and trained to wage war against fellow human beings without feeling much remorse. More specifically, I want to make clear how the same kind of dehumanizing, depersonalising, and objectifying language is used in army boot camps, but this time with a totally different outcome: inclusion in a total institution with the character of a family, a clan or a brotherhood. In other words, I want to demonstrate how the same kind of corrupted language can have diametrically opposed effects: radical exclusion on the one hand and radical inclusion on the other. As I shall argue below, the two effects indeed condition each other in some remarkable ways.

It is not easy, however, to show that this kind of language can, under specific circumstances, also lead to constructing instead of destructing a group, for there are not many studies which address the issue of language in military training camps. There is no systematic study, as yet, on how corrupted language in these camps can lead to an at least temporary implosion of the grammars of alterity and how this, in turn, leads to a situation governed by the unmitigated, often expressly violent binarism between the drill instructors as the 'good guys' and the recruits as the 'bad guys'. True, military terminology and soldiers' jargon have been studied rather extensively (cf., for instance, Karlson and Judersleben 1994 and Buschmann 1995).

Yet in the literature consulted for the present purpose, I only found a very small amount of explicit material on the use of corruptive language during the military training of recruits, and of army men wanting to become officers or members of special units or task forces.[6] Most of my sources only implied this use without being specific on its nature. Before I will briefly deal with a few of them, I present a short general remark about the nature of the socialization of recruits in boot camps since the Second World.[7] Although I have only seen data pertaining to their training in the American, Canadian, British, and Israeli armies, I nevertheless think that the following generalizing remarks are valid ones.

The transformation of civilians into soldiers implies, in a sense, a shock treatment within a limited span of time. First they are 'broken down,' then they are 'rebuilt from scratch' and 'taught to be human' again (Ben-Ari forthcoming: 4; Winslow 1997: 62; Bourke 1999: 79). Next to a whole series of military skills and knowledge about weaponry, they have to learn the basic ingredients of military culture such as its language, ceremonies and rituals, symbols, history of their unit and, above all, a collection of core values such as obedience, discipline, loyalty, duty, honor, cooperation and sacrifice (cf. Winslow 1997: 65; see also Wamsley 1972: 401). In fact they have to develop a whole new habitus that makes them, if necessary, ready for immediate combat. From a heterogeneous collection of individuals with different sociocultural backgrounds and no knowledge of military skills and army culture, recruits in boot camps are, at least ideally, transformed into a kind of highly trained, inward-looking brotherhood with a proper fighting spirit.[8] In general the period in boot camps is described and experienced as a sort of infernal, disgusting and extremely humiliating ordeal because of all the hazing, gigging and bracing.[9] Notorious during the Second World War, for example, was the 'blood and hate' training in the British army, which included visits to abattoirs and the use of animal blood intended to inoculate troops against battlefield gore (Place 2000: 447). The psychologist Brewster Smith, who himself went through officer candidate training wrote:

> The hopeful candidate is subjected to a nearly catastrophic experience, which breaks down to a large extent his previous personality organization. His previous valuations fail him and in order to find a basis for self-respect, he must adopt new standards or escape from the field. (...) The catastrophic experience provides a kind of purgatory, a definite demarcation from the candidate's enlisted incarnation that puts a barrier between the new officer and his enlisted memories. It has some of the characteristics of a conversion experience, or the ordeal of the medieval knight. (...) The constant threat of 'washing out' of O[fficer] C[andidate] S[chool] serves to increase subjective pressure and provide a most effective punishment for stamping in correct behavior. Other features of the ordeal are an extremely 'GI' atmosphere, gigging, hazing, 'bracing', and a general apotheosis of 'chicken' (that is, petty detail)'. (Stouffer et al. 1950: 389/90)

Though the inculcation of military skills and army culture takes place in diverse ways such as heavy physical exercise, drill and all kinds of instructions, in all these cases the spoken word of the instructors plays a tremendous role.[10] And this spoken word is very often of a very specific nature. Let me try briefly to illustrate this.

A British soldier who was trained in the 1920s described his training as a nightmare involving 'constant humiliation and the use of indecent phrases' and 'indecent names' (quoted in Bourke 1999: 80). Though Samuel Stouffer et al. present a plethora of quotes in their famous study *The American Soldier*, I only found one, in the whole of volume I, which directly quoted a sergeant using an insulting and humiliating way of speaking. The sergeant, in this instance, said to a soldier: 'By Jesus, you haven't any more brains than a frog on a railroad track' (1950: 397). For the rest, the study offers rather implicit quotes from recruits, but these occur regularly enough and are telling. One recruit describes how '[t]he recruit is warned and threatened, *shouted at and sworn at*, punished and promised further punishments, with such frequency and from so many sides that he gets to be like the rat in the neurosis production experiment. He soon comes to fear the Army and his superiors who represent it' (412, italics mine). This testimony shows a strong family resemblance with the following by an Israeli recruit: 'From the first moment they started to treat us very strictly. They ordered us to run, using various forms of harassment and humiliation... *They used very rough language*... When a soldier answered a question, the commander would say something like: "Don't throw up in my ear"' (Lieblich quoted in Ben-Ari forthcoming: 4, italics mine). Gary Wamsley, who used the method of participant observation to find out more about the nature of military socialization in two different contexts, noticed how in one new cadets, called 'raunchies', were savagely abused by 'upperclassmen', called 'White Gloves'. These 'raunchies' were 'constantly and caustically told they were "nothing", "nobody", spastic, slovenly, gross, and, worst of all, "casual"' (Wamsley 1972: 406). Some people who could no longer bear this degrading treatment attempted suicide or became mentally deranged. Charles Levy, a sociologist who interviewed Vietnam veterans, mentions the fact that it was rather usual for drill instructors in marine boot camps to call recruits 'faggots': 'By compelling these men to accept such labels, the drill instructors achieved on a psychological level the same control that they had on a physical level when, for example, the men were not allowed to defecate during the first week of boot camp' (1974: 52). The (dis)qualification of recruits as 'faggots', 'poufs', 'queers,' 'sissies' and 'pussies' or worse seems to (have) be(en) a widespread practice in armies. According to William Miller, 'to call someone a "sissy" or a "pussy" is really to create a new entity, not woman, not man, but a womanly man, an un-man' (2000: 234). I think that the use of these degrading designations for recruits can be interpreted in this sense, for in the eyes of their instructors they were absolutely a kind of 'in-between-persons'. Another factor that further serves the labelling of recruits as a detestable bunch of homosexuals is put forward by Donna Winslow, who notices the following curious aspect of basic training: 'the emphasis on traditionally female activities such as grooming, cleaning, washing, folding linen, making beds, etc.' (1997: 62). Finally I want to point to Levy's (1974) observation that the accusation of being a contemptible homosexual had not so much to do with really being thought one, but more with the fact that homosexuality represented a lack of all the aggressive characteristics that were thought to comprise masculinity. This connection between passivity and homosexuality was vivid to the marines in boot camp since they were unable to combat the label and the activities surrounding it. When a recruit mentioned that he and a friend had been separated in violation of the 'buddy system' under which they joined, the drill instructor is reported to have asked, 'Do you like Private X?' The next question was: 'Do you want to fuck him?' (1974).[11]

Exactly this kind of verbal harassment by drill instructors is very vividly presented in (war) films when depicting the situation of recruits in boot camps.[12] Taylor Hackford's movie *An Officer and a Gentleman* (1982) introduces such a tough drill instructor, Sgt. Foley (played by Louis Gossett jr.). This man repeatedly calls the recruits 'slimy worms' not worth looking their superiors in the eye. When a recruit says 'you' to him he sarcastically replies: 'I am not a "ewe", boy! A "ewe" is a female sheep. Sweet pea, will you fuck me in the ass? Is that it why you called me a "ewe"?' The instructor is constantly insinuating that the recruits are 'queers': 'Uh, you are from Oklahoma. Two things come from Oklahoma: steers and queers. What are you? I don't see horns, so you must be a queer'. Almost exactly the same kind of humiliating talk is used by the drill instructor in Kubrick's *Full Metal Jacket* (1987).[13] What makes this film so interesting is that this instructor, Sgt. Hartman, is played by Lee Ermey who before he became Kubrick's technical advisor had really been a Marine DI. So this man was just doing in the film what he had done for years in the army, and one can thus consider him as a kind of 'key informant' providing authenticated data on the kind of dehumanizing language used by DIs in the army. Here follows a short list of Ermey's alias Hartman's degrading vocabulary: 'maggots', 'ladies', 'pukes', 'scumbags,' 'you are not human', 'you are nothing', 'pieces of amphibian shit', 'ugly ape', 'shit-kicker,' 'disgusting fatbody', 'ten-percenter', 'shit-bird', 'gutless piece of shit', 'pig' and 'animals'. We are confronted here in a frank and plain manner with the kind of corrupted language used for recruits which is frequently hinted at by social scientists who studied the situation in boot camps.[14]

The kind of dehumanizing and depersonalising classifications recruits are faced with during their training shows a great family resemblance with the kind of corrupted language applied to particular groups and categories of others in the wider society who are thought to threaten its purity and orderliness.[15] In both cases this a-social linguistic turn implies an implosion of the grammars of alterity and an explosion of more or less violent behaviour toward both recruits and despised Others. In the latter case, however, the effect is often an entirely different one from that in the former. Despised others are often radically excluded, even exterminated, as in the case of the Jews and Gypsies during the Second World War. By contrast, recruits who succeed in surviving their mental and physical mistreatment are radically included in the total institution that is the army. In their case, this double mistreatment serves a selection process. This leads to the creation of a loyal and aggressive 'band of brothers' that is able and prepared to kill putative enemies of the (national) social body, whenever ordered to do so.In this context, the following statement is revealing, coming from drill instructor Ermey alias Hartman in *Full Metal Jacket* at the end of the terrible training period: 'Today you people are no longer maggots. Today you are Marines. You're part of a brotherhood. From now on, until the day you die, wherever you are, every Marine is your brother. Every Marine will be ready to give his life for you, and you will be ready to give yours'.

Harsh Language, Bonding, and Rebounding Violence

Experts have often compared the harsh training of recruits with the initiation ceremonies of so-called primitive peoples. Ben-Ari, for instance, does so explicitly in his study on the Israeli army (Ben-Ari 1998 and forthcoming). Completely in line with Van Gennep's three-phase theory of initiation rituals, their stay in boot camps is seen as the liminal in-between stage in which the initiands are often subjected to a whole series of mental and physical ordeals.[16] Maurice Bloch has stressed the significance of this practice during *rites de passage* because it generates what he calls 'rebounding violence'. One consequence of being exposed to violent treatment by initiators is, as Bloch argues, 'the legitimation of expansionism, which itself takes one of two forms; (a) it may be internally directed, in which case it legitimates social hierarchy or (b) *it may be externally directed and become an encouragement to aggression against neighbors*' (1992: 98, italics mine). The violent verbal and physical treatment of recruits in boot camps resulting in a solid team of potential killers seems to me to form a perfect illustration of Bloch's 'prey-into-hunter' thesis.[17] During the Vietnamese War, likewise, the humiliating, degrading and frustrating training practices of American Marines and airborne forces were very much inspired by the idea that the rage they engendered would be 'transformed and channeled…into fury at the enemy' (Ben-Ari 1998:85).[18] In this connection it is also important to realize that extremely rough and heavy training, as it often occurs in elite forces, not only results in a high drop out rate (sometimes in the form of suicide), but also in the formation of units whose members tend to be or become noticeably alienated and xenophobic. Winslow, for instance, keenly remarks in her study on the Canadian Airborne Regiment: 'As the individual becomes progressively hyper invested in the group identity, his capacity to relate to others outside of the group becomes significantly diminished and the potential for xenophobia increases. Thus, the individual becomes enmeshed in his or her group and alienated from those outside the group. (…) [T]his is very adaptive in a war situation where the self needs to be sufficiently alienated from the enemy in order to allow the soldier to live with the destruction of this enemy' (1997: 86). This brings me to a final question: what is the role that corrupted language about enemies, in the form of an extremely degrading and dehumanizing terminology, fulfills with regard to the eagerness of soldiers to kill these enemies ?

The general idea is that '[C]ombat soldiers must be emotionally detached from their enemies in order to kill them, a task assisted by negative racial and cultural stereotypes' (Miller and Moskos in Winslow 1997: 137–38). It would be easy to present here a long list of the kind of dehumanizing disqualifications used for enemies in wars, revolutions and other conflicts, but that would be rather boring, for it seems that they are largely variations on a few themes, with very high scores for animals and insects. What is more interesting is what Ben-Ari has brought forward in this respect. Like many others he claims that dehumanization of enemies by soldiers before and during wars helps them to ease the killing process. In this connection he signals an interesting difference between Americans and Israelis. The former tend to `vilify' and 'demonize' enemies, whereas the latter tend to 'objectify' them, turn them into killable things or obstacles.[19] But that is not all, for in order to kill the 'demons' or to get rid of the 'obstacles' soldiers also need to dehumanize themselves to some extent. In the case of the Israeli soldiers this happens, according to Ben-Ari, by seeing themselves as a kind of 'machine' (1998: 87). So in their case it is matter of 'things' killing 'things'. I agree that corrupted designations can make it easier for soldiers to kill the people who have been so denigrated, because dehumanizing language not only originates in hatred but can also intensify hatred. Yet at the same time I think that we should not exaggerate this factor. It seems that another factor is at least equally important or even more so. That is the rage which is generated when a fellow soldier or a 'brother' is killed by an enemy, whether this enemy is qualified as human or not. In the literature one very often comes across this almost incomprehensible love for a 'buddy' as the main source for the wish to kill (cf., for instance, Bourke 1999: 170; Marvin and Ingle 1999: 112). We are confronted here with a direct effect of the extreme solidarity, which for a large part was and still is created by the use of corrupted language and temporarily dehumanizing training practices in boot camps. In this connection the following statement in a Canadian army document is revealing: 'Briefly, the soldier must want his Regiment, his comrades and those around him to survive. The Regiment is his family, where he is not alone. (…) The Regiment provides the opportunity for him to become the best soldier in the world; he fights for something more than himself; he fights for his comrades and the regiment; and indirectly, for his home and his family' (in Winslow 1997: 74). No reference is made here to a fight against a despised enemy. But in order to kill the killer of a 'brother', denigrating and degrading epithets of the type used by drill instructors, such as 'amphibian piece of shit' or 'devil,' helped to find the proper distance to eliminate.

There is thus nothing gratuitous or incidental in the fact that dehumanizing language is not reserved to creating an other radically different from the self. On the contrary, dehumanization appears to work as a double-edged sword, as is witnessed by its systematic use in military training camps, in certain rites of passage, or in other social contexts aimed at a radical inclusion of the self into an overpowering 'us'. This double-edged character can best be understood, perhaps, by referring back to the double-edged character of fantasy as I have discussed it above. Certain kinds of fantasy distort not only the other, but they also distort the self. This is not a moralist argument, but rather an argument that further clarifies the slash that we have placed between identity/alterity, selfing/othering and inclusion/exclusion. Fantasy is rooted in the self as much as generated from, or projected onto, the other. Fantas(ma)tic representations are both hiding places and shapers of desire, and in both these roles they hide and shape the image of the other as much as they hide and shape the grasp of the self.

Notes

1. Very much to the point Jeggle remarks: 'The mouth of the party and the ears of the people had entered a very strange relationship. The ears were not addressed with words to work through, but with a kind of language ballet – or perhaps merely a simple ribbon dance – in any case an action [planned] in parallel to the optical spectacles and rallies. It was a cultic use of language, a kind of incantation – and the ears, prone to be deceived, gave credence to the litanies (*Singsang*). In the process, effective use was made of the modern techniques of acoustics, of microphones and loudspeakers' (1986: 121, trans. mine).
2. See, for instance, Rawson who deals with 'the language of punitive castigation (God destroying mankind "from the face of the earth" in the Deluge), the *façons de parler* of personal or group hatred ("they ought to be shot", "exterminate all the brutes"), and the stark realities of mass-killing' which all share the same vocabulary (2001: 12).
3. I realize that what is considered to be positive and negative depends on one's position and perspective.

4. 'In short, what really bothers us about the "other" is the peculiar way [we imagine or fantasize – JV] it [sic! – JV] organizes its enjoyment: precisely the surplus, the "excess" that pertains to it – the smell of their food, their "noisy" songs and dances, their strange manners, their attitude to work…' (Žižek 1990: 54; see also Žižek 1992: 165).
5. What I deem particularly relevant here is that Žižek mentions the sensorial experience of the Other, his (bodily) smells and sounds. I think that such experiences should play a much more prominent role in research on both violent and non-violent inclusion and, especially, exclusion processes all over the world.
6. I did not come across many studies by social scientists, especially sociologists and anthropologists, of the nature and type of military training processes generally. It seems that this has been more a field of (social) psychologists, who were and still are rather less interested in ethnographic details or the social and cultural aspects of these processes. But see Marvin and Ingle (1999).
7. I have not found material on this topic of an earlier date.
8. If one wants to know more of the nature of military socialization I can recommend the studies by Winslow (1997) on the Canadian Airborne and Ben-Ari (1998) on the Israeli army. Though both anthropologists pay attention to military language – Ben-Ari more than Winslow – they do not say very much on the language used in training camps. See also Marvin and Ingle who write: 'In boot camp civilians are transformed from "maggots" and "nasty things", Marine Corps jargon for the profane, unholy, and grotesque, into initiated members of the totem class' (1999: 104).
9. An airborne soldier interviewed by Winslow said, for instance, 'You got to go through the hazing ritual. Which is degrading and demoralizing and disgusting to get to that' (1997: 130). And Beaumont (cited in Winslow 1997: 127) wrote about elite forces: 'Entrance to these units was often through the surviving of an ordeal…requiring tolerance of pain or danger and subsequent dedication to a hazardous role'.
10. But not only of the drill instructors, for sometimes buddies can be rather rough in word and deed too (see, for example, Winslow 1997: 63).
11. On the role of homosexuality in the German army, see Theweleit (1985).
12. I have not scrutinized war novels on passages describing the corrupted language in use for recruits, but I am sure that they form just as rich a source as war movies.
13. '"Sir, I'm not lying to you.' – '"EWE", "EWE," "EWE"? Did you say "EWE"? Do you know what a ewe is? A ewe is a female sheep. A female sheep is for fucking!' – 'Sir…' – 'Why do you want to fuck your drill instructor???'
14. There are many other (war) movies in which rough drill instructors are staged. A few examples: *G.I Jane* (1997) by Ridley Scott, *Men of Honor* (2000) by George Tillman jr. and *Band of Brothers* (2001) by David Frankel. Revealing is the way in which Joel Schumacher's film *Tigerland* (2000) is advertised: 'The system wanted them to become soldiers. One soldier just wanted to be human'. In this connection it is good to realize that films are not only interesting because they reflect reality, but also because they figure as sources of inspiration for soldiers. Winslow makes it perfectly clear how airborne soldiers found their 'performative models' in such movies as *Rambo* and *Platoon* (1997:136/37).
15. Since a number of years the use of insults and severe physical harassment during military training is officially forbidden within the U.S. Marine Corps (Marvin and Ingle 1999:108; see also Eijsvogel 1999). This does not mean, however, that they belong to the past.
16. Winslow also uses Van Gennep's ideas, but she applies them only to what happens in a particular stage of the training (1997: 95/96).
17. I still do not know if I can agree with Bloch's idea that the aggressiveness of humans is no innate propensity, but instead something that is the result 'of the attempt to create the transcendental in religion and politics' (1992: 7).
18. It is interesting that Ben-Ari regularly emphasizes that humiliating training practices do not occur in the Israeli army.
19. This does not happen always in the same manner and degree. During the Second World War, for example, there was a rather great difference between the ways in which the American sol-

diers 'demonized' their German and Japanese opponents. The latter were much less seen as human than the former.

References

Ben-Ari, Eyal. 1998. *Mastering Soldiers. Conflict, Emotions, and the Enemy in an Israeli Military Unit*. New York: Berghahn Books.
——. (with the assistance of Galeet Dardashti). forthcoming. 'Tests of Soldierhood, Trials of Manhood: Military Service and Male Ideals in Israel', in *War, Politics and Society in Israel: Theoretical and Comparative Perspectives*, eds. Daniel Maman, Zeev Rosenhek and Eyal Ben-Ari. New Brunswick, N.J.: Transaction Publishers.
Bloch, Maurice. 1992. *Prey into Hunter. The Politics of Religious Experience*. Cambridge: Cambridge University Press.
Bourke, Joanna. 1999. *An Intimate History of Killing. Face-to-Face Killing in Twentieth-Century Warfare*. London: Granta Books.
Buschmann, M. 1995. 'Zur militarischen Onomastik und Terminologie', *Muttersprache* 105 (3): 210–26.
Eijsvogel, Juurd. 1999. 'Trots is voorgoed. De Spartaanse vorming van Amerikaanse mariniers op Parris Island', *NRC Handelsblad*, 20 March 1999.
Fowler, Roger. 1991. *Language in the News. Discourse and Ideology in the Press*. London, New York: Routledge.
Jeggle, Utz. 1986. *Der Kopf des Körpers. Eine volkskundliche Anatomie*. Weinheim and Berlin: Quadriga Verlag.
Karlson, H.J. and J. Judersleben. 1994. 'Die Soldatensprache der NVA. Eine Wortschatzbetrachtung', *Muttersprache* 104 (2): 143–64.
Klemperer, Victor. 1999 [1957]. *LTI. Notizbuch eines Philologen*, eighteenth edition. Leipzig: Reclam.
Koenigsberg, Richard. 1995. 'Content Analysis of the Writings and Speeches of Hitler: How manifest content reveals latent meaning', *The Psychoanalytic Psychotherapy Review* 6 (2-3): 79–86.
Labrie, Arnold. 2001. *Zuiverheid en decadentie. Over de grenzen van de burgerlijke cultuur in West-Europa 1870-1914*. Amsterdam: Uitgeverij Bert Bakker.
Lévi-Strauss, Claude. 1967. 'The Story of Asdiwal', in *The Structural Study of Myth and Totemism*, ed. Edmund Leach. London: Tavistock, 1–49.
Levy, Charles J. 1974. *Spoils of War*. Boston: Houghton Mifflin Company.
Marvin, Carolyn, and David W. Ingle. 1999. *Blood Sacrifice and the Nation. Totem Rituals and the American Flag*. Cambridge: Cambridge University Press.
Miller, William Ian. 2000. *The Mystery of Courage*. Cambridge, Mass.: Harvard University Press.
Moore jr., Barrington. 2000. *Moral Purity and Persecution in History*. Princeton: Princeton University Press.
Place, Tim Harrison. 2000. 'Lionel Wigram, Battle Drill and the British Army in the Second World War', *War in History* 7 (4): 442–62.
Rawson, Claude. 2001. *God, Gulliver, and Genocide. Barbarism and the European Imagination, 1492–1945*. Oxford: Oxford University Press.
Stouffer, Samuel A. et al. 1950. *The American Soldier: Adjustment During Army Life*, volume 1, second printing. Princeton, N.J.: Princeton University Press.
Theweleit, Klaus. 1985. *Männerphantasien. 2. Männerkörper. Zur Psychoanalyse des weissen Terrors*. Basel: Stroemfeld/Roter Stern.

Verrips, Jojada. 2001. 'The State and the Empire of Evil', in *Powers of Good and Evil. Social transformation and Popular Belief*, eds. Paul Clough and Jon P. Mitchell. New York: Berghahn Books, 185–210.

Wamsley, Gary L. 1972. 'Contrasting Institutions of Air Force Socialization: Happenstance or Bellwether?' *American Journal of Sociology* 78 (2): 399–417.

White, David G. 1991. *Myths of the Dogman*. Chicago and London: The University of Chicago Press.

Winslow, Donna. 1997. *The Canadian Airborne Regiment in Somalia. A Sociocultural Inquiry*. Ottawa: Canadian Government Publishing.

Žižek, Slavoj. 1990. 'Eastern Europe's Republics of Gilead', *New Left Review* 183: 50–63.

———. 1992. *Looking Awry. An Introduction to Jacques Lacan through Popular Culture*. Cambridge, Mass.: The MIT Press.

———. 1996. 'Fantasy as a Political Category: A Lacanian Approach', *Journal for the Psychoanalysis of Culture and Society* 1 (2): 77–86.

Step IV

From Testing Grammars to Widening the Debate

Chapter 9 Between Structure and Agency: From the *langue* of *Hindutva* Identity Construction to the *parole* of Lived Experience
Christian Karner

Chapter 10 Encompassment and its Discontents: The Rmeet and the Lowland Lao
Guido Sprenger

Chapter 11 Debating Grammars: Arguments and Prospects
Gerd Baumann and Andre Gingrich

Chapter 9
Between Structure and Agency
From the *langue* of *Hindutva* Identity Construction to the *parole* of Lived Experience

Christian Karner

A synchronic bias and the reductionist treatment of cultural meaning as epiphenomenal to structure may be the most commonly identified flaws in the structuralist paradigm (see Champagne 1990; Craib 1992; Douglas 1976; Wilden 1972). In this chapter I take two further limitations of the Lévi-Straussian framework, which are particularly relevant to the study of identity formation or negotiation, as my conceptual starting points: firstly, the assumption that an entire discourse may be reducible to a single grammar of identity reflected in terms such as 'cultural principle of order' (Descola 1992) or 'structural equation' or 'logic' (Kunin 1995, 1998). Secondly, I will challenge the common structuralist overemphasis on the deterministic power of 'system' (or *langue* in the Saussurian terminology) through a complementary analysis of individual social actors' reception, decoding or – as it will turn out – selective and contextual appropriation of a discourse constructing a particular Hindu 'self' and its various 'others'. In doing so, I will complement other contributions to this book that similarly draw attention to ideological struggles over classificatory grids. Agency, resistance, and (individual) *parole* are thus reintroduced into the discussion of self/other relations and their underlying cognitive patterns.

The argument presented here will draw on data concerning Hindu nationalism (*Hindutva*) as a transnationally circulating ideology. Although research was carried out both in northern India (Delhi, Rajasthan, UP) and among the Hindu diaspora in the British East Midlands, I will here predominantly refer to data from the British setting. Hindu nationalism is most widely associated with the BJP (*Bharatiya Janata Party*), the party currently heading the

National Democratic Alliance government of India. As the political offshoot of the RSS (*Rashtriya Swayamsevak Sangh*), a cultural revivalist organization founded in 1925 and concerned with a national re-awakening through bodily and ideological discipline, the BJP also entertains 'symbiotic organizational connections' (Andersen and Damle 1987) to the VHP (or World Hindu Council). The latter is best known for a series of mass-scale ritual campaigns of ethno-religious mobilisation during the 1980s and 1990s centred on the northern Indian town of Ayodhya, the mythological birthplace of the Hindu deity Ram (see Jaffrelot 1996; Hansen 1999; Rajagopal 2001). *Hindutva*'s most infamous manifestation occurred in December 1992, when a Hindu mob of *kar sevaks* (or volunteers) stormed and demolished the *Babri Masjid* of Ayodhya in Uttar Pradesh. According to the Hindu nationalist construction of history, Babar – founder of the Mughal dynasty – had erected the mosque in 1528 on the ruins of a Ram temple. The reconstruction or liberation of the temple was the declared aim of the *Ramjanmabhoomi* movement, in which the *sangh parivar* – or family of some eighty organizations affiliated to the RSS (McDonald 1999) – played a crucial ideological and organizational role. The death toll of the ensuing wave of communal (Hindu-Muslim) violence that swept across India during December 1992 and January 1993 has been estimated as high as 3000. Recent events in Gujarat, such as the arson attack on a train returning from Ayodhya and the retaliatory anti-Muslim pogroms costing many more lives, testified to the passions the temple/mosque controversy continues to evoke.

The transnational significance of Hindu nationalism has been reflected in the organizational diffusion of the *sangh parivar* to Hindus living in East Africa, South East Asia, Trinidad and Mauritius as well as North America and Western Europe. In Britain, the HSS (*Hindu Swayamsevak Sangh*) was established as an RSS offshoot in 1966, followed by the VHP (U.K.) in 1972 and a series of other (student, women and charity) organizations. Significantly, the HSS emulates the RSS methodology of local branches (*shakhas*) meeting regularly for the purposes of exercise, ideological 'education' and devotion to the organization's saffron flag (*Bhagwa Dwaj*). There are approximately sixty HSS *shakhas* in the U.K. today (Bhatt 2000: 559), with full-time workers being frequently 'supplied' by the RSS and British-born enthusiasts encouraged to attend Instructor or Officer Training Camps in Britain as well as in India. *Hindutva*'s ideological presence in the U.K. – beyond an innermost circle of volunteers (*swayamsevaks*) regularly attending their local units – was most clearly reflected in a two-day ritual gathering known as the *Virat Hindu Sammelan* in the town of Milton Keynes north of London in August 1989. Organized by the VHP (U.K.), the HSS and 350 other organizations affiliated or sympathetic to the *sangh parivar*, this gathering was attended by an officially estimated 50000 people.[1] Its message was predominantly one of Hindu unity, an attempt to transcend internal differences of caste, class, region, devotional and linguistic background and the construction of a unifying and global 'Hindu platform'. Echoing another one of the VHP's central concerns, the idea that *Hindu dharma* could 'ennoble the world' and that diaspora Hindus had a particularly important role to play in this context was also articulated during the event (see *Virat Hindu Sammelan* 1989). However, alongside such messages of seeming harmony, inclusivism and tolerance, the *Sammelan* was also part of one of the *sangh*'s antagonistic ritual campaigns unfolding throughout India and the diaspora at the time (Bhatt 2000; Mukta 2000). Known as the 'Bricks for Lord Ram campaign', money and stones were collected locally and then sent to Ayodhya for the purposes of reconstructing Ram's temple, thus illustrating both the *sangh parivar*'s organizational strength and the transnational appeal of its ideological message of the re-awakening Hindu nation.

In what follows I analyse selected articulations of the *Hindutva* discourse as encountered in the ideas and writings of some of its key ideologues.[2] The grammars of identity thus extrapolated will be shown to be varied, with 'orientalizing', 'ternary', 'hierarchical', and what may be termed 'asymmetrical Aristotelian' or 'anti-grammatical' self/other category relations coexisting within Hindu nationalism. By analysing some informants' engagement with this 'discursive formation' (Hall 1996), the second part of this paper will highlight its indeterminacy and contingency.

Hindutva's Heterogeneous *langue*

The articulation of Hindu nationalism has been relatively widely observed to be context- and audience-dependent (e.g., Jaffrelot 1996; Manor 1998; Jenkins 1998; Hansen 1999; Rajagopal 2001). The *sangh parivar*'s transnational presence underlines its varied objectives, ranging from the BJP's nationalist aims in India – using Eriksens's definition of nationalism as an ethnic ideology concerned with state power (1993) – to the *sangh*'s diasporic presence within ethnic associations/communities (Handelman 1977). Yet, the aforementioned *Virat Hindu Sammelan* in Milton Keynes was only one illustration of the organizational and ideological interconnectedness of these divergent contexts. Discursively, the attempt to construct and reify a particular Hindu identity, and to mobilise and awaken the Hindu nation on the basis of this identity, may be usefully taken as *Hindutva*'s defining characteristic. However, the articulation of this discourse utilizes, as we shall now see, several grammars of identity.

Despite some of its obvious weaknesses and rigidities discussed above, structuralism as a 'science of [categories and] relations' remains of 'considerable interest to students of categorisation and classification' (Saler 2000: 14). Identity construction, so the first two chapters in this book remind us, relies on the two intrinsically interrelated categories of 'self' and 'other'. Echoing Saussure's premise that the meaning of any sign is relational to, and thus a matter of difference from, other signs within a given semiotic system, the structuralist methodology extrapolates constitutive units from a symbolic system and investigates their interrelations, thus revealing an underlying equation, logic, principle, or grammar (e.g., Lévi-Strauss [1958] 1993; Leach 1970; Kunin 1998).

Emulating this programme, we may approach Hindu nationalism by extrapolating the categories or ideological building blocks of Hindu 'self' and (Muslim, Christian, Marxist) 'other' from its discourse and by investigating their interrelations as defined in the texts, documents and statements analysed. Supporting my analysis with some models/theories of categorisation from the cognitive sciences,[3] the following grammars of identity can be discerned.

Orientalizing Structures of Opposition

Ideological bifurcation, Manicheism, a dualistic or binary *Weltanschauung* (e.g., Pandey 1993; Frykenberg 1994; Almond et al. 1995), 'externally antagonistic and internally homogenizing' (van der Veer 1994: 105): such are the most common descriptions of the logic informing Hindu nationalism. Even a brief look at some of its key texts reveals the operation of a grammar based on mutually exclusive and antagonistic categories. The Hindu 'self' is thus frequently constructed as fundamentally opposed to, and by, a series of (foreign) others, including Muslims, Christians, Marxists and Western-styled Indian secularists. As the following statements by the RSS ideologue and second supreme guide (*sarsanghchalak*) M.S. Golwalkar illustrate, this oppositional grammar allows for no movement or ambiguity between the categories of 'self' and 'other':

> The invaders who came during the last ten or twelve centuries could not be driven out. They could not be absorbed either. They remained a separate entity and ruled as foreigners in this land. (Golwalkar 1966: 138)
> We, Hindus, are at war at once with the Moslems and the British. (Golwalkar 1947)
> A person can either be a Hindu or a Communist, he cannot be both. (Golwalkar 1966: 53)
> Partition [...] meant an acknowledgement that the Muslims formed a distinct and antagonistic national community [...] in this land [of] the Hindu Nation and that [they] had won for themselves a distinct state by vivisection of the country. (Golwalkar 1966: 432)

Idioms of war and the idea of Hindus 'under siege' were re-appropriated for a diaspora audience in an article published by the Nottingham and Manchester branches of the VHP (U.K.) in 1997:

> The image of Hindus and Hinduism that prevails in the information age is created by non-Hindus and by anti-Hindu forces. [...] *Sanatana Dharma* is being eroded, particularly in the minds of young Hindus [...] who find it denigrated in the media. [...] The front line of the battle in the world today is no longer on any particular battlefield. It lies now in the media and information field, which can be quite as deadly and poisoning in its results as any battlefield. (Frawley and Rao 1997, 3–5)

Many articulations of this oppositional grammar are informed by what psychologists call 'essentialist thinking' and define as the cognitive assumption that there is an 'underlying nature, or category essence, [that] is thought to be the causal mechanism that results in those properties that we can see' (Gelman et al. 1994, 344). In the case of Hindu nationalism, such essentialism manifests itself in frequent allusions to what are termed the Hindu and Muslim 'race spirit' respectively:

> Let us remember that this unity is ingrained in our blood from our very birth, because we are all born as Hindus. (Golwalkar 1966: 118)
> It is just like dressing himself in various garments [...]. The man does not change on that account. (Golwalkar 1966: 111)
> After all, it is in the nature of predatory nations to overrun, plunder and destroy other countries. (Golwalkar 1966: 206)

The 'innate nature' attributed to Hindus, however, is constructed as the binary opposite to 'the Muslims'. The RSS newspaper *Organiser* thus recently stated that 'not mere tolerance but respect for others is ingrained in the blood of Hindus' (10 December 2000). A brief look at Golwalkar's most controversial, and to my mind repugnant, statement, similarly shows that the belief in an unalterable essence can inform orientalizing/oppositional grammars of identity:

> To keep up the purity of the Race and its culture, Germany shocked the world by purging [sic] the country of the semitic Races [...]. Race pride at its highest [sic] has been manifested [t]here. Germany has also shown how well nigh impossible it is for Races and cultures, having differences going to the root, to be assimilated into one united whole [...]. (Golwalkar 1947: 43)

Positive and Negative Ternary Structures

The cognitive linguist George Lakoff defines the 'classical view' of categories as follows:

> Things are in the same category only if they have certain properties in common. Those properties are necessary and sufficient conditions for defining the category. (1987: xiv)

V.D. Savarkar, the ideological founding father of *Hindutva*, articulates two such necessary and sufficient criteria in his influential definition of 'the Hindu':

> A Hindu is a person who regards this land [...] from the Indus to the Seas as his Father-Land and his Holy-Land that is the cradle of his religion. (1942: i)

The insistence on the *two* criteria of considering India *both* fatherland *and* sacred space as defining characteristics of the Hindu 'self' create the structural possibility of liminal social groups.[4] Two such groups, those who regard India as either 'fatherland' or 'holyland' but not both, are addressed and dealt with very differently in the discourse of Hindu nationalism. Indian Muslims and

Christians are widely conceptualised as located on the fuzzy, ambiguous edges of the nation (Pandey 1999) and are evaluated in distinctly negative terms. Frequently accused of harbouring extra-territorial loyalties – be they to Pakistan, Saudi Arabia, the Vatican or international Communism – Indian Muslims, Christians and Marxists are portrayed by Hindu nationalists as posing a threat to the advocated unity and integrity of the Hindu nation. A recent example of the *Hindutva* perception of these structurally ambiguous social groups as powerful and dangerous, an outside force to be domesticated and controlled, was provided by the current RSS *sarsanghchalak*, K.S. Sudarshan, and his view of Indian Christians:

> Why should those people, who do not consider other ways of worship equal […] be allowed to work and enter India? We need to have an Indian national Church for the Indian Christians […] while throwing all other foreign churches out of the country. (*Organizer*, 15 October 2000)

On the other hand, diasporic Hindus, who may think of India as sacred space though no longer as their fatherland or country of action (*karmabhoomi*) (Raj 2000: 546), are structurally evaluated in positive terms. Diaspora Hindus' financial and cultural capital is constructed as a source of power to the reawakening *Hindu rashtra* (nation) and they themselves as part of it. Prime Minister A.B. Vajpayee was thus recently quoted as saying:

> People of Indian Origin and Non-Resident Indians should be partners in the country's efforts to become a major global player. We do not merely seek investment and asset transfer. What we seek is a broader relationship, a partnership among all children of Mother India. (*Organizer*, 21 January 2001)

Importantly then, the *Hindutva* discourse distinguishes between two different types of ternary structures: firstly, a negative or threatening version associated with non-Hindu Indians, whose 'mythology and Godmen, ideas and heroes are not the children of this soil' (Savarkar 1942: 92) and who are thus presumed to harbour extra-territorial loyalties; secondly, positive liminality is frequently attributed to diaspora Hindus, whose knowledge and experience of the outside world is portrayed as an asset in the revival of the *Hindu rashtra*.

Encompassing Hierarchies

The next grammar of identity to be extrapolated from Hindu nationalism is hierarchical insofar as it postulates the existence of an (all-)inclusive and internally stratified category. One manifestation of such hierarchical thinking was encountered in the RSS's opposition to the announcement, in August 1990, of the then Indian Prime Minister V.P. Singh, that 27 per cent of public sector jobs would be reserved for the so-called 'Other Backward Classes' (OBCs). Although the *sangh parivar* often prides itself in its alleged organizational and ideological egalitarianism (e.g., Seshadri 1988), the upper castes and urban middle classes have historically been over-represented both in its organizational ranks and in the policies advocated by the BJP as well as the *Jana Sangh* as its predecessor. RSS opposition to V.P. Singh's plans for affirmative action on behalf of the OBCs drew on an organicist social philosophy based on an idealised conception of a hierarchically unified and harmonious Hindu nation. This social philosophy not only legitimates an idealised caste (*varna*) system, but also naturalises social hierarchy and lends itself as an ideological tool of brahminical hegemony. Positive discrimination favouring OBCs was thus constructed as a direct affront to the Hindu nation and its allegedly *dharmic* hierarchies (*Organizer* 26 August 1990).

A hierarchical grammar also underlies frequently encountered constructions of Hinduism and its relation to other religious traditions:

> Hindu thought [...] has exhausted the very possibilities of human speculation as to the nature of the unknown. [...] Are you a monist, a monotheist, a pantheist, an atheist, an agnostic? Here is ample room for you [...] in this Temple of temples. (Savarkar 1942: 93)

This portrayal of Hindu thought as 'the Temple of temples' implies a hierarchical conceptualisation of its relationship to other religions, *Hindu dharma* being clearly defined as superior to the others. Religious differences are therefore in certain contexts seen to constitute differences of degree rather than kind. Within the cognitive sciences, such a conceptualisation may be accounted for by what is known as prototype theory, according to which membership in certain categories is graded, rather than an all-or-nothing phenomenon, depending on the degree of fit, or number of characteristics shared, with an ideal or prototypical case (Rosch 1978, Medin and Wattenmaker 1987). Such prototypical reasoning can also illuminate Hindu nationalist definitions of the 'Hindu fold' as including Jainism, Buddhism and Sikhism as religions of Indian origin. In the context of the Ayodhya controversy, Ram devotionalism (*bhakti*) came to be widely construed as the ideal or prototypical manifestation of a 'national Hinduism' (Hansen 1999). As for the other gradations within the category of the Hindu 'self', Sikhism, due to its history of self-assertion and martial values, is discursively constructed as somewhat superior to Buddhism. Importantly however, *Hindutva* ideologues portray both traditions as mere 'sects' within the *Hindu rashtra*:

> The formation of many of these sects served another useful purpose. They helped maintain the integrity of our people. The Sikh sect, for example, came into being to contain the spread of Islam in Punjab. (Golwalkar 1966: 102f.)
> Sikhs are very much a part and parcel of Hindu society. (Deoras 1984: 12)
> We yield to none in our love and respect for the Buddha. Buddhism has conquests to claim but they belong to a world far removed from this matter-of-fact world. (...) What was the use of a universal faith that instead of soothing the brutal egoism of other nations only excited their lust by leaving India defenceless and unsuspecting? The only safeguards in the future were valour and strength that could be born of a national self-consciousness. (Savarkar 1942: 17f.)

Asymmetrical 'Aristotelianism' or Anti-grammar?

Alongside such structures of opposition, liminality and encompassment, Hindu nationalism also appears to operate with a forth discursive configuration, which conceptualises and advocates the full metamorphosis of difference into sameness. Significantly, this forth type differs from the notion of hierarchical encompassment insofar as it conceptualises movement from one category to another as a diachronic process and the resulting transformation as total and complete. During many hours of interviews, a full-time RSS organizer referred to Islam as 'Muslim *dharma*' and declared that in the future Hindu nation Muslims would still be 'allowed' to worship in mosques but that their attitudes would be 'relatively more enlightened and pro-India' (interview 30 November 2000). Given the Hindu connotations of the term *dharma* as a polysemic concept referring both to a cosmic order and the individual's social duties, the notion of 'Muslim *dharma*' epitomises the grammar of encompassment. Through it, the 'other' is incorporated into an overarching category (i.e., *dharma*), within which hierarchical differences in degree continue to be reproduced (i.e., 'Muslim *dharma*' as allegedly inferior to Hindu *dharma*).

Yet beside this logic, and in an even more radical vein, Hindu nationalism also conceptualises transformations that are total and result in the complete erasure of difference. Importantly, the 'direction' of the transformation is of paramount importance in determining its discursive/structural evaluation. Consequently, there is a fundamental asymmetry between transformations of the 'other' into the 'self', which are encouraged, and the opposite process of the 'self' becoming the 'other', which is strongly condemned. Thus, *Hindutva*'s ideologues advocate, on occasion, the conversion of Indian Muslims/Christians to Hinduism and their full assimilation into a Hindu dominated social order:

> Mere common residence in a particular territory cannot forge a unified national society. [...] The Muslims and Christians here should bring about a *total* [my italics] metamorphosis in their life-attitudes and take rebirth in [our] ancient national lineage. [They] should give up their present foreign mental complexion and merge in the common stream of our national life. (Golwalkar 1966: 129f.)
>
> All those who fall outside [...] can have no place in the national life, unless they abandon their differences and completely merge themselves in the National Race [...] culturally [and] linguistically. [...] In short, they must be 'naturalized' in the country by being assimilated in the Nation wholly. (Golwalkar 1947: 53–55)

On the other hand, the transformation of the Hindu 'self' into the 'other', whether in the shape of religious conversion to Islam or Christianity or in the form of adopting Western ideologies, carries a clearly negative structural value and evokes the very different terminology of 'apostasy' or 'treason':

> Together with the change in their faith, gone are the spirit of love and devotion for the nation. They have developed an identification with the enemies of this land.

They look to some foreign lands as their holy places [...] [and they have] mentally merged themselves with the aggressors. [...] What else is it, if not treason, to join the camp of the enemy? (Golwalkar 1966: 128)

Every man going out of the Hindu pale is not only a man less but also an enemy the more (Seshadri 1988: 8).

Two alternative interpretations of this data appear to be possible. On the one hand, we may liken the conceptualisation of movement from one category to another to Maurice Bloch's notion of an 'Aristotelian logic', according to which identities are thought to be malleable. Unchanging (Platonic) *Formen* or essences thus give way to a 'transformational dialectic' (Bloch 1998: 71). Crucially, however, Hindu nationalism shows a profound asymmetry in its discursive evaluation of such diachronic transformations. As we have seen, only the 'other's' transformation into the 'self' is deemed permissible in the *Hindutva* discourse. Building on Bloch, we may thus speak of an 'asymmetrical Aristotelianism' as another possible grammar of identity.

On the other hand, the intense sentiments evoked by such transformations suggest certain parallels with other contributions to this volume (see the chapters by Müller, Postert, Verrips and Arnaut), which theorize the implosion of grammars and the resulting 'anti-grammars'. Advocating the forcible assimilation of all 'others' as well as the utter condemnation of all 'conversions away' may then be seen as symptoms or moments of an anti-grammatical disorder that recognizes no differences as legitimate but aims for their complete annihilation. Such anti-grammar may further be seen as a necessary, though not in itself sufficient condition for the demolition of the *Babri Masjid* in *Ayodhya* in December 1992 when hundreds of *kar sevaks* clearly believed that a mosque had to be turned into a temple as part of the imminent 'Hinduisation' of India. Anti-grammar thus appears to underlie a discourse of non-difference, which constructs the 'self' as the only legitimate 'reality'. The existence of all 'others' is only acknowledged as a prelude to their full, and if necessary forced, assimilation into the all-consuming category of 'us'.

Instances of Social Actors' *parole*

In his comprehensive study of '*The Saffron Wave*' of Hindu nationalism sweeping across India during the late 1980s and into the 1990s, Thomas Blom Hansen observes a seemingly inevitable discrepancy between *Hindutva*'s ideological/cognitive order and the complexities of the social world. He thus speaks of the 'incompleteness of taxonomic schemes of classification incapable of comprehending the richness of [...] social life [and] the incapacity of any narration of the self [...] to disclose fully the identity it purports to portray' (1999: 23). In the remainder of this chapter, I will draw attention to three ethnographic instances of contestation of the 'grammars of identity' extrapolated in the previous section. My attempt to make theoretical sense of such an ideological struggle in line with the Saussurian framework will draw on relevant work from within cultural studies.

Anti-essentialist approaches to the study of identities have been strongly influenced by Stuart Hall. Emphasizing the strategic and situational construction of identities as well as their perpetually processual 'nature', Hall argues that identities are not about 'who we are' or our 'roots' but about 'what we might become' and the 'routes' we follow to get there. Defining identities as 'temporary points of *suture*' or 'attachment to the subject positions which discursive practices construct for us' (Hall 1996: 5f.), his thinking implies a two-sided process that involves power and discourse as well as the subject and (a degree of) agency. Translated into the terms of our discussion, Hindu nationalism constitutes an ideological *langue* or a discourse seeking to construct particular subject positions and to 'attach' social actors to them. Not surprisingly however, people's lived experiences and their engagement with this discourse can give rise to ideological inconsistencies and 'oppositional decodings' (Hall 1980).

Peter Gottschalk's recent ethnography of the village of Arampur (Bihar) provides valuable insights into cross-cutting loyalties and multiple identities, and it thus challenges any simple juxtaposition of orientalizing grammars applied by Hindus to Muslims or vice versa. Of particular relevance to this discussion is Gottschalk's description of a local *swayamsevak*:

> Although he works as a primary organizer of the local RSS and is never reluctant to criticize Muslims, Sitaram Sharma joins his family at the side of a [Sufi] saint's tomb near Singhpur [...]. There they place a garland or orange flowers atop embroidered sheets draped on the concrete-surfaced barrow of the tomb. [...] One of the elder family members explains that [...] his family does this *puja* once a year in honour of this man who once helped them. (Gottschalk 2000: 49)

Gottschalk's observations corroborate existing arguments about Sufi shrines as places of religious syncretism providing mediatory space for transcending communal divides (van der Veer 1994, Sikand 2000). With regards to the RSS, this data illustrates that the ritual practices and lived experiences of *swayamsevaks*, especially in everyday activities outside the local *shakha*, may complicate and contradict the RSS official classification and evaluation of social groups and identities. Gottschalk's informant thus turns out contextually to defy the reifying subject position articulated by the Hindu nationalist discourse. In line with Hall's processual model of identities, this long-term *swayamsevak* is shown to be 'fixed' by RSS discursive practices in certain contexts, but far more ambiguous, syncretistic and eclectic in others, including his family's performance of *puja* at a local Sufi shrine. On the level of social practice, or identity *parole*, devotion to *Bharat Mata* (Mother India) and the *Bhagwa Dhwaj* appear not to preclude this social actor's contextual association with the threatening liminality widely attributed to Indian Islam and such contextual participation in Muslim rituals. The clearly defined role of the *swayamsevak* thus constitutes only one among several available and relevant 'identity-slots' (Hansen 1999).[5]

In much the same vein, my own data, too, support a contextual and actor-orientated reading of *Hindutva*'s orientalizing grammar of identity. When I conducted an interview at the Hindu *mandir* (temple) in Nottingham, which entertains strong organizational links to the HSS/RSS/VHP, it revealed a striking instance of ideological resistance:

> CK: Religion teaches us how to be good people, and still it causes all this conflict, like in the Middle East.
> I: Do you think (that) religion directly causes all this violence?
> CK: No, you see, it's people interpreting religion wrongly. In essence all religions have the same principles, all religions teach us how to be good people. Why do I have to see you as different? Why do people think, "he's a Muslim, so he's bad and violent"? It's not true. In essence all religion is good. Hindu, Sikh, Muslim, Christian, they're all good, potentially. (interview conducted 26 October 2000)

This stood in stark contrast to the opinions expressed by a *brahmin* at the same *mandir* who had described Islam as allegedly 'ignorant of all principles of tolerance and forgiveness' and hence as 'completely different' from *Hindu dharma* (13 October 2000). Yet less than two weeks later, my above-quoted informant who revered this very same *brahmin* as 'a man of great wisdom and religious learning' rejected such a dichotomous view based on an orientalizing grammar of identity to replace it with a decidedly more inclusivist account.[6] This, too, underlines the point that relations of power and authority do not confer or impose identities and opinions in any straightforward manner. The successful 'ideological articulation' – to re-appropriate an argument made by Abercrombie (1980, 1996) – of a given grammar of identity therefore remains a matter of contingency and an empirical question to be investigated contextually.

A final instance of ideological *parole* to be discussed here concerns *Hindutva*'s hierarchical grammar of identity, particularly the discursive inclusion of Sikhs within the 'Hindu fold'. A second-generation, U.K.-born Sikh informant of mine reflected on a recent holiday trip to India as follows:

> Going to *gurdwara* is a crucial part of life over there, not just something you do every Thursday or Sunday. [...] What was very strange though was going to shops and seeing pictures of Guru Nanak right next to pictures of [Hindu deities]. It made me feel strange. Even though there are some shared cultural roots, religiously Hinduism and Sikhism are entirely separate! It's very weird hearing about Hindus getting married in a *gurdwara*. I really feel that religiously we're entirely different, one is monotheistic, the other is polytheistic. (interview conducted 4 December 2000)

This informant was, over a period of many months, particularly consistent and vehement in his rejection of the idea, frequently espoused by Hindu nationalists, of Sikhism as a sect within, and part of, the Hindu nation. He would criticize the often permeable boundaries between Sikh and Hindu practices. Similarly, when told about the images of the Sikh gurus being displayed in the VHP *Bharat Mata mandir* in Hardwar, he categorically rejected the validity of such eclecticism (21 April 2001). In the theoretical terms of this discussion, he contested and rejected the 'subject position' – as defined by

Hindutva discursive practices – of Sikhs as part of the *Hindu rashtra* and the hierarchical grammar of identity implicit in it. Significantly, he also took issue with the often ambiguous or multiple identities encountered on the level of lived experience or 'discursive *parole*'. He thus told me about two girls he knew in Bradford 'who would go to the *gurdwara* on Thursdays and to the *mandir* on Sundays' (29 October 2000) in terms that revealed his disapproval of such fluid or multiple identities. In opposing any blurring of the Sikh 'self' with the Hindu 'other', my informant frequently drew on another readily available interpretative repertoire and its own orientalizing grammar of identity: the alternative discursive construction of Sikhs as an entirely separate, distinctive and internally unified religious community.[7] Remarkably however, the very same informant who felt so uneasy about the ambiguities of lived identities, 'admitted' on a separate occasion to the seeming inevitability of context-specific *parole*. Situationally 'detaching' himself from any one discursive practice, he once referred to the various aspects of his identity: religious (Sikh), cultural (Punjabi), pan-'Asian' in certain contexts, but also decidedly northern English. Articulating a meta-narrative of identity construction, he went on to declare that 'you sometimes only use those parts of your culture which fit the situation' (5 August 2000).

Concluding Remarks

Andrew Tudor has commented on the complementary concerns with *langue* and *parole* as follows:

> Structuralism and the various post-structuralisms were marked by a conceptual tension. [...] On one hand, structuralism [was] committed to understanding the constraints imposed by structures of whatever kind. But on the other hand, as Saussure had before them [sic], they also recognised the social relativity of semiotic systems, their inbuilt potential for polysemy, and the inventive capacity of social agents. [...] The codes through which *langue* functioned had to be understood before it was possible to approach questions of *parole*. (Tudor 1999: 165f.)

The line of argument presented in this chapter has largely corresponded to this broad history of structuralism. Approaching the discourse of Hindu nationalism in an attempt to extrapolate its underlying constructions of identity, the first part of my analysis has focused on the ideological *langue* of the discourse of *Hindutva* as it was articulated by the *sangh parivar* both in India and in the diaspora. In extrapolating different types of grammars coexisting in Hindu nationalism, this analysis could take distance from the more rigid, monolithic and reifying conceptions of structure implicit in some traditional structuralist work (e.g., Lévi-Strauss 1970, 1976; Kunin 1998, Descola 1992). I went on to investigate the social actors' own reception, their (partial) appropriation as well as their contextual contestation of the *Hindutva* discourse. While the discussion of category relations and grammars of identity drew on (categorization) models from the cognitive sciences, my discussion of fragmented/ experienced identities was informed by Stuart Hall's definition of identity as a never-completed process. In terms of identity construction, the tension between discursive practices aimed at fixing identities and the relative instability or fluidity of lived identifications theorized by Stuart Hall has been confirmed by the data. Undoubtedly, 'there are limits to the extent to which identities can become free-floating and self-selected' (Gillespie 1995: 17), most importantly unequal power relations or contextually available and meaningful cultural practices that might serve as repertoires for identity construction. Within those limits, however, the processes involved appear to be open-ended, with discursively defined subject-positions being contested by alternative discursive practices (and their grammars of identity), as in the case of my Sikh informant. All along, social actors' lived experiences and often-ambiguous identities defy and complicate the reifications any of these discourses seek to impose on the articulation of a particular identity.

Discursive *parole* has thus been shown to be underdetermined, though inevitably constrained and informed by the frameworks of meaning and identity available. The grammars of identity discussed in this book may be said to furnish widely circulating structures of classification. Their ideological 'orderliness' may be undermined by social actors' switching or manoeuvering amidst competing repertoires and therefore stands in some contrast to the ambiguities of social practice.

Notes

1. This is not to imply that people's presence at, or participation in, a ritual (gathering) translates into their automatic internalisation of the organizers' ideological agenda. The possibility of alternative ritual decodings or oppositional constructions of meaning is touched upon in the second part of this paper and constitutes a question in need of further ethnographic investigation.
2. The following extracts have been chosen from a vast (and steadily growing) body of ideological writings, documents, statements, etc. Given the scope of this chapter, I have had to be highly selective in my choice of quotations and I have attempted to include some that are particularly illustrative of the various 'grammars of identity' discussed here.
3. Lakoff has defined the cognitive sciences as 'a new field that brings together what is known about the mind from many academic disciplines: psychology, linguistics, anthropology, philosophy, and computer science' (1987: xi).
4. Also see M. Douglas on 'ethnic anomalies' (1966), V. Turner on 'betwixt and between' categories (1967), Eriksen (1993), chapter 3 in Bauman (2000) and Rajagopal (2001: 237–70) for related discussions.
5. For a similar and highly relevant argument, also see Baumann's ethnography of Southall (1996).
6. Such inclusivism may, of course, have partly served the purposes of impression management *vis-à-vis* the curious (researching) outsider. However, such strategic rhetoric would constitute a particularly striking example of discursive *parole* (or utterance) rather than contradicting the argument presented here.
7. For an empirical deconstruction of the ideal – particularly widespread in the Sikh diaspora – of such alleged '*panthic* unity', see Ballard 1994: 88ff.

References

Abercrombie, Nicholas, Stephen Hill and Bryan S. Turner, eds. 1980. *The Dominant Ideology Thesis*. London: Unwin Hyman.
——. 1996. *Television and Society*. Oxford: Polity Press.
Almond, Gabriel A. 1995. 'Fundamentalism: Genus and Species', in *Fundamentalisms Comprehended*, eds. Martin E. Marty and Scott R. Appleby. Chicago: University of Chicago Press, 399–425.
Andersen, Walter K. and S.D. Damle. 1987. *The Brotherhood in Saffron: The Rashtriya Swayamsevak Sangh and Hindu Revivalism*. Colorado: Westview.
Ballard, Roger. 1994. 'Differentiation and Disjunction among the Sikhs', in *Desh Pardesh: The South Asian Presence in Britain*, ed. Roger Ballard. London: Hurst, 88–116.
Bauman, Zygmunt. 2000. *Vom Nutzen der Soziologie*. Frankfurt: Suhrkamp.
Baumann, Gerd. 1996. *Contesting Culture: Discourses of Identity in Multi-Ethnic London*. Cambridge: Cambridge University Press.
Bhatt, Chetan. 2000. 'Dharmo Rakshati Rakshitah: Hindutva Movements in the U.K.', *Ethnic and Racial Studies* 23 (3): 559–93.
Bloch, Maurice. 1998. *How We Think They Think*. Oxford: Westview.
Champagne, Roland A. 1990. *French Structuralism*. Boston: Twayne Publishers.
Craib, Ian. 1992. *Modern Social Theory: From Parsons to Habermas*. London: Harvester/ Wheatsheaf.
Deoras, Balasaheb. 1984. *Answers, Questions*. Bangalore: Sahitya Sindhu.
Descola, Philip. 1992. 'Societies of Nature and the Nature of Society' in *Conceptualizing Society*, ed. Adam Kuper. London: Routledge, 107–126.
Douglas, Mary. 1966. *Purity and Danger*. London: Routledge.
——. 1976. 'The Meaning of Myth', in *The Structural Study of Myth and Totemism*, ed. Edmund Leach. London: Tavistock, 49–69.
Eriksen, Thomas. H. 1993. *Ethnicity and Nationalism: Anthropological Perspectives*. London: Pluto Press.
Frawley, David and T.R.N Rao. 1997. *Role of Intellectuals in Sanatan Dharma*. Nottingham and Manchester: Vishwa Hindu Parishad (U.K.).
Frykenberg, Robert E. 1994. 'Accounting for Fundamentalisms in South Asia: Ideologies and Institutions in Historical Perspective' in *Accounting for Fundamentalisms*, eds. Martin E. Marty and Scott R. Appleby. Chicago: University of Chicago Press, 591–617.
Gelman, Susan A. et al. 1994. 'Essentialist Beliefs in Children: The Acquisition of Concepts and Theories' in *Mapping the Mind: Domain Specificity in Cognition and Culture*, eds. Lawrence A. Hirschfeld, and Susan A. Gelman. Cambridge: Cambridge University Press, 341–62.
Gillespie, Marie. 1995. *Television, Ethnicity and Cultural Change*. London: Routledge.
Golwalkar, Madhav S. 1947. *We or Our Nationhood Defined*, 4th edition. Nagpur: M.N. Kale.
——. 1966 *Bunch of Thoughts,* 2nd edition. Bangalore: Jagarana Prakashana.
Gottschalk, Peter. 2000. *Beyond Hindu and Muslim*. London: Oxford University Press.
Hall, Stuart. 1980. 'Encoding/Decoding', in *Culture, Media, Language* ed. Stuart Hall et al. London: Hutchinson, 128–38.

———. 1996. 'Introduction: Who Needs Identity?' in *Questions of Cultural Identity*, eds. Stuart Hall and Paul du Gay. London: Sage, 1–17.
Handelman, Dietmar. 1977. 'The Organization of Ethnicity', *Ethnic Groups* 1: 187–200.
Hansen, Thomas B. 1999. *The Saffron Wave: Hindu Nationalism and Democracy in Modern India*. Princeton: Princeton University Press.
Hansen, Thomas B. and Christophe Jaffrelot, eds. 1998. *The BJP and the Compulsions of Politics in India*. Delhi: Oxford University Press.
Jaffrelot, Christophe. 1996. *The Hindu Nationalist Movement and Indian Politics*. London: Hurst.
Jenkins, Rob. 1998. 'Rajput Hindutva, Caste Politics, Regional Identity and Hindu Nationalism in Contemporary Rajasthan', in *The BJP and the Compulsions of Politics in India*, eds. Thomas B. Hansen and Christophe Jaffrelot. Delhi: Oxford University Press, 101–120.
Kunin, Seth D. 1995. *The Logic of Incest*. Sheffield: Academic Press.
———. 1998. *God's Place in the World*. London: Cassell.
Lakoff, George. 1987. *Women, Fire and Dangerous Things*. Chicago: University of Chicago Press.
Leach, Edmund. 1970. *Lévi-Strauss*. Fontana: Collin.
Lévi-Strauss, Claude. 1970. *The Raw and the Cooked: Introduction to a Science of Mythology*. London: Cape.
———. 1976. 'The Story of Asdiwal', in *The Structural Study of Myth and Totemism*, ed. Edmund Leach. London: Tavistock, 1–48.
———. [1958] 1993. *Structural Anthropology 1*. London: Penguin.
Manor, James. 1998. 'Southern Discomfort: The BJP in Karnataka', in *The BJP and the Compulsions of Politics in India*, eds. Thomas B. Hansen and Christophe Jaffrelot. Delhi: Oxford University Press, 163–201.
McDonald, Ian. 1999. "Physiological Patriots'? The Politics of Physical Culture and Hindu Nationalism in India.' *International Review for the Sociology of Sport* 34 (4): 343–58.
Medin, Douglas and Wattenmaker, William. 1987. 'Category Cohesiveness, Theories, and Cognitive Archaeology', in *Concepts and Conceptual Development: Ecological and Intellectual Factors in Categorization*, ed. Ulrich Neisser. New York: Cambridge University Press, 25–62.
MU.K.ta, Parita. 2000. 'The Public Face of Hindu Nationalism.' *Ethnic and Racial Studies* 23 (3): 442–66.
Pandey, Gyanendra. 1999. 'Can a Muslim be an Indian?' *Comparative Studies in Society and History*, 41 (4): 608–30.
Pandey, Gyanendra, ed. 1993. *Hindus and Others: The question of Identity in India Today*. Delhi: Viking.
Raj, Dhooleka S. 2000. '"Who the hell do you think you are?" Promoting Religious Identity Among Young Hindus in Britain.' *Ethnic and Racial Studies* 23 (3): 535–58.
Rajagopal, Arvind. 2001. *Politics after Television: Hindu Nationalism and the Reshaping of the Public in India*. Cambridge: University Press.
Rosch, Eleanor. 1978. 'Principles of Categorization', in *Cognition and Categorization*, eds. Eleanor Rosch and B.B. Lloyd. Hillsdale: Erlbaum, 27–48.
Saler, Benson. 2000. *Conceptualizing Religion*. New York: Berghahn Books.
Savarkar, Vinayak D. 1942. *Hindutva: Who is a Hindu*, second edition. Poona City: S.R. Date.

Seshadri, H.V. 1988. *RSS: A Vision in Action.* Bangalore: Jagarana Prakashana.
Sikand, Yoginder. 2000. 'Popular Beliefs and the Dialogue of the Everyday Life: Inter-religious Interaction at the Sufi Shrines of Jammu', *Studies in Interreligious Dialogue* 10 (2): 135–47.
Tudor, Andrew. 1999. *Decoding Culture: Theory and Method in Cultural Studies.* London: Sage.
Turner, Victor. 1967. *The Forest of Symbols.* Ithaca: Cornell University Press.
Van der Veer, Peter. 1994. *Religious Nationalism.* Berkeley: University of California Press.
Virat Hindu Sammelan. 1989. *Let Us Ennoble the World (Souvenir, Milton Keynes).* Chatham: Chatham Printers.
Wilden, Anthony. 1972. *System and Structure: Essays in Communication and Exchange.* London: Tavistock.

Chapter 10
Encompassment and its Discontents
The Rmeet and the Lowland Lao

Guido Sprenger

This chapter explores certain features of Baumann's three grammars of alterity/identity and relates them to their consequences in social practice. The argument expands in two ways: first, certain features are derived from the structure of each grammar which are not explicitly mentioned by Baumann. The validity of the grammars as theoretical models is tested by linking these features to ethnographic data from Northern Laos. The central question to be asked, both of the models as theoretical abstractions and of the data to be analysed, is: how much and what kind of dialogue is made possible by each grammar?

The second trajectory of the argument is its focus on encompassment, as this type of grammar appears to be the most asymmetric kind, i.e., the one least prone to dialogue and reversibility. In theory and in practice, encompassment poses particular problems. In a theoretical discourse, the model of an encompassment grammar should be assigned its proper field of application within contact situations between culturally diverging groups; the kind of grand social theory in which Louis Dumont introduced the term is beyond its scope. It is indeed one of the strong points of the grammars model that it does not position itself within any grand theory; it is an effective means to classify and analyse particular communicative acts and render visible their implications for political and social practice. It keeps its theoretical points of reference open and flexible and thus embodies the kind of epistemological difference it attempts to describe.

In practice, issues of hegemony and political power come into focus more obtrusively in the encompassment model than in the other grammars. While segmentary and orientalizing grammars are dialogic, encompassment can be described as non-dialogic. As the example of the Rmeet will show in this article, encompassment grammars are only enacted as monologues or in contexts involving a clear-cut power relation. In the present case, those power relations are identified between the Lao nation-state and the minorities. While the grammars model will enable us to consider this particular relationship and its correlates in discourse more closely, it also points to a curious asymmetry: state/minority relations usually are seen in terms of encompassment by the Lao majority. By contrast, Rmeet minority members stress nominal equality in many contexts, originally professed by government ideology itself. This context allows local concepts of sociality to become discernible.

Baumann and Dumont

As Baumann states in this volume, the encompassment model of selfing/othering is only loosely inspired by Louis Dumont. Still, the differences need to be made more explicit, in order to shed light on the problems that this particular grammar engenders.

First of all, Dumont's notions of hierarchy and encompassment were designed to describe ideologies as integrated wholes, always referring to a system of values within a particular culture. By way of contrast, in Baumann's model the three grammars are like tools that are to be employed according to context and need; encompassment is just one among them. The interrelationship between the three grammars is not a subject of Baumann's model, they are implicitly treated as equally valid and not integrated into some overarching system of values. This integration is what Dumont's theory demands of any relationship, and this is also what constitutes the basic difference between Dumont and Baumann: Dumont's model describes societies – specifically those he calls 'traditional' – and their values as hierarchic, each social position or representation gaining its value from its particular relationship to the whole. His model is thus hierarchic and encompassing in itself, and furthermore assumes the ideological unity of a society (Dumont 1980: 20, 343, n. 1a).

Baumann's model, on the other hand, is somewhat individualising: it is not premised on ideological unity, but rather on the differences between the groups under scrutiny. This does not mean by itself that Baumann and Dumont are incompatible, although I will not try to reconcile them here. The important point, however, is this: Dumont's theory needs a certain kind of flexibility in regard to the definition of its terms, in order to work on the scale it was designed for; the application of Baumann's encompassment grammar is comparatively narrow and thus has to be defined in a much more precise way. Let me elaborate the point by way of two examples. Among the classic demonstrations that Dumont gave for his theory are the examples of the right hand and the left hand and the relation between man and woman in Genesis. The right hand is (in particular cultures) of higher value than the left hand because it has a privileged relation to the body as a whole: for example it is more active or performs acts of purity. Both hands are differentially related to the whole and are therefore not equal first and valued later. For Dumont, value is part of their definition as parts of a whole (Dumont 1986: 228). Still, the difference between part and whole, body and hand, is maintained. On the other hand, in the biblical example, the difference is virtually denied on a higher level, rather as in Baumann's examples: Man is, on one hand, opposite to Woman, but as Eve stemmed from Adam's body, it is Man-as-humankind which is actually identical with the whole: Man becomes the defining category of the whole (Dumont 1980: 239–40), just as Hindus claim to be the defining category of a whole that includes Sikhs (Baumann, this volume; see figure 10.1).

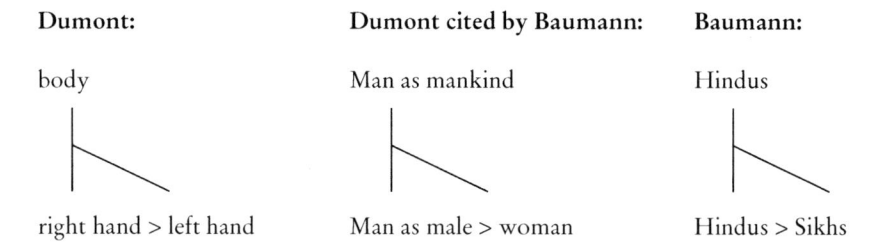

Dumont:	Dumont cited by Baumann:	Baumann:
body	Man as mankind	Hindus
right hand > left hand	Man as male > woman	Hindus > Sikhs

Figure 10.1 Contrasting Examples of Encompassment

While in Dumont's thinking, and for his purposes, right/left hand and Man/Woman are examples of the same basic idea, I propose that they are different in the model of grammars of alterity. The right hand/left hand kind of division would, if transferred to discourses about culturally defined groups, be rather a case of a segmentary grammar. For Dumont, the privileged position of the right hand vis-à-vis the left is inseparable from its relation to the body and the entire system. For Baumann's grammars, this value difference would be a secondary phenomenon – otherwise one would have to describe most or even all cases of segmentary grammars in terms of encompassment: The relationship of two different entities to a whole, to which they both belong, is in practice always different, and thus the elements will be differentially valued with respect to each other. Yet the grammars model does not refer to the ideology of societies in their entirety: it analyses particular discursive strategies and their consequences in situations between representatives of different ideologies who need not share a central value. At this level, value-free segmentation as an idea does exist, even if the use of this concept in the *analysis* of societies is debatable.[1] Thus, for the purpose of this chapter, I will use Baumann's encompassment in a rather strict sense. Defining an other by encompassment means that one of the two categories is opposed to the other on a lower level, but is identified with their unity on a higher level, notably without losing its peculiar identity. The right hand is not the body, and a Nuer lineage is not a clan; but Hindus are still Hindus, even when they encompass Sikhs.

Grammars Dialogic and Non-Dialogic

With this distinction in mind, one may classify the three grammars in a different way. The orientalizing grammar and the segmentary one are dialogic, while encompassment is a denial of dialogue – at least if we refer to dialogue between (representatives of) groups with discernibly different identities;[2] in this respect encompassment resembles the anti-grammar, a point to which I shall return in the final section.

The potential for dialogue is derived from the type of difference constructed by each grammar. In each case that the grammars model can be applied to, certain generalisations are used to define the characteristics of groups or categories of people and these comprise the kind of difference conceived between these groups. The grammars model explicitly describes these types of differences, but it also implies certain properties of the terms that are used, or rather, it implies (discursively assigned) qualities of the units that are linked and defined by those differences. Let me trace these implications for each grammar.

Orientalizing grammars often involve a disparagement of the other, but just as often an appreciation. This type of conceiving the other is based on binary classifications, and while this binarism usually involves a degree of generalization that most people would find unacceptable on closer scrutiny, it may be used as a consensual base for communication. The binary terms of the classification – like 'rational/emotional', 'peaceful/aggressive' – refer to putatively inherent characteristics of groups or categories of persons. Although the complementarity of the terms betrays their relational nature, they appear to describe 'substantial' features. As the binary categories are usually based on the language and understanding of just one of the groups, the acceptance of these categories for dialogue often involves hegemony. While two groups may orientalize each other, dialogue is only possible when (members of) both groups agree on a particular set of criteria employed to talk about their difference. Usually, the influence of one of the parties will be more dominant in determining this set of terms for communication. Still, the degree of influence, and in particular the balance of disparagement and appreciation, may significantly change in the course of the dialogue.

Segmentary grammars raise the least obstacles to dialogue. The only thing that the two groups have to agree upon is their affiliation with a third category that is not identical with one of them but is situated on a different level of classification. They do not even have to conceive of their differences as substantial features of their respective groups; the opposition between Nuer lineages or between fans of rival football teams is purely a matter of social structure, not of inherent characteristics of their members or the organization of the group. Indeed, segmentary grammars may be distinguished by their ontological identification of the groups. Being nominally equal parts of an overarching category, their internal structure may be conceived to be identical – which is what Evans-Pritchard's classical use of the notion entails (1940: 135). I will return to this point in the section on the nation-state. Admittedly, this structural opposition may be used as a basis for 'substantial' oppositions, and this is not uncommon. Binary terms taken from orientalizing contexts may be transferred to segmentary contexts. Still, this is not a defining feature of segmentary grammars, and 'substantial' differences may be devalued in actual dialogue. Those particular contexts in which segmentary grammars are used stress the sameness of the social units under consideration. Even when differences between these units in their relation to the higher level seem obvious (like majority/minority), segmentary grammars privilege sameness over valorisation.

While segmentary grammars, by their way of classification, do thus not impede dialogue, and while the obstacles inherent in orientalizing grammars may be overcome, the case is more difficult with encompassment as a grammar. It is the most asymmetric type of the three, and this creates a logical problem when dialogue is initiated in terms of encompassment. The first step in conceiving an other is identifying certain features that differ between the self and the other. Encompassment, in the definition used here, implies that the other is defined as a variety of the self that differs not substantially but only in context and the other's self-definition. For the encompassing ones, this is not a problem; for the encompassed ones, by contrast, it would require crediting the encompassers with a higher level of truth. It means, paradoxically, that those features that made the other different in the first place become part of the self-definition, of the identity of the encompassed ones: things different become things identical. Thus encompassment denies the other the right to be different, and it demands that the encompassed others define themselves by the very same features as those defined by and defining the encompasser. From purely logical reasoning, one could predict two consequences: first, the relation should be precluded from violence for the encompassers should not fight a part of themselves; secondly, encompassment precludes dialogue.

Still, both violence and dialogue may occur under certain circumstances in relationships of encompassment. Violence may occur in situations in which the encompassed ones demand to be recognized as a separate category, often implying political autonomy from a powerful encompassing group. An example is the way the Turkish government used to treat Kurds as 'Mountain Turks'. Those Kurds who would not approve of such encompassment could be denounced as criminals and separatists, then to become victims of violence and persecution. Dialogue may occur in those narrowly defined contexts in which the power of the encompassing group is immediately felt, but conflict is avoided. One example are the Hmong village officials who, when in direct contact with Lao officials, agree with the view that the Hmong, not ethnically Lao, are a kind of *Lao* as members of the Lao-dominated nation (see Postert in this volume). As Hmong village officials depend on the Lao administration for their offices, power relations are particularly emphasized. Since dialogue is restricted to those rare situations in which these two parties meet, the acceptance of encompassment is highly situation-specific, and not applicable to the self-definition of the Hmong majority in most other contexts.

From this we can derive the key factor that separates an entirely monologic use of encompassment on the one hand from violence or dialogue on the other; and this leads us back to Dumont. What made Western scholars feel so uneasy about hierarchy and encompassment, so Dumont argued, was their confusion of value hierarchy with power hierarchy (Dumont 1980: 19). Dumont's analysis rests on the condition that value hierarchies (hierarchy proper in his terms) could work on a different level than power hierarchies (political or economic relations), and that therefore the nominally powerless Brahmins could be superior in terms of value to the powerful rulers and kings – because both shared a similar conception of a cosmological whole that valorised their differential relationship. In the field which Baumann's model was designed for, however, the kind of silent agreement on the concept of the whole between encompassers and encompassed, as assumed by Dumont, does not exist. Acted out, an encompassment grammar always involves questions of power, be it in the form of dialogue, with power relations silencing the articulation of difference, or in the form of violence, with power suppressing difference.

Perhaps Baumann's model was conceived in view of an urban society in which ethnic or cultural groups live in close vicinity or the same community. To test the model in regard to non-urban societies, Mainland Southeast Asia is particularly well suited. Beginning with Leach (1964 [1954]) and Moerman (1965), many researchers have stressed that ethnic identity is subject to permanent negotiation and relational re-definition in this part of the world.

The Rmeet Setting

The Rmeet, called Lamet in the older literature, number about 16,000 people and live in three mountainous northern provinces of Laos: Luang Nam Tha, Bokeo and Udomsai. Their villages are situated on mountain slopes and ridges and thus remote from trade routes and administrative centres. The Rmeet speak a Mon-Khmer language and therefore represent what is probably the oldest wave of immigration still extant in Laos, along with their culturally closest neighbours, the Khmu, a much larger group. Like other ethnic groups belonging to this language family in Laos, they do not possess a type of organization above village level. Their point of reference for supra-village or state organization are the polities of the surrounding Tai speaking groups, first of all the Lao.

During the colonial period and until the victory of the socialist *Pathet Lao*, the area of research was part of the Kingdom of Laos, and the Rmeet paid taxes to the king via their village headmen. Otherwise, the relation between the Rmeet villages and the state used to be quite tenuous; most of the Rmeet were afraid of the lowlanders and refused learning to write.[3] On the other hand, there was regular economic exchange with the lowlands, as we know from ethnographic data from the 1930s. Being excellent rice farmers, the Rmeet descended once a year to the lowlands to sell their surplus to traders. In addition, young men would often go to Thailand for a few years of wage labour (Izikowitz 1951: 310, 351).

The relationship to the state became closer after the downfall of the kingdom and the victory of the socialist *Pathet Lao* party in 1975. In the village where I did research, a school was founded shortly after the *Pathet Lao* started to control the area. Relations to the representatives of the nation-state are nowadays managed by village headmen, an office that did not originate within Rmeet society but was introduced by French colonial and earlier Siamese rule (112). Nowadays, officials of the district administration visit the remote villages about once every six weeks for various types of work.

Economic ties to the lowland are today of basically the same kind as sixty-five years ago, although they have intensified considerably. In order to sell rice, livestock and forest produce, the villagers have to descend to the Nam Tha river, which is a five-hour walk away. There is a monthly market on the bank of the Nam Tha, where villagers buy petrol, zinc sheets, clothing, batteries and other household items. Traders only rarely go to the mountain villages, and if they do, the purpose is to arrange meetings with villagers on the Nam Tha in order to buy forest produce. As in the 1930s, the Rmeet consider Thailand as the 'land of possibilities' (Izikowitz 1951: 351), and young men and sometimes women would spend one to five years there on wage labour, some of them never to come back, some of them only to return decades later. Thus, while the everyday life of the Rmeet hardly involves contact with lowlanders and their institutions, they are fully dependent on the lowlands for their external trade. This makes the lowlands the most important category of reference for Rmeet cultural identity. This category is designated by the word *yam* which covers the lowlands as a geographic area; the Tai-Kadai-speaking ethnic groups like Lue and Lao, not all of them living in the lowlands; and the livelihood, culture and language of these groups. To a lesser degree, the term includes state representatives, who in most cases are members of the lowland groups, although usually they will be described as coming from the respective administrative centre of the district (*muang*) or the province (*kweeng*).

Different meanings of the word *yam* are assigned to particular contexts. Thus the Khmu are usually considered a highland group, but a Rmeet man who had emigrated to a lowland village of practising Buddhists, and who had married a Khmu woman there, told me that his wife was *yam*. Conversely, those Rmeet who turned away from their language and rituals after their emigration are said to have 'become *yam*'.

Another point is the role of *chlo yam*, lowland language, in ritual. Most verses recited by shamans during healing rituals are unintelligible even to those fluent in Lao, but are identified as *chlo yam*. This is not because shamanism was introduced from the lowlands, at least not from a Rmeet perspective. These healing traditions are said to be of local origin, while the lowland shamans only master a diminished version of highland rituals. The point is that *chlo yam* is the language of the spirits in general. Thus, *yam* is not simply an essentialist category of land and people, but a certain cultural context that is defined by specific contrasts to Rmeet culture.

Contexts for Grammars in Northern Laos

How can the relationship to *yam* and its various aspects be described by the grammars of alterity? In fact, all three grammars are employed in respect to different aspects of the relationship.

In the orientalizing grammar, 'substantial' binary oppositions are stressed between the Rmeet and the *yam*. The most fundamental point for the Rmeet[4] is knowledge and education. A common reply to the question about the most distinctive feature of the Rmeet is that the Rmeet do not know anything: they do not know writing, nor how to build a car or an airplane, not how to build machines, nor how to handle money. They also emphasized that they are ugly, due to their dark skin, while the white complexion of the lowlanders was far more beautiful. Furthermore, lowlanders are able to practise wet rice cultivation, which is much less laboursome than dry rice shifting cultivation. They also have much less trouble with spirits, as the lowland spirits are assembled in Buddhist temples where monks take care of them.

The positive aspects of this orientalizing construction of opposites only rarely come to the fore – at least in relations with me, the foreign, white-skinned anthropologist. In an 'orientalist positive' mode, the Rmeet see themselves as more sociable, they love and care for each other, a relation designated by the verb *kho am po*. One young man, who had been working in Thailand for two years, expressed this opinion very pointedly in a somewhat different context: 'In Thailand you have to be afraid of robbers, among the Rmeet you have to be afraid of spirits'. Still, this positive orientalizing terminology is partially a function of social divisions. With most informants adressing this issue, it was not clear whether the unfriendliness of the lowlanders was seen as an essential part of their sociality, or if it was implied that dealing with lowlanders was unpleasant because their sociality categorically excluded the Rmeet.

Moreover, a grammar of segmentation is also being used, with the Lao nation-state as an overarching point of reference. There are two contexts in which the community of the Rmeet and the *yam* are evoked as different but equal members of the nation-state. The first context has been indicated already: in the contrast to Thailand, a much wealthier and more developed country, the features of the Rmeet and the Lao are conflated. This means, while the Thai are seen as unsociable, the term *kho am po* is used to describe the community of all the citizens of Laos. The primary experience of most Rmeet with Thai is with policemen and border guards, representatives of state bureaucracy, whereby they are considered to be permanently suspicious about illegal trade and immigration. In contrast, relations with Lao lowlanders in similar positions are much easier, a fact interpreted in terms of belonging together and caring for each other. Most informants would emphasize similar points about knowledge and abilities when talking about the opposition of Laos and Thailand, as when they would speak about the Rmeet and the lowlanders. Thus, almost the same rhetoric of difference that is employed in the orientalizing division is transferred to a higher level of social organisation in the segmentary division – here, orientalizing values infuse the ideally equalizing, value-neutral language of segmentation.

What makes the two discourses incompatible is the impossibility to overcome the 'ugliness' of the Rmeet, a feature that cannot be transferred to the Thai/Lao discourse. Physical beauty as a measure to evaluate persons and peoples should not be underrated in the Laotian context, and this contrast remains an essential feature of the orientalizing grammar. The second context for a segmentation view concerns a historical perspective. Under the reign of the king, the Rmeet were called *kha* by the lowlanders, a term understood by the Rmeet to mean 'to kill'. The explanation brought forward for this is a myth about an ancient king of Laos who was Rmeet. The lowlanders enticed the Rmeet to fight their own king and kill him. Actually, *kha* in Lao is a term for 'serf'.[5] In any case, the term is considered an insult by the Rmeet. The term *kha* indeed became the hallmark of the highlanders' marginalisation in a modernising Lao Kingdom after the Second World War. The success of the *Pathet Lao* in 1975 was partially based on the ideology of equality of lowlanders and highlanders professed by the communists (Stuart-Fox 1997: 79–80). This equality became part of the official government rhetoric after 1975;[6] and as such it was adopted by many Rmeet when they refer to their lowland acquaintances: 'Before they called us *kha*, but now we are friends, we are all Lao' – but by inference, not *yam*.

In both these grammars, the orientalizing stress on (partly essential) oppositions and the segmentary reference to the Lao Nation that subdues some of these differences, the Rmeet see themselves on the disadvantaged side of difference: they are the ugly ones, the uneducated, the insulted. Within the contexts described by the orientalizing and the segmentary grammar, the Rmeet show a mixture of admiration and mistrust, coupled with a tendency to adopt the dominant lowlanders' evaluation of their situation, an attitude found among several highland groups in mainland Southeast Asia (Kammerer 1988: 261).

This picture is reversed when we come to consider encompassment. The origin myths of the Rmeet describe them as the original ancestors of all the people in the world, and the original owners of those items of wealth that nowadays have to be obtained by trade. The most telling of these origin myths is the story of the flood, and this is said to be *pawadsaad priim*, 'old history', considered a true historical event by storytellers. The story involves a man who digs up a bamboo rat from a hole in the ground. The bamboo rat asks to be released, as a flood will soon come and destroy all humankind. The man builds a wooden drum, and, after some reflection, he decides to abandon his wife and to take his sister with him. The waters rise and kill everyone except the sibling couple. After the flood has receded, they look for partners but always meet up with each other. They finally decide to become husband and wife, and the girl gives birth to a gourd. The gourd grows bigger and bigger, and after the couple hears voices from inside, they cut it open. From the gourd emerge all the peoples of the earth, starting with the Rmeet and the Khmu, then the Lao, the French, Americans, Germans and so on. In this myth, the

Rmeet claim priority, not only in the order of emergence, but in a truly encompassing manner. The first couple represents the unity of humankind which is later split up into numerous ethnolinguistic groups. Although it is not mentioned in the text of the myth itself, all storytellers would readily add that this primordial couple was Rmeet. Thus, the term that is part of a multitude of similar units on a lower level, represents all of them on a higher one, creating the part-whole relationship characteristic of encompassment.

Yet this claim to priority is not accepted by the groups thus encompassed. The story is one of many variants found in the area, each placing the storyteller's own ethnic group at the apex of the ancestral line (Dang Nghiem Van 1993). Cosmologies always tend to be encompassing, and in highland Southeast Asia, ethnic diversity is a part of cosmology. This creates the seemingly paradoxical configuration of an ethnic landscape in which changes of identity and intercultural exchange are frequent (see Leach [1954] 1964; Hinton 1983), but in which each group claims cosmological priority over the others. The underlying assumption that all the others are just parts removed from one's own group may facilitate these identity changes and borrowings. Elements that moved away from the original unity are being re-integrated. In this respect, the encompassing myth becomes the foundation of cross-ethnic integration – but, paradoxically, only insofar as it is not introduced into dialogue.

The only instance I recorded of the myth being brought into dialogue ended in a slight compromise: an elderly Rmeet told the story in the presence of a young schoolteacher who was Khmu. The Khmu are divided into several regional subgroups called *tmooy*. Sometimes, Khmu would categorize the Rmeet as a *tmooy*, Khmu Rmeet (Simana 1997: 1–2, fn. 8). This categorization is rejected by the Rmeet, although the Khmu are considered their closest cultural relatives. Yet the Khmu versions of the flood story are very similar to the Rmeet versions (Ferlus 1972; Lindell et al. 1976). When I asked which group the primordial couple came from, the Rmeet storyteller answered: 'Rmeet'. The schoolteacher hastened to add: 'Khmu Rmeet', and the storyteller repeated this in approval. In this case, the two parties were recognizing the similarity of their traditions and their position vis-à-vis other ethnic groups. From the perspective of traditional Lao (and highlanders') ethnohistory, the Mon-Khmer-speaking groups, foremostly represented by their largest group, the Khmu, are the predecessors of the lowlanders and the original owners of the land. It was the particular situation which made this example of 'double encompassment' temporarily acceptable: the Rmeet encompass everybody, and the Khmu encompass the Rmeet.

Orientalizing:

Rmeet		*yam* (Lowlanders)
uneducated, ugly	<	educated, beautiful
unsuccessful with money	<	successful with money
sociable	>	unsociable

Segmentation:

People's Dem. Rep. of Laos　　　　　　Thailand

```
           uneducated    <    educated
           sociable      >    unsociable
  Rmeet    yam (Lowlanders)
```

Encompassment:

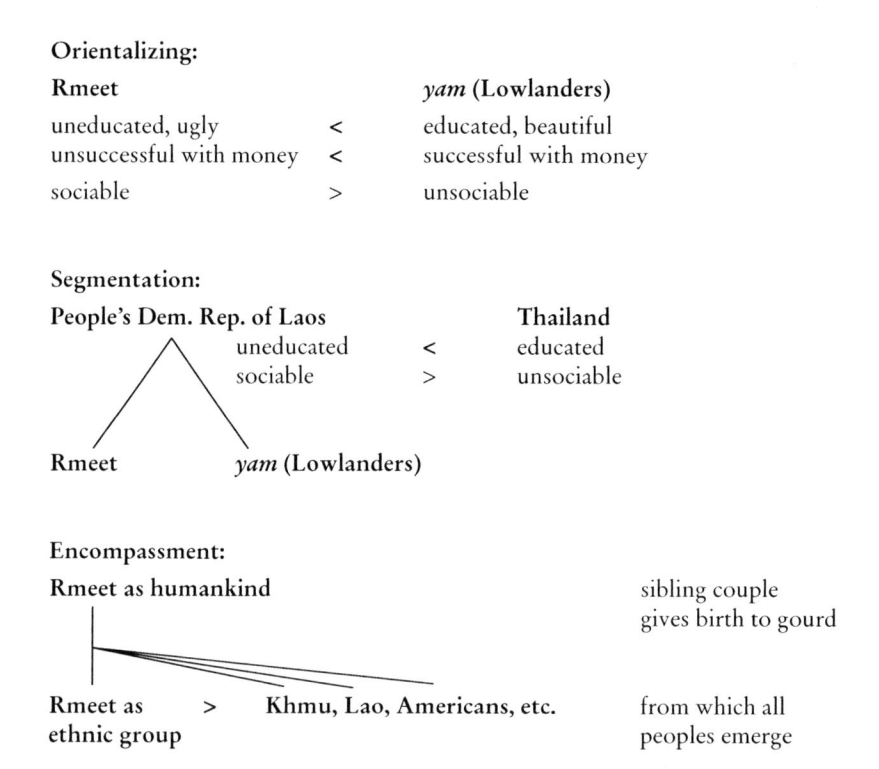

Rmeet as humankind　　　　　　　　　　sibling couple
　　　　　　　　　　　　　　　　　　　gives birth to gourd

Rmeet as　　>　Khmu, Lao, Americans, etc.　　from which all
ethnic group　　　　　　　　　　　　　　　　peoples emerge

Figure 10.2 The Three Grammars in Rmeet Usage

Grammars and the Nation-State

One of the problems that fuelled the crafting of this chapter into its present form was the claim that the relationship to the state is seen in terms of a segmentary structure by the Rmeet. This demands some further discussion, as it could easily be argued that it is indeed a case of acceptance of being encompassed. The major ethnonym associated with lowlanders is *Lao*, which is also part of the name of the state; therefore, identifying as citizens of the Lao nation-state would mean accepting encompassment by the *Lao* as an ethnolinguistic group. But I have no proof for this acceptance; rather, when the Rmeet identify *Lao*-as-ethnolinguistic-group with *Lao*-as-defining-the-state, they still conceive of the *Lao* sociality as a structurally equal other. Although they accept being Laotians in respect to being subject to state administration, they still regard *Lao*-as-*yam* as an entity opposite to themselves.

This point should be subject of further debates, as it is not simply some juggling with theoretical models whose value has still to be proven. The question is of importance for the analysis of state/minority relations. As usual in modern states, the dominant ethnic group is associated with founding and running the polity, often providing it with its name. In most cases, this is combined with a particularly modernist tendency to stress ethnic unity in nation-states, turning minorities into marked categories of citizens (or, as in the case of Thailand and Burma, denying them citizenship in the first place). This leads to conflicts with those minorities that refuse to be included in the state's ethnic self-definition. A more recent tendency to rewrite constitutions and policies in order to accord with the plural realities of some of these states was developed as an attempt to provide a base for solutions to these conflicts. The question is: what kind of plurality is it? How do nation-states and dominant groups define this term, and how do minorities perceive it? If the distinction of unmarked majorities and marked minorities is universal to modern nation-states, how is the relationship conceived in different cultural contexts?

Encompassment in Dumont's sense, implying shared acceptance of an ideology and differential relations to central values and institutions, was a way of integration in traditional polities; but these ideologies conflict with the notion of, at least nominal, equality in modernist nation-states (Platenkamp 2002). In modernist contexts, encompassment rather takes the form of Baumann's examples: a denial of difference. Encompassment as a denial of difference is indeed a tendency in the Lao nation's attitude to minorities (Postert, this volume, Evans 1998: 150–51); but in spite of the attempts to transmit this point to the minorities, this view is not shared by them.

The Lao People's Democratic Republic is a multi-ethnic nation-state that recruits the majority of state officials and high-level representatives from a single ethnolinguistic group, the Lao. The relationship with the minority groups has been changed in the course of the twentieth century. During the rule of the Lao King, the polity was defined exclusively as a product of Lao and Buddhist culture. Still, the mountain populations speaking Mon-Khmer languages were considered to be the original owners of the land and confirmed in this role during the New Year rituals in the royal capital, Luang Prabang (Evans 1998: 144), a ritual that the Rmeet, living in another province, did not participate in. They were thus included into the realm, and their differential role within it was recognized; in all aspects except ritual ones, however, they were marginalised and disparaged.

This situation was changed by the Lao independence movement when it introduced a trinomial classification for the minority groups. It came to be widely used under the Socialist party *Pathet Lao* and is ascribed to the new government by the Rmeet. Thus the lowlanders and Tai-Kadai-speakers were identified as 'Lowland Lao' (*Lao Loum*), the Mon-Khmer speakers as 'Lao of the Slopes' (*Lao Theung*), and the speakers of Sino-Tibetan and Miao-Yao languages that had immigrated since the mid-nineteenth century as 'Lao of the Peaks' (*Lao Soung*) (see Postert, this volume, for further discussion of the classification). Although this was dismissed as 'anti-revolutionary' a few years after the revolution, the Lao government only recently made an attempt to replace it by a classification into four language families (Pholsena 2002: 184–85; Simana 2001). Still, the trinomial classification is common usage in conversations of officials. This 'republican' classification had a double edge.

First, it was designed to negate the strict separation of lowlanders at the power centres and highlanders at the margins. As Evans (1998: 144–45, 148–49) observed, this categorization of 'marginal' and 'central' does not necessarily mean a relationship of oppression, as it was interpreted by the *Pathet Lao*; yet it pointed at a socio-cosmic hierarchy that the *Pathet Lao* aimed to replace with a concept of common and equal citizenship. Their particular strategy of managing the majority-minority relation consisted of marking all ethnic groups – even the majority, which was no longer just Lao but '*Lao* of the Lowlands'.

The difference between the Lao/*kha* classification and that of '*Lao* of the Lowlands, Slopes, or Peaks' demarcates a shift between two concepts of polity. The earlier one is a 'cosmological' idea of state that clearly defines the relations of certain sociocultural groups to the polity as a whole. By contrast, the more recent classification is a 'democratic' structure in which belonging to a particular group is not supposed to predict an individual's relation to the polity (Evans 1998: 143; Platenkamp 2001). At this point, the trinomial classification turns against the integration of cultural minorities. In practice, this means that the actual differences between cultural groups remain in existence, but they are considered as obstacles to national integration: there is no way to assign these differences a positive value in the polity.

Cultural differences within a state of the type of the Lao PDR tend to be devalued and reduced to mere folklore (Evans 1998: 152). This is mirrored in the classification: Differences between *Lao Loum*, *Lao Theung* and *Lao Soung* are reduced to geographical denotations within an encompassing notion of 'Lao', a concept that even comprises the linguistic category Tai (Rajah 1990: 326). Although local 'customs and traditions' (*hidgoong babpeni*) regularly are evoked in official rhetorical discourse, cultural differences are hardly considered by government policies – and this is not a failure of a specific government in Laos, but a general problem of modern state ideology.

From the point of view of the Lao, the two meanings of Lao as lowlanders and as state cannot be separated. The Lao as ethnic group figure as the creators of the polity that was transformed from kingdom to nation-state. For the Lao lowlanders and state officials, the use of 'Lao of the Slopes' and 'of the Peaks' certainly means a way to encompass minorities. But how do the Rmeet view this identification of culture and state? In which aspects do they see themselves as part of, and in which sense as structurally differentiated from Lao sociality?

Let me return here to the argument above that segmentary grammars imply structural identity of units (at least) on the lower level. The argument implicit for those conceiving the identity is that similar structural positions imply similarities in internal organization. Segmentation is stressed when the Rmeet not only consider their relations with the lowlanders as a group of individuals, but when they compare their respective societies. In this comparison, the identification of societies is made explicitly in respect to the *yam*, when the Rmeet single out and compare certain key features that define a community. For the Rmeet, Lao sociality is identified by two features: Buddhism and the state. The state is defined by an overarching ruler, and important in this context are the images and ideas of both kingship and the president's office, although to the Rmeet they represent different types of rulership: one ritualised and exclusive to its community, the other non-ritual and relating to other communities. Further, every single village or city ward (*baan*) of the Lao is centred around a Buddhist temple.

For all these features the Rmeet find equivalents within their own community structure. The Buddhist temples are seen as equivalents to the *cuong läh*, the small community house where villagers communicate with the village spirit.[7] The person responsible for this ritual communication is the *taa samaan*, the village priest, who is identified with the king. Although his office only relates to a single village, he shares an important characteristic with the king in that his office, too, is hereditary. Although it is not entirely clear if the Rmeet also acknowledge the cosmological function of the king in ritual, he is distinguished from a 'secular' concept of rulership. The present government is known not to deal with spirits, and accordingly it is the village headman, a non-hereditary office transferred by elections and reconfirmed by the state administration, that is likened to the president and plays no role in village rituals.

These equations were made in contexts when Rmeet informants explained their own community, but not when explicitly talking about their relation to the lowlanders. In those contexts, they were assessing similarities and differences at the same time. A *cuong läh* is very different from a Buddhist temple. While the lowland religion is called *sadsanaa pud* (Buddhist religion), highland cosmologies are said to be *sadsanaa phi* (spirit religion); what separates the two is not so much the veneration of the Buddha, but the way in which ancestors and local spirits are treated. Furthermore, the Rmeet know from historical experience that a king and a president are mutually exclusive to a single community. But by comparing the structuring and centralising features of their community with those of the Lao polity, they were claiming a similar type of sociality: one similar enough to be considered a unity equal to the ethnically specific Lao community. The distinct types of rulership that coexist in Rmeet society today, however, historically were separate in Lao society. The ritual house and a king/priest are concepts that differentiate communities and ethnic groups from each other: By contrast, the idea of presidency/village headmanship represents unifying forces of a 'nation-state' type. Ritual houses, priests, kings and temples only refer to a single, centralised community; presidents and village headmen ensure equality between communities and segmentary relations between different levels of organization. The same kind of exchangeability, based on election, defines presidents defines the village headmen; the kind of specificity particular to kings and temples (of spirits and of hereditary lines) is claimed for village priests and ritual houses.

What we find here is a strategy somewhere in-between grammars, but best understood in terms of segmentation. The state is at once situated at a level above the *yam*/Rmeet contrast, turning individual villages into parts of an administrative whole. As far as the state is representative of (lowland) Lao sociality, it is seen as a segmentary, nominally equal other. The state's sociality is seen as similar to the Rmeet village sociality in structure, and in particular in respect to the presidency, but as different in content. An acknowledgement of the Lao sociality encompassing the Rmeet sociality via the state, however, is still rejected.

Encompassment and 'the Anti-Grammar'

As I hope to have demonstrated, the grammar of encompassment does not lend itself easily to balanced dialogue between self and other. It actually denies otherness, just as Baumann's 'anti-grammar' denies the other his/her physical presence. Dialogue may only occur in narrowly defined contexts of strong hegemonic or political power. True, the denial implicit in encompassment is a matter of categorization: it does not necessarily turn into violence. But if certain structural similarities between one of the grammars and the 'anti-grammar' are recognized, what does that mean for the understanding of the anti-grammar?

Baumann's model seems to imply a fundamental and substantial difference between grammars and the anti-grammar. On one side, there are grammars designed for communication in social situations; on the other side, there is physical destruction and intellectual degeneration: the rule of 'the baby grammar'. The strong line drawn between them demarcates a change in quality, and this qualitative shift is implicitly measured against a humanistic background: peace and tolerance, so this ideology says in short, are features of a fully realized, truly human being, while destruction and violence are a move back to immaturity, explained by a degradation of what makes people human. If I may slip back to Dumontian terminology, the idea-value 'grammars' is closer to the central value of 'humanism' than the idea-value 'anti-grammar' (see Dumont 1986: 252). Of course, 'humanism' here is a concept native to modern European societies, and admittedly it is essential for shaping and understanding modern policies. Nonetheless, I propose that anthropologists should make the uncomfortable step away from this concept, in order to theorize cultural situations, whether foreign or indigenous to Western modernity, in which 'humanism' is not a leading value.

This does not blow up the difference between grammars and the anti-grammar, but it does change the relationship between them. What separates grammars and the anti-grammar is not the way others are conceived, but the way others are treated. The three grammars are differentiated from each other by the structure of their code, not by social practice. Whether an orientalizing grammar goes along with imperialism or with a respectful attempt to communicate, is not predicted by its definition. Each grammar implies the possibility of social practices contrary to the 'humanist' idea-value, and one should open up the question how this happens by thinking of anti-grammars in the plural.

True, anti-grammars are of a different kind from grammars: they are exclusively defined by violence and persecution. Violent exclusion of others is accompanied by particular changes in discourse, and as Müller and Verrips (both this volume) demonstrate, discourse changes can be consciously designed to prepare violence and exclusion. But as Arnaut (this volume) points out, hate speech and acts of reconciliation, violence and communication may coexist. The question of whether violence can be validly predicted from these discourse changes demands more research: discourse changes where, initiated by whom, and received in what way?

The model to be tested in this volume – including its gradual movement from grammars to anti-grammar – presumes that the difference between grammars is of a lower-order kind than that between grammars and anti-grammar. These differences are indeed of a different order. The differences between grammars are structural and discursive, the difference between grammars and anti-grammar is mostly practical and enacted. But the differences between grammars are not of an equal kind; grammars cannot be exchanged for each other in practice; as I have shown, the relation of the encompassment grammar to the practice of dialogue is very different from the other grammars. On the other hand, any grammar has a potential to pave the way to destruction. I would therefore propose to modify the original model. This modification assumes that anti-grammars in the plural are no less structured than grammars and that may indeed they use the same codes as grammars (Figure 10.3).

The original model (Baumann)

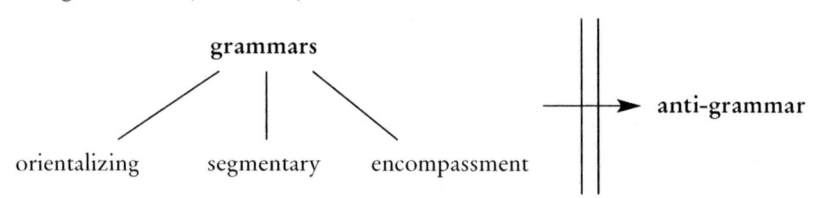

```
                    grammars
                   /    |    \
                  /     |     \              ‖
                 /      |      \             ‖ ⟶ anti-grammar
                /       |       \            ‖
         orientalizing  segmentary  encompassment
```

The modified model

orientalizing grammar	segmentary grammar	encompassment grammar
↓	↓	↓
anti-grammar	anti-grammar	anti-grammar

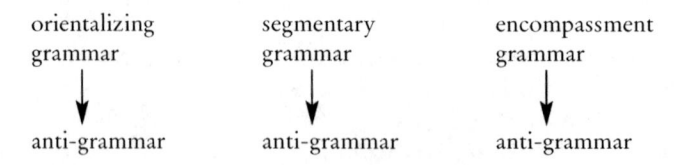

Figure 10.3: Two Schemata of Models for Anti-Grammars

Anti-grammars, although not supposed to entail dialogue, still involve communication. This may sound counter-intuitive, as most common definitions of communication describe it as exchange. But communication covers all transfer of messages, even those which are not meant to be answered. Even monologues need listeners, real or imagined; and even strategies of persecution and escape need a clearly perceived image of the other and his/her behaviour. The gain of integrating anti-grammars in the plural into the grammars is twofold. First, phenomena like pogroms and genocide will not simply be defined in the negative, by the absence of something. To define phenomena by the absence of certain features betrays in almost all cases a moral rather than an analytical stance; in this case, a 'humanistic' set of assumptions threatens to hinder, rather than help us in understanding more about the ideological processes involved. This, then, would be the second gain. We would be able to develop a language to talk about strategies of alterity in a context of physical violence and political persecution. Genocide and pogrom, frightening but not out-of-the-human, are still phenomena to be described in a unified theory that addresses all types of self/other-relationships.

Notes

Research was conducted in 2000–2001 and in spring 2002 in Luang Nam Tha Province, Laos, in the framework of the Research Group of the German Research Council, 'Cultural diversity and the construction of polity in Southeast Asia'. I want to express my gratitude to the members of the Institute of Cultural Research, Vientiane, its Director, Houmpanh Rattanavong, and Suksavang Simana, for making research possible. I am also grateful to Gerd Baumann, Andre Gingrich and the participants in the 2002 EASA workshop for their comments and questions, as well as to Jos Platenkamp.

1. To elaborate on this argument, it is difficult to consider the right/left-hand type of difference as an example of encompassment and apply this to the grammars model. It would actually blow up the model or at least would deprive it of its capability to classify discourses. The argument consists of three steps (see Dumont 1986: 230–33): one, the ascription of differences to separate entities cannot be separated from their description in qualitative terms. Two, the description of differences cannot be separated from their valorisation: all terms of a difference are always better or worse, more or less powerful, more or less pure etc., according to context; and there are no value-free contexts. Third, the valorization refers to a higher level, a central, encompassing value. Differences are never conceived as between two terms, but at least between two terms differentially related to a value representing the whole: 'purity', 'individualism', 'the body'. The idea of value-neutral contexts, i.e., unvalorised difference, is particular to modernity and its bureaucratic organization.

   When applied to the grammars model, this line of argument would resolve some problems, but create others. Baumann describes orientalizing grammars as 'going ternary' by splitting up the other into subcategories and thereby undermining the binary structure that characterizes this grammar. It is not self-evident, however, that the 'staggering' process has to involve three categories (why not four or five?) or that it has to be employed in any case. From the perspective elaborated above, the ternary character of orientalizing becomes clear. An orientalizing argument like 'Islam is aggressive, Christianity is peace-loving' is never merely descriptive. In each context where it appears, there is an underlying evaluation according to the third, encompassing term, e.g., an idea of human nature. If 'man as competing for survival' were the higher value, Islam might score better, if it were 'man as cooperating for survival', Christianity might. The same valorising relationship of parts to whole is inherent in segmentary grammars. Lower-level units may be claimed equal, but in actuality, their differences still entail a different relationship to the whole: the football team that wins the district league will represent all districts of its province in the provincial league. Dumont (1971: 58–60) argued this case with respect to the Nuer.

This argument, too, would entail problems for the grammars model: it would make all differences between grammars appear as minor variations of a single scheme of encompassment. The grammars model theorizes the variance in the style of dialogue or non-dialogue between groups, the ways they formulate claims to judgment, representation, the application of rules, and the particularities of identity construction. All of these have consequences for the ways in which groups manage their interactions. Reducing all three grammars to being varieties of encompassment, however, would remove these dynamics from systematic description and would privilege a single undifferentiated model.

2. Encompassment may also be accepted if single individuals or families cut off from their origin become integrated into the community. The issue of incompatible group identities may be bypassed in these cases.
3. For a similar account from the same area, see Tayanin 1994: 42–3.
4. Most of my Rmeet informants on these issues were adult men, heads of households, and fathers; it is their point of view which I generalize when I talk about 'the Rmeet' in the following.
5. The term *kha* carries numerous ambiguities. At once, it refers to highlanders as inferior and subjects of the Lao, but in another respect, highlanders used to perform an important role in the new year rituals of the Lao King. In these rituals, a representative of Khasak (a group of Mon-Khmer speakers from the Luang Prabang area) became king for a brief moment, only to be succeeded by the actual Lao King. For an analysis of this complex relationship, see Aijmer (1979).
6. Actual participation of minorities in the government still falls short of expectations, and the marginal status of minorities remains a problem for development and education.
7. The large community houses with several hearths and sleeping places for bachelors, as described by Izikowitz (1943), have disappeared, probably forty to fifty years ago.

References

Aijmer, Göran. 1979. 'Reconciling Power with Authority: An Aspect of Statecraft in Traditional Laos', *Man N.S.* 14: 734–49.

Dang Nghiem Van. 1993. 'The flood myth and the origin of ethnic groups in Southeast Asia.' *Journal of American Folklore*, 106, 304–37.

Dumont, Louis. 1971. *Introduction à deux théories d'anthropologie sociale*. Paris: Mouton.

———. 1980. *Homo hierarchicus: The Caste System and its Implications*. Chicago: University of Chicago Press.

———. 1986. *Essays on Individualism: Modern Ideology in Anthropological Perspective*. Chicago: University of Chicago Press.

Evans, Grant. 1998. *The Politics of Ritual and Remembrance: Laos since 1975*. Chiang Mai: Silkworm Press.

Evans-Pritchard, E.E.1940. *The Nuer: The Description of the Modes of Livelihood and Political Institutions of a Nilotic people*. Oxford: Clarendon.

Ferlus, Michel. 1972 . 'La cosmogonie selon la tradition Khmou', in *Langues et techniques, nature et culture. T. 1: Approche linguistique*, edited by Jacqueline M.C. Thomas and Lucien Bernot. Paris: Klincksieck, 277–82.

Hinton, Peter. 1983. 'Do the Karen Really Exist?' in *Highlanders of Thailand*, edited by John McKinnon and Wanat Bhrusastri. Kuala Lumpur: Oxford University Press, 155–68.

Izikowitz, Karl Gustav. 1943. 'The Community House of the Lamet', *Ethnos* 8: 19–60.

———. [1951] 1959. *Lamet: Hill Peasants in French Indochina*. New York: AMS Press.

Kammerer, Cornelia Ann. 1988. 'Territorial Imperatives: Akha Ethnic Identity and Thailand's National Integration, in *Ethnicities and Nations: Processes of Interethnic Relations in Latin America, Southeast Asia, and the Pacific*', edited by R. Guidieri, F. Pellizzi, and S. Tambiah. Austin: University of Texas Press, 259–92.

Leach, Edmund. [1954] 1964. *Political Systems of Highland Burma*. London: Bell.

Lindell, Kristina, Jan-Öjvind Swahn and Damrong Tayanin. 1976. 'The Flood: Three Northern Kammu Versions of the Story of Creation.' *Acta Orientalia* (Copenhagen) 37: 183–200.

Moerman, Michael. 1965. 'Ethnic Identification in a Complex Society: Who are the Lue?' *American Anthropologist* 67: 1215–30.

Pholsena, Vatthana. 2002. 'Nation/Representation: Ethnic Classification and Mapping Nationhood in Contemporary Laos.' *Asian Ethnicity* 3 (2): 175–97.

Platenkamp, J.D.M. 2001. 'Intercultural Conflicts in Indonesia.' Paper read at the Symposium 'Integrating Others: the Appropriation of Modernity', University of Münster.

———. 2002. 'Changing Models of Sovereignty in Southeast Asia.' Unpub. ms., University of Münster.

Rajah, Ananda. 1990. 'Orientalism, Commensurability and the Construction of Identity: A Comment on the Notion of Lao Identity' *Sojourn* 5 (2): 308–33.

Simana, Suksavang.1997. *Kmhmu' Livelihood: Farming the Forest*. Vientiane: Ministry for Information and Culture.

———. 2001. 'The Ethnic Groups of the Lao P.D.R.' Paper presented at the 'Symposium on Globalization and its Impact on the Asia Pacific Region', Luang Prabang.

Stuart-Fox, Martin. 1997. *A History of Laos*. Cambridge: Cambridge University Press.

Tayanin, Damrong. 1994. *Being Kammu: My Village, My Life*. Southeast Asian Program Series 14. Ithaca, NY: Cornell University Press.

Chapter 11

Debating Grammars

Arguments and Prospects

Gerd Baumann and Andre Gingrich

The cross-examination of the three grammars has exemplified an analytic approach pragmatically based on a 'weak' rather than an essentialised conception of identity/alterity. Identity and alterity were seen as mutually constitutive. The project, conducted in a dialogical manner, has traced four steps of enquiry. The first step proceeded from a critique of essentialist and moralist ideas of identity and othering to a differentiation of the three grammars. As these grammars are articulated in social interactions, they inevitably involve dimensions of hegemony, hierarchy and power, and thus the second step has analysed these in ethnographic studies and comparisons. When hierarchy and power are expressed by physical force, one comes up against the limitations imposed on the use of the grammars. Violence, so it was argued in the third step, not only limits the use of the grammars, but its inherent delegitimization of grammatical otherings in turn furthers the rule of anti-grammatical otherings. Our last angle of enquiry, the fourth step, has attempted to widen the debate by revisiting the problem of structure versus agency and by questioning the relationship between grammatical and anti-grammatical otherings. In taking these four steps, we have suggested answers to some questions and tried to reformulate others.

Attempting now to pull together the main strands of argument that arose, we proceed from the questions answered by the project to questions raised about it, in order then to turn to the reformulations that a differentiation of grammars makes possible. Finally, we will consider the possible remit of a grammars approach when applied to questions not privileged in this volume. These include the understanding of gender and sexuality, of aesthetics, and of global processes and power dynamics.

Among the questions answered, an important one concerns the potential of the grammars for comparative purposes. We have seen comparisons across time, as in Müller's analysis of the German material, across vast cultural space as in Sjørslev's Brazilian and Danish material, across transnational space as in Karner's analysis of Hindu nationalism, across regional variations as in Postert's and Sprenger's analyses of the data from Laos, and across discursive techniques as in Arnaut's Ivorian data. The comparative dimension, however, is inherent in the grammars approach even when its application is not explicitly aimed at comparison. The mere idea of differentiating among several grammars of identity/alterity throws into starker relief the otherwise invisible gradations as well as the otherwise irreconcileable extremes that any ethnography of identity/alterity constellations is faced with. Well beyond merely 'tidying' the analysis of formations of identity/alterity, this inherent comparative potential of the grammars approach has produced new and sharpened ethnographic insights in all the ethnographic test cases examined in this book.

Two critical questions have been raised by the ethnographic test cases about the project itself. One asks whether the grammars proposed may not entail an unwarranted individualist bias, as indicated by Postert's exposition of his Laotian material; the other asks whether the distinction between the three grammars and a singular anti-grammar may not harbour an element of ethnocentrism, as raised in Sprenger's examination of other data from Laos. Both of these questions merit detailed consideration, not least because they, too, confirm the creative potential of this unusual experiment to collaborate on the basis of one hypothesis, but not to homogenize the voices until each contributor thumps the same *ostinato*.

In considering the charge of an undue individualism, our reply can only appeal to a weighing up of losses as against gains. The traces of methodological individualism identified by both Postert and Sprenger may well be the price to pay for a heightened attention to agency, as exemplified by Karner's analysis of Hindu nationalism. In stressing that individual actors make choices – be they between different grammars or be they through instrumentalising one grammar for decision-making processes – one may indeed give an individualist twist to the grammars approach. Basically, however, grammars have been proposed here in the sense of classificatory structures with normative implications. In that sense, they do not primarily focus on any kind of individual action and interaction, but on those forms of agency that constitute relations between human groups. While the grammars discussed in this volume are thus in no way ' immune' towards an individualist interpretation, the main thrust of their conceptualisation is directed towards social agency rather than individual action.

In adapting Dumont in this manner, we have perhaps allowed for a higher tolerance threshold towards individualism than Dumont himself would have been ready to accept. Yet something similar applies to all our sources of inspiration. This point emphasizes all the more that the three grammars proposed here have been adapted freely, rather than adopted ready-made, from their original architects. In adapting Said, we have laid more stress than he did on the potentially self-critical and self-relativising dimension inherent in orientalizing the other. In adapting Evans-Pritchard, we have stressed more than he did the room for conflict on how to define the apex or the intervening levels of a segmentary grammar. Whether or not the three masters would forgive us is, alas now, 'a question too late for the asking'.

In considering the second charge, that of ethnocentrism, we must ask whether the proposition to differentiate among different grammars has placed too stark a dividing line between the grammars and the anti-grammar or, as Sprenger suggests, the anti-grammars in the plural.

The argument that brought Sprenger to raise the point is certainly a valid one: different grammars do entail different directions and degrees of dialogical potential. The observation was made in Baumann's chapter two, it could be traced again in Mühlich's chapter three and in Müller's chapter four, and it was explicitly discussed in Sjørslev's chapter five. Implicitly or explicitly, all contributors raise the question whether some grammars might be 'better' in moral terms or 'better suited' for different purposes. None of us have seen the grammars proposition as a value-free or *l'art pour l'art* exercise in improving on one or another school of structuralism. On the contrary and in general, each and every ethnographic test, be it of the grammars proposition or any other, is informed by social values implicitly held or, hopefully as one may add, explicitly voiced by the analyst. Social science, after all, is a social activity, and no social activity is ever value-free. By necessity, then, the differentiation of different grammars must give rise to questions of evaluation. Interestingly – and we think of this as a productive outcome – these questions cannot be answered in the abstract. On an abstract level, the formal properties of these grammars will merely allow for minimalist statements. Encompassment tends toward a monologue in that the 'we' encompasses the 'them', whether the 'them' agree to it or not. Segmentation tends toward dialogue among those perceived as 'equivalent', in that identity and alterity are defined as dependent on contexts and levels; but it does exclude those who cannot be accommodated under the same apex. Orientalizing, finally, stands somewhere in-between the monological and the dialogical in so far as its more intelligent versions do harbour the potential of self-critique and of mirroring the self in the other. That said, however, the tempting question of the moral values to be assigned to one or another grammar cannot be answered by way of an abstract minimalism, and more importantly, it cannot even be posed regardless of context and agency. The grammars, to sum up this argument about values, are not better or worse in themselves, but relatively better or relatively worse, depending on agency in context.

◆ ◆ ◆ ◆ ◆

The division between grammatical selfings/otherings and anti-grammatical selfings/otherings, however, cannot be treated in the same way.

In debating the problem of what we have agreed to call 'extreme violence' and have exemplified by ethnocide and genocide, we face the problem of evaluation the other way round. None of our contributors, and presumably none of our readers, are happy with genocidal movements as traced back in Müller's diachronic analysis of German sources, with categorical killings as alluded to in Sjørslev's discussion of street children, with sectarian murders committed by religious nationalists as studied by Karner, or with the soldiers turned into killing machines by the violent inclusion analysed by Verrips. Here, then, the shoe is on the other foot: now, it is not the grammars proposition that needs to stand the test of ethnocentrism or value relativism; instead, it is our shared disgust and horror at systematic and categorical mass murder that can appeal to the grammars to help us define what we actually mean by genocide or ethnocide. Arnaut's analysis of the mass media discourses in a state preparing itself for a genocide has raised the question at its most chilling: how many human beings dead in a ditch does it take for something to 'count' as a genocide? Clearly and evidently, the answer must be qualitative, rather than quantitative, and we thus propose to use the grammars proposition to reformulate a question that has been haunting anthropology since its beginnings ('warrior tribes'), but particularly over the past twenty years (the anthropology of violence). In considering this question, we turn to the first of the two reformulations that may be helped by the grammars approach.

Violence is indeed the most pressing problem that each of our contributors has addressed by way of the grammars proposition. Scape-goating, as exemplified by Mühlich's data from Nepal, does not by itself constitute a case of anti-grammar, unless it is accompanied and exacerbated by dehumanization, as exemplified by Arnaut's data from Côte d'Ivoire and by Verrips' analysis of extreme coercive inclusion. Müller and Sjørslev also specifically address the problem of violence by tracing the genesis of preparing people's cognitive ways toward acquiescing in categorical killings. Postert and Sprenger, too, explicitly consider the grammars proposition on the background of the violence manifested by colonialism and the Vietnam war, and references to Klemperer run through this book like an invisible red thread. Clearly, all of us have implied that grammatical otherings are fundamentally different from the anti-grammar of categorical killing, and Arnaut and Verrips have analysed what is involved in transforming grammmatical otherings into ungrammatical ones. But let us return to the critique at hand, the critique of an implicitly ethnocentric stress on a 'Western' form of humanism.

In trying to reformulate the distinction between violence as an extreme form of communication and violence as a total and dehumanizing annihilation of the other, we dare suggest a qualitative distinction that is not as immediately counter-intuitive as the questionable view of violence as if it were merely spam on your e-mail: unwanted communication, but communication nonetheless. On the one hand, so we suggest, there is system-immanent or system-maintaining violence. On the other hand, there is the exceptional violence of irretrievably anti-grammatical selfings/otherings that not only aim to annihilate the other, but implicitly and compulsively abolish the former self.

While all systems of inequality will involve a certain intensity of system-immanent violence, a distinction between the three grammars and the rule of anti-grammar is indispensable. The rule of anti-grammatical otherings clearly prepares and legitimizes major forms of manifest physical violence against whole categories of people now defined as cohesive groups that must be systematically excluded or even annihilated in their entirety. Whatever they do or say in their defence, they are wrong and will not be accommodated within any of the established grammars. As the victim Klemperer observed so sharply, first the German Jews got killed because they were made out to be too rich; then the Polish Jews got killed because they were portrayed in the genocidal propaganda as being too poor (Klemperer [1957] 1999).

What we have agreed here to call 'exceptional violence' is hardly ever a feature in the long-term maintenance of any social system. Whether it be in Nazi-occupied Europe, in former Yugoslavia or in Rwanda, genocide not only kills the other, but it also eradicates the former self as it once was. Genocide, which represents the outcome of complex agencies in complex phases of local and wider crises (Wolf 1999), will involve indiscriminate and categorical, as opposed to selective, state violence, state terror, non-state terrorism, war, genocide or any combination of these. Such phases of exceptional violence, as well as the crises to which they claim to respond may, admittedly, be linked to the more normal and routinised phases of social and systemic interaction. While state terror is not identical with state terrorism, both state terrorism and non-state terrorist movements share one interest at heart: to sell exceptional violence as system-maintaining violence. 'Exceptional' and 'systemic routine' violence are thus often connected with each other, and anthropologists are faced with fluid gradations between the two. It seems important to us, nonetheless, to emphasize the difference of quality between the two polarities.

Intentionally directed against entire categories of people, exceptional violence cannot be engineered without exceptional mechanisms of internal mobilisation – an observation most explicitly discussed by Arnaut and Verrips in this volume. Such mobilisations are rare, for they need to legitimize extraordinary uses of brutal force as inevitable and justified by denying any right to human existence of those targeted as victims. This is the minimum contents of anti-grammatical otherings which are linked, as we see them, to the specific conditions of intermittent crises and result in exceptional violence. Rhetorically and even psychoanalytically, it may be tempting to accommodate the rule of anti-grammatical otherings and exceptional violence in a very abstract category of 'human communication.' Both anthropologically and morally, however, this appears to us, as to most of our contributors, to be a highly implausible strategy.

By contrast to genocidal violence, the more 'normal' forms of system-immanent violence tend to maximise those routinised forms that are covert, while explicit physical violence is reserved for special fields of routine only, such as legal punishment or combat training. Anthropological studies have demonstrated this for a vast spectrum of cases. They range from tribal feuding (Jamous 1992) via the state forms of imprisoning people (Asad 1997) to violence against women and children among the urban poor (Scheper-Hughes 1992; see also Sjørslev in this volume). Consequently, dominant ideologies and normative discourses of 'normal' violence tend either flatly to deny the existence of system-immanent violence, or else they tend to treat it as a necessary but negligible by-product of a primarily peaceful maintenance of order. The proposition of the grammars as it has been tested here can easily accommodate both versions of the routine lie about system-immanent violence, be it the official denial of violence as a system-maintaining force or the ideological representation of violence as an unintended but necessary by-product of maintaining 'social order'. In short, while anti-grammatical otherings must explicitly mobilize people for the alleged necessity of manifest categorical violence, grammatical otherings tend be operated in such routinised and taken-for-granted ways that they appear as basically self-understood and non-violent, however violent their consequences in the maintenance of any one social system. To strengthen this effect, some particular aspects of system-immanent violence are represented as belonging only to special and exceptional domains. Some of these special domains may then indeed be represented in dominant discourses as a form of dialogue or communication, as in cases where 'negative reciprocity' comes into play in feuds for honour, or when the rule of law claims that it makes prisoners 'pay back' what they 'owe to society'. We may add, further to emphasize the difference between system-immanent and exceptional violence, that the system-immanent or system-maintaining varieties leave intact the categories of self and other as they have previously been defined. Exceptional violence, by contrast, cannot but abolish, inadvertently or even willingly, its very definition of the self, for it is now bereft of its former other.

With this reformulation, our argument has in some ways come back full circle. It started with an anthropological critique of two opposite, but complementary versions of an unwarrantably 'strong' concept of identity: on the one hand, Heidegger's legacy of viewing difference as external to identity and on the other hand, both Lacan's and Spivak's tendency toward an *a priori* subject-centred concept of identity. In the place of these ' strong' conceptions of identity, the proposition argued for a 'soft', or in philosophical parlance 'weak', conception that envisages identity and alterity as mutually constitutive categories of thought. The grammars as proposed answered to this desideratum in their different ways, and it was shown how it was only at the threshold of empowering the anti-grammar of dehumanization that identity and alterity ceased to be conceivable as mutually constitutive or potentially dialogical. When the altrocidal murder entails the egocidal suicide or, as we express it less individualistically here, when each potentially dialogical grammar of identity/alterity is collapsed into the anti-grammar of a system self-programmed for self-destruction, then that threshold is qualitative. With these suggestions, we can now turn to the second reformulation that the grammars approach allows us to propose.

This second reformulation concerns the old division between a purported primacy of structures and the helpless reduction of all social facts to contextual contingency. The heuristic pursuit of grammars in action may allow us to bridge that divide theoretically, but with due attention to the subtleties of agency in context.

As we argued in our Foreword to explain our use of the term 'grammars', one dimension of the grammars relates to norms. The case studies, comparisons and theoretical reflections that followed may allow us to move this argument one step further. The ethnographic tests in fact confirmed a normative understanding of the grammars, but they also suggested a further differentiation. The distinction we have in mind here is that between descriptive and prescriptive norms, that is, between those norms that describe the purportedly 'normal' and those other norms that articulate moral postulates or standards (Cialdini 1996). As we know, moral standards do not determine behaviour, but yet one can recognize behind culturally sanctioned behaviours an obvious dynamic of standardization. Without that standardization, even deviance would be an unthinkable concept. By the same token then, grammars, in the sense of classificatory structures with a normative dimension, do not do things or cause actions to happen; rather, it is people in action who do things with grammars. Social actors in their contexts can shift from a segmentary grammar to an encompassing one, sometimes in the same sentence, and they can pitch an orientalizing grammar against somebody else's claim to segmentary equality, just before proceeding to a patronizing gesture of encompassing the other.

The repertoire of grammars, so far as we have explored it here, is tiny, for we have only been able to identify three of them, and there may be more of course. Yet this limitation may have theoretical reasons as well as empirical ones. The theoretical reason leads back to the theory of tropes, one of the guiding insights that informed both structural linguistics and structural anthropology from their beginnings. The theory of tropes identifies no more than four basic modalities of figurative language and thinking: metaphor, metonymy, synecdoche, and irony or – as one may add – self-irony. There are internecine debates, of course, whether synecdoche is merely a subcategory of metonymy, and whether irony is a trope that can exist independently of either metaphor or metonymy. We can muster enough self-irony to excuse ourselves from resolving these debates. The limitation of the repertoire of tropes, however, may be suggestive so far as the limited repertoire of our grammars is concerned. As Hayden White's famous structural account of *The Historical Imagination* (1973) argues, the metaphoric trope ('My love is a rose') compares two wholes, metonymy plays with the wholeness of a part and the part-ness of that whole ('fifty sail' as fifty ships), and synecdoche reduces a whole to a part ('He is all mouth'). These three options bear a striking resemblance, respectively, to the orientalizing grammar that posits two wholes, the segmentary grammar that negotiates between wholes as parts and parts as wholes, and the encompassing grammar of reducing othered wholes to parts. So far as the fourth trope is concerned, that of irony or self-irony, it may be useful to consider it as a modality based either on a tongue-in-cheek reversal of orientalizing contrasts ('the lucidity of Nostradamus') or on seeing oneself through the eyes of the other. A pertinent example of the latter is given in the 'realm of aesthetics' by Guido Sprenger (chapter 10) when he describes how the Rmeet of Laos consider themselves irredeemably ugly on dominant Lao standards of beauty.[1]

There may thus be good logical reasons why such a limited repertoire of only three grammars of identity/alterity can be offered as a useful analytical tool. Thinking of wholes and parts, of selfings and otherings, only three permutations appear to be possible: whole vs. whole (orientalization), whole as part and part as whole (segmentation), and whole as part (encompassment).

Turning from theoretical answers to empirical ones, the limited repertoire of only three grammars is more than enough to get on with, since their uses and permutations are of an astonishing contextual flexibility. One part of that flexibility may well reside in the fact, or better perhaps in the heuristic assumption, that all three grammars are, in principle, available to all at all times and in all situations. To illustrate the point, even the full-time orientalist travelling through the Maghreb is capable, in contexts that he or she deems suitable, to encompass the oriental other by an exoticizing embrace or to place the once-exotic Call to Prayer in a segmentary order together with church bells at home and piped Christmas carols in the shopping mall. Even in situations ruled by the anti-grammar of genocide, most people do not lose their capacity of thinking of at least some of the others, usually neighbours or colleagues, in terms of encompassment (Klemperer [1957] 1999). The proposition of the grammars, defined as socially shared and normatively endowed classificatory structures, does not preclude attention to agency and context. On the contrary, it sharpens our attention to agency in context. Without attention to context and 'opportunity structures', after all, a deification of an abstract power of agency can only lead to unrealistic beliefs in agency regardless of structures. The agency then postulated can only take recourse to fictions such as 'rational choice' without testing these fictions against the structurally possible. Assessing that degree of subjective or intersubjective possibility, however, is impossible without due regard to structures, be they social or cognitive.

◆ ◆ ◆ ◆ ◆

On this basis, it seems possible, and even promising, to consider expanding the remit of the grammars proposition beyond the focal points of ethnic and national identities that were privileged in this volume. At least three such fields come to mind.

The field of gender and sexuality studies designates one of these growth points, as already hinted at by most contributors to this book, but most notably perhaps by Mühlich and Verrips. Clearly, the grammar of orientalizing the other carries message of the highest relevance for gender-related topics: 'What is good in us is lacking in them,' so the orientalizing grammar insinuated, but it equally implied a subordinate reversal: 'what is lacking in us is (still) present in them'. This adaptation of Said's seminal thought can easily support and confirm basic representations of gender relations among us, such as 'virtue,' 'health,' or 'complementarity,' which may be opposed to 'unruliness,' 'sickness, perversion,' or 'constant conflict' as metaphors for gender relations among 'them.' In their reversed form, these orientalizing otherings may also entail exoticising notions that could be paraphrased as: 'what is (unfortunately, now) forbidden to us is (still, and desirably) permitted there.' Western colonialist sexual phantasies about 'the harem' and about paedophilia and homophilia in the Middle East are cases in point mentioned by Said (1978). Interestingly, they occur likewise in medieval Arabic literature about gender relations among peripheral tribal groups such as Ibn al-Mujawir (Löfgren 1951; Gingrich 1997).

Beside the grammar of orientalization, those of segmentation and encompassement also deserve detailed consideration with regard to gender relations. It might be worth exploring, for instance, how far different feminist and female interest groups pursue a segmentary logic by their different versions of recognition as 'distinct but equivalent'. At the other end of the spectrum, there seems to be a grammar of encompassment at work wherever it is regarded as a legitimate normality that 'adult males only' represent 'the rest' of society. Under these conditions, that 'rest' then includes all women, who on this normative level are often seen as an inferior and distinct part of the social whole. On a more specific level, however, this frequently goes hand-in-hand with representing women as 'the centre of the house', to which at this level the men are in fact represented as peripheral (Gingrich 1997). Future explorations into the gender relevance of the grammars might well want to consider further such logics of 'inversion' between general and more specific levels of normative representations of gender.

In a similar vein, the grammars may serve to systematise and compare certain shifts in the conceptualisation of sexual orientation. Clearly, it is the orientalizing grammar that has the longest track record of being used to classify a heterosexual or a homosexual self in relation to a homo- or heterosexual other. Much as in the case of gender relations, it offers ideas of hierarchy but it allows one to admit a certain complementarity of the two parties that mutually orientalize each other. 'We heterosexuals are normal and natural, yet they, the homosexuals, are redeemed by a certain propensity', be it for the arts in some cultures, for healing gifts in others, or for risqué entertainment in yet others. Conversely, 'we homosexuals practise a far more liberated life-style than those thoughtless breeders, but they, too, have their redeeming functions and virtues'. The more recent idea that heterosexuality and homosexuality are but two extremes connected by a continuum of subtle gradations and transitory forms appeals more strongly to a segmentary order. Who is 'us' or 'them' is no longer conceived of as a fixed categorical divide, but as a matter of contextual fission and fusion, and like all segmentary grammars it holds out at least the normative aspiration towards equal worth and equal treatment. Strange, from the grammatical point of view, is the most recent development, the subsumption by encompassment of officially registered gay and lesbian partnerships under the legal rubric of 'marriage' or marriage-like institutions. As with so many cases of encompassment, there are people happy to be so encompassed, and others, including one of the editors, who refuse this as a retrograde denial of their right to difference.

A second field of studies where an analysis in terms of the grammars may offer some analytic and comparative insights seems to us to lie in the study of aesthetics, a long-lost love of many anthropologists, media scholars, and students of culture in general. In this volume, the topic has been raised by Baumann in relation to poetry, drama and music, by Mühlich and Sjørslev in relation to ritual and religion, and by Sprenger in relation to ideas of physical beauty or self-ascribed ugliness. What these aesthetic considerations add to the argument looks like an intangible difference at first. Aesthetic appropriations of things belonging to others, be they rituals, styles, or criteria of beauty, always play with all three grammars at the same time. For appropriation to make sense at all, the other must be regarded as a suitable donor, that is, a partner fit for exchange within a segmentary order of equals or near-equals. At the same time, the definition of what is the other's, and what of the other's is to be appropriated, usually involves an act of exoticising and thus orientalizing. In the act of appropriation, the grammar used most commonly is that of encompassment: elements originating with the other are hierarchically subsumed under forms, styles, or criteria of beauty super-defining the self. The exceptions are famous, for they are those works or performances that transcend appropriation and can make one listen or see or apprehend what is strange through the senses of the other. They thus create a new aesthetic apex in which that of oneself and that of the other are merged in ever-changing relations of fusion and fission. A musician may think here of Stravinsky as opposed to Debussy; a painter may think of Max Ernst as opposed to the primitivists; and an observer of ritual may think of condomblé as opposed to the pick-and-mix of 'multiculti folklore' events. What these exceptions can achieve are an emotional impact and an aesthetic integrity that amount to a new form of selfing the other and othering the self. This dialogical engagement with the other transcends simplistic orientalism as well as the self-affirming grammar of encompassment, and it establishes a new segmentary equality of fission and fusion. In the process, the recognition thus given to the originally 'other' grows well beyond the 'recognition' that Charles Taylor speaks of in his famous essay on 'Multiculturalism'(1994). It is no longer concerned with recognizing the so-called other as legitimate or illegitimate, but is now concerned with recognizing others as sources of a transformed and self-transforming self (see Appiah 1994; Baumann 1999: 135–48).

A third possibility to widen the remit of the grammars proposition concerns the macrolevel of global interactions, such as we know it from international and postcolonial relations in the contemporary world.

The highly contested fields of global interaction between forces from Western countries and from Muslim countries quite often highlight the uses and, more tellingly, the abuses of segmentary grammars. A well-known example in this context was U.S. President Bush's call, in 2001, for a 'War against Terrorism', when he insisted that any country not supporting that policy would be treated as an enemy. This argument established a clear-cut global divide, which separated countries into supporters in the war against terrorism, and enemies of various degrees with an 'axis of evil' at their centre. When, in 2002, Germany was the first E.U. country to refuse any active participation in war preparations against Iraq, a cornerstone in President Bush's 'axis of evil', that country suddenly found itself threatened with ejection from the purportedly segmentary, but effectively encompassing, order of the American-led coalition.

Grammars of encompassment can often be recognized in the processes of E.U. enlargement. Non-E.U. countries negotiating their entry procedures into the E.U. are frequently represented and treated by E.U. institutions as if they really were 'part of us' but on an inferior hierarchical level, long before and during these negotiations. Finally, a central argument in the dominant logic of 'development' emphasizes 'free trade' and privatisation that 'developing' countries, according to this rhetoric, allegedly have not yet pursued enough. Critically to assess these dominant paradigms as versions of orientalization and of encompassment thus might represent one important anthropological contribution to current debates about globalization.

In fact, globalization also provides a 'presentist' rationale for merging the fieldwork dimension with anthropology's comparative aspirations, when we consider further the potentials for working with these grammars of identity/alterity. If global and transnational forces increasingly interact with people's lives, then this introduces an additional research impetus to compare, namely, how far these interactions may differ, and how far they may resemble each other. Apart from this 'presentist' rationale, further empirical and comparative corroboration always represents by itself a second, more 'methodological' rationale for the same purpose. The new plurality of comparative methods, as recently discussed by many anthropologists (see Gingrich and Fox 2002), offers a number of suggestions that may also be useful for further presentist and methodological inquiries into the potentials and limits of these grammars. The new plurality of comparative methods, in a nutshell, includes a variety of explicit procedures, such as micro- and macro-comparison along either temporal or spatial dimensions, or in a number of combinations. In some contributions to this volume, authors have already anticipated the directions of such comparative dimensions in exploring the grammars, and a grammars approach is certainly capable of generating new and creative comparative axes.

Combining, as our contributors have done, a fieldwork-based, contextually sensitive examination of grammars and anti-grammars with these new pluralities of comparative methods will be a methodological help further to broaden the empirical basis. It will also enable us to address pressing issues of the present world in a more wide-ranging manner than through singular examples only. By strengthening the existing comparative dimension in elaborating these grammars, we have moved from the general proposition, through a broad series of case studies and their thorough reflexive consideration, on to the level of medium-range theorizing. Such empirically and comparatively saturated theorizing from an anthropological perspective will in turn give additional momentum to our wider interdisciplinary engagement within the social sciences, with cultural studies, and with the humanities at large.

Note

1. For these two related points, we wish to thank our colleagues Peter van Rooden in Amsterdam and Ernst Halbmayer in Vienna.

References

Appiah, K. Anthony. 1994. 'Identity, Authenticity, Survival: Multicultural Societies and Social Reproduction', in *Multiculturalism: Examining the Politics of Recognition*, ed. A. Gutmann. Princeton, NJ: Princeton University Press: 149–64.
Asad, Talal. 1997. 'On Torture, or Cruel, Inhuman, and Degrading Treatment', in *Social Suffering*, eds. Arthur Kleinman, Veena Das and Margaret Lock. Berkeley, Los Angeles, London: University of California Press: 285–308.
Baumann, Gerd 1999. *The Multicultural Riddle. Re-Thinking National, Ethnic and Religious Identities*. New York: Routledge.
Cialdini, Robert B. 1996. 'Norms', in *The Social Science Encyclopedia*, eds. Adam Kuper and Jessica Kuper. London: Routledge: 574.
Gingrich, Andre. 1997. 'Inside an "Exhausted Community": An essay on case- reconstructive research about peripheral and other moralities', in *The Anthropology of Moralities*, ed. Signe Howell. London, New York: Routledge: 152–77.
Gingrich, Andre and Richard G. Fox. 2002. *Anthropology, by Comparison*. London, New York: Routledge.
Ibn al-Mujawir. [n.d.] 1951: *Descriptio Arabiae Meridionalis (Ta'rib al-Mustabsir)*, ed. Oscar Löfgren. Leiden: Brill.
Jamous, Raymond. 1992. 'From the Death of Men to the Peace of God: Violence and peace- making in the Rif', in *Honor and Grace in Anthropology*, eds. J.G. Peristiany and Julian Pitt- Rivers. Cambridge, New York: Cambridge University Press: 167–92.
Klemperer, Victor. [1957] 1999. *LTI: Notizbuch eines Philologen*. Leipzig: Reclam.
Said, Edward. 1978. *Orientalism*. New York: Pantheon.
Scheper-Hughes, Nancy. 1992. *Death Without Weeping: The Violence of Everyday Life in Brazil*. Berkeley, Los Angeles, London: University of California Press.
Taylor, Charles. 1994. 'The Politics of Recognition' in *Multiculturalism: Examining the Politics of Recognition*, ed. Amy Gutmann. Princeton, NJ: Princeton University Press: 25–74.
White, Hayden. 1973. *Metahistory: The Historical Imagination in Nineteenth-Century Europe*. Baltimore and London: The Johns Hopkins University Press.
Wolf, Eric. 1999. *Envisioning Power. Ideologies of Dominance and Crisis*. Berkeley: University of California Press.

Notes on Contributors

Karel Arnaut works at the Department of African Languages and Cultures, Ghent University. He did field research on masquerading traditions and Islamic public festivals in the Bondoukou region of Côte d'Ivoire; made field collections of Bedu masks for ethnographic museums in Britain; and wrote about the collecting and representation of contemporary African art objects. His current work analyses identity and violence in public performances in Bondoukou and Abidjan, and it also extends to the study of, and participation in, Ivorian and African civil society in Belgium and Europe.

Gerd Baumann works at the Research Centre for Religion & Politics at the University of Amsterdam and at the Amsterdam School of Social Science Research. His first fieldwork in the Sudan led to the ethnography: *National Integration and Local Integrity: The Miri of the Nuba Mountains in the Sudan* (Oxford University Press 1986), his second fieldwork to the monograph: *Contesting Culture: Discourses of Identity in Multi-Ethnic London* (Cambridge University Press 1996). His more recent books include: *The Multicultural Riddle: Re-thinking National, Ethnic and Religious Identities* (New York: Routledge 1999).

Andre Gingrich works at the Austrian Academy of Sciences where, as the laureate of the Wittgenstein Prize 2000, he directs the research centre 'Local Identities and Wider Influences', and at the Department of Social and Cultural Anthropology of the University of Vienna. He has done field research in Tibet as well as in Saudi Arabia and Yemen, and is also engaged in work on gender and on neo-nationalist movements in Europe. His publications include a volume co-edited with Richard G. Fox, entitled *Anthropology, by Comparison* (New York: Routledge 2002) and a volume co-authored with Frederik Barth, Robert Parkin and Sydel Silverman, entitled *Four Traditions in Anthropology: The Halle Lectures* (Chicago: University of Chicago Press, forthcoming).

Christian Karner works at the School of Sociology and Social Policy, University of Nottingham. His fieldwork among Hindu communities in the British East Midlands was complemented by research in northwestern India and resulted in his thesis entitled 'The Categories of Hindu Nationalism: A Neo-Structuralist Analysis of the Discourse of Hindutva' (2002). He is currently a Lecturer and Leverhulme Research Fellow in the School of Sociology and Social Policy at the University of Nottingham, working on a two-year project investigating (counter-)hegemonic national identities in Central Europe. His publications also include work on Austrian nationalism and discursive resistance to it (*Sociological Research Online*, vol.6, issue 4).

Michael Mühlich has done research for several years in Nepal, in 1991/93 on the culture of the Sherpas and in 1997/98 on informal and traditional credit relations. He worked as an assistant in the Museum of Ethnology in Berlin (1996/97) and has taught at the universities of Berlin and Leipzig on subjects including ritual and economy. He is currently working as an IT consultant in Frankfurt/Main. His publications include *Traditionelle Opposition: Individualität und Weltbild der Sherpa* (Pfaffenweiler: Centaurus Verlag 1996) and *Credit and Culture: A Substantivist Perspective on Credit Relations in Nepal* (Berlin: Dietrich Reimer Verlag 2001).

Anne Friederike Müller, currently at the Department of German at King's College London, studied history and social anthropology at the universities of Tübingen, Paris, and Cambridge. She has worked on the historical anthropology of early modern France and on popular political culture in Germany since 1871. Her research interests include the history of anthropology, social theory, the memory of war crimes, and the cultural history of basic rights in post-1945 Europe. Recent publications include 'Old Men and the Past: Personifications of German History after 1989', in *Memory Traces: 1989 and the Question of German Cultural Identity*, edited by Silke Arnold-de Simine (Oxford: Peter Lang, 2004).

Christian Postert, currently at the Department of Social Anthropology at the University of Münster, has studied both Social Anthropology and Human Medicine and has been engaged in field research, from 2000 to 2002, among the Hmong in Laos. His latest publication (in press) is 'From "Culture Circle" to "Cultural Ecology": The Hmong/ Miao Reflected in German and Austrian Anthropology', to appear in *The Hmong/ Miao in Asia*, edited by N. Tapp, N., G.Y. Lee, J. Michaud, and C. Culas (Chiang Mai: Silkworm Press).

Inger Sjørslev, working at the Department of Anthropology at Copenhagen University, did her main fieldwork on Afro-Brazilian religions in the regions of Bahia and Sao Paulo, respectively. She has worked with Brazilian popular culture as a Keeper at the National Museum of Denmark, and has been engaged as an NGO activist on indigenous issues. Her main book on the Afro-Brazilian religions was published in Danish as *Gudernes rum* (Copenhagen: Gyldendal 1998) and in German as *Glaube und Bessessenheit: Ein Bericht über die Candomblé Religion in Brasilien* (Gifkendorf: Merlin Verlag 1999). Recently, she has worked on political culture in Denmark and co-edited, with Finn Sivert Nielsen, the collection *Folkets repræsentanter* (Arhus: Arhus Universitetsforlag 2002).

Guido Sprenger is affiliated to the Institute of Ethnology, University of Münster, Germany. He has studied Social Anthropology, Political Science and History in Münster and Leiden. In 2000–2002 he did fieldwork on the social and ritual system of the Rmeet (Lamet) in Northern Laos. He has also published on the Trobriand Islands: *Erotik und Kultur in Melanesien: eine kritische Analyse von Malinowskis* The Sexual Life of Savages (Münster/Hamburg: LitVerlag 1997) and on music: 'Two Ears each Head Has: Structure and the Unknown in the Music of Asmus Tietchens' in *Monography Asmus Tietchens*, edited by Kai U. Jürgens (Münster/Bochum: AufAbwegen 1999).

Jojada Verrips works at the Department of Cultural Anthropology at the University of Amsterdam and has carried out research on a Dutch farming community (1970), among Dutch bargees (1980), and among Ghanaian fishermen (1991, 1996). He is co-editor of *MAST*, an international journal on maritime anthropology founded in 1988. Among his books are: *En boven de polder de hemel* (Groningen: Wolters-Noordhoff 1983), a study of a Dutch village 1850–1971, and *Als het tij verloopt* (Amsterdam: Spinhuis 1991) on bargees and their trade unions. He is currently working on a book entitled *The Wild (in the) West*, concerned with the abject and the horrendous in Western popular culture.

Subject Index

Abidjan, 112, 130, 133–34. *See also* Côte d'Ivoire
acephalous system, 23
aesthetics, xiv, 18, 27, 31–35, 40, 42, 47, 192, 201
Afro-Caribbean's, 26
agency, x–xi, 5, 13, 30, 96, 157–69, 192–93, 196, 198, 199
Alsace-Lorraine, 65
ambiguity, xi, 30, 53, 59, 168–69
An Officer and a Gentleman (film), 148
anti-essentialist approach, xiv, 166
anti-grammar, xii, 19, 42, 46, 96, 117, 159, 164–65, 176, 187–88, 192, 194–96, 199.
 See also dehumanization, difference
antimodern, 8, 12, 72
anti-Semitism, 8. *See also* National-Socialists
aristotelanism, asymmetrical, 164–65
Austria, 70
Ayodhya, 157–59, 163. *See also* India
Aztecs, 43

Barcelona, 29. *See also* Spain
Basque, 28. *See also* Spain
Beijing, 5. *See also* China
Belgium, 28, 65
Bharatiya Janata Party (BJP). *See* India
binarism, 36–37, 39, 47, 115, 142, 146, 160, 177, 180. *See also* classification, grammar
Bio-Mythology, 143
bootcamps, 145–50
 transformation into soldiers in, 146–47
Bosnia, 45
Brazil, 32, 79–89, 95–96. *See also* grammars
 carnival in, 81, 84–89
 cultural and racial politics in, 80–85, 89
 Afro-Brazilian religions, 80–81, 84, 87–88
 grammar of encompassment in, 80–84, 87–89
 grammar of orientalization in, 87–89
 Grupo Cultural Afro Reggae, 85–86
 'the mimetic nation', 88
 segmentary grammar in, 85–86, 87–89

 social exclusion/inclusion in, 82–84, 86–89, 96
British Empire, 21–23, 120. *See also* colonialism
Buddhism, 29, 107, 163, 179–80, 184–86
Burkina Faso, 121

Carpathian Mountains, 37
caste system, 25–26, 38, 54, 56, 59
Catalonia, 28. *See also* European Union
Catholics, 29, 65–66
China, 5, 34, 101, 108
Christianity/Christians, 25–26, 30, 40, 60, 160, 162, 164, 189n. 1.
citizenship, 79, 83–86, 89, 93–95, 127, 184–85
civilisation, 70
civil rights, 44, 123
clan. *See* Nuer
classification, ix–x, xii, 16, 18, 35, 60, 159, 165, 169, 177, 199. *See also* ambiguity, grammars
 binary classifications, 176
 classificatory levels, 24, 28–29, 47, 157
 trinominal classification in Laos, 104, 184–85
code-crossing, 118–19, 125, 128–33, 136
code-switching, 126, 137n. 6.
cognitive, 41–42, 47, 165, 199
 role of language, 47
 sciences, 160, 168, 169n. 3.
colonialism, 11, 13, 38–39, 44, 49n. 3., 65, 108–10, 117, 121–23. *See also* British Empire, France, French-Indochina, imperialism
Confucianism, 30
concentration camp, 44. *See also* Holocaust
Côte d'Ivoire, 112–38
 concept of *ivoirité*, 119, 123–25, 127–128, 136, 137n. 7.
 grammar implosions in, 115–19, 133–37
 grammar of encompassment in, 118, 125, 131, 136
 grammar of orientalization in, 118, 125, 128, 132

identity politics in, 113
'Jula' tribe of, 113–14, 116, 119–36
mass grave in Yopougon, 112–14, 116–17
movie '*Côte d'Ivoire, poudrière identitaire*', 112–14, 117, 134, 179
segmentary grammar in, 118, 125, 126–28, 131
creolization, xi. See also *métissage*
Croatia, 45
cultural fundamentalism, 93–96
cultural relativism, 10, 12, 14–15, 45, 94
Cultural Studies, 5–6, 12, 165, 203
'Culture and Personality' School, 10, 14

dehumanization, 115, 118, 195, 197. See also anti-grammar, difference, language
Denmark, 79, 89–97
  concept of *hygge* in, 91–92
  Danish People's Party, 90, 93–94
  grammar of encompassment in, 90, 91–94
  grammar of orientalization in, 93–94
  mechanisms of inclusion/exclusion in, 90, 93, 96
  political participation of immigrants in, 90–92
  segmentary grammar in, 94
dialogue, 36, 92, 115, 136, 173, 182, 187–88, 197
  dialogical relationship, 4, 6
  and grammars, 46, 73, 176–78, 189n. 3., 201
dichotomy, 4–5, 13, 167
Die Gartenlaube, 68, 71
différance, 6
difference, 8–9, 13, 47, 181, 186, 189n. 1.
  between descriptive and prescriptive norms, 198
  cultural differences, 103, 185
  essentialising difference, 3–16
  of grammars and anti-grammar, 187–88
  and identity, 4, 11, 118
  and racism, 9, 91, 93
Don Giovanni, 31
Don Quixote, 31

East Germany, 27
eclecticism, 167
ecumenism, 29
Egypt, 24
elites, 20, 30, 63, 73, 80, 84, 85, 122, 126, 150
England, 31, 41, 157–58, 168
  literature, 32–33
encompassment, xi–xii, 25–26, 60, 173–90
  and anti-grammar, 187–88
  genocidal encompassment, 125

grammar of encompassment, x–xi, 25–35, 38, 47–48, 58–60, 73–74, 173–74, 176–78, 187–88, 194, 198–203. See also Brazil, Côte d'Ivoire, Denmark, Germany, *Hindutva*, Laos, Nepal
  traced diachronically, 64–65
Enlightenment, 7, 40, 43
Eritrea, 24
esprit, 71
essentialism, x, 3–16, 76n. 2., 85, 89, 107, 160, 192. See also anti-essentialist approach, difference
ETA, 5
ethics, 63–77
ethnocentrism, 193–95
ethnocide, 42, 45, 96, 195. See also genocide
European Union, 28, 38, 202
equality, 30, 48, 83, 86, 90, 95, 97n. 2., 174, 181, 184, 186, 198, 201. See also inequality, power
exoticism, 33–34, 201

falsification, 18, 40–42
fantasy, 143–45, 151
fascism, 49n. 3., 95–96, 97n. 1. See also National-Socialists
favelas, 84. See also Brazil
federalism, xii, 23–24, 28, 38, 46
feminism, 10, 200. See also gender
fission, 34, 200–201. See also segmentation
Flemish, 46. See also Belgium
Folklore Studies, 72
fotonovelas, 32. See also Brazil
France, 29, 64, 66, 69–70
  French colonies 120, 122, 129, 179
Freemason, xii, 30
French-Indochina, 101, 108–10
Full Metal Jacket (film), 142, 148
fusion, 34, 200–201. See also segmentation

gadjos, 37. See also Gypsies
Geist, 71
gender, xiv, 10, 192, 199–200
  gendered comparison, 64–65
genealogies, 76
Genesis, 174. See also Old Testament
genocide, xi, 18, 23, 42–47, 63, 73–76, 96, 195–96, 199. See also ethnocide, violence
  poiesis of 112–38
Germany, 7–8, 27, 38, 43–45, 48, 143, 161, 202. See also Prussia
  barbaric stereotype, 66–68, 70, 72, 74, 76n. 3.
  concept of *Kultur*, 70, 73, 77n. 8.

German romanticism, 71, 75
grammar of encompassment in, 64–65, 73–74
grammar of orientalization in, 65–73
nation building and genocide, 63–77
philosophical tradition, 8, 14
segmentary grammar in, 64, 73
globalization, xiv, 24, 192, 201–2
grammars, ix–xii, 16, 18–50, 53, 63, 75, 110, 142, 157, 159, 165, 167–68, 173–74. *See also* difference, encompassment, hegemony, hierarchy, orientalism, segmentation
   binary grammar, 19, 35–37, 136
   complexity of grammars in Brazil, 79–89, 96
   debating grammars, 192–203
   dialogic and non-dialogic, 176–78
   grammar of tripartition, 36
   'grammars of Us and Them', 19–27
   grammatical dilemma, 34
   hidden grammars in Denmark, 89–97
   implosion of grammars, 142–46, 149, 165
   modernist grammatology, 6
   and the Nation-State, 183–87
   n+1 challenge of, 40–46, 108
   ternary grammars, 35–40, 137, 159, 161–62, 189n. 1.
Great Britain, 65–66. *See also* British Empire
Greece, 67–68
Gujarat. *See* India
Gypsies, 36–37, 48, 149

Hallstein Doctrine, 27
hegemony, xi, , 87–88, 95, 101, 122, 136, 176, 192. *See also* encompassment, hierarchy
   brahminical hegemony, 163
   hegemonic encompassment, 34, 84–85, 173
   hegemonic rationalities, 7
hermeneutics, 71
hierarchy, 10, 29, 38, 58, 60, 83–84,93, 185, 192. *See also* encompassment, hegemony, *Hindutva*
   hierarchical distances, 15
   hierarchical encompassment, 25, 34, 162–63, 174, 178
   hierarchical grammar, 159, 167–68, 200
   racial hierarchies, 117
Hinduism/Hindus, xii, 26, 29–30, 38, 175. *See also Hindutva*
Hindutva, 157–169. *See also* India
   grammar of encompassment in, 162–63
   grammar of orientalization in, 159–161, 166–67
   hierarchical grammar of, 159, 167–68
   ternary structures of, 161–62
Hmong. *See* Laos
Holocaust, 42, 45, 143
Hungary, 48
humanism, 47, 66, 187, 195
Humanities, 7, 12, 14, 71, 203
hybridization. *See* creolization, *métissage*
hyphenated identity, xi

immigrants, 39, 93, 97n. 1., 123, 180. *See also* Denmark
imperialism, 10–11, 187. *See also* colonialism
India, 25–26, 34, 61n. 8., 157–59, 161–65. *See also Hindutva*
individualism, 29, 60, 84, 110, 193
inequality, 35, 45–46, 82, 196. *See also* equality, hierarchy, rights
interdisciplinarity, 3, 9, 203. *See also* transdisciplinarity
intertextuality, 136
Iraq, 202
Islam, 29, 123, 164, 166–67, 189n. 1. *See also* Muslims
Italy, 66–67, 69, 72

Jainism, 163
Java, 34
Jazz. *See* music
Jews, 43–44, 48, 73–76, 149, 196
Judaism, 29–30

Kathmandu, 56. *See also* Nepal
Kurds, 177
Kwakiutl, 43

language, 42–47, 74, 76, 96, 115, 119–23, 125–31, 179, 181, 184, 198. *See also langue*, linguistics, *parole*
   dehumanizing language, 117–18, 181–93
language-object, 38
langue, 18, 42, 45, 157–70
Laos, 101–11, 173–90
   construction of transethnic group identities in, 102–5
   contexts for grammars in Northern, 180–83
   'contextual absolute' identity/alterity in, 107
   grammar of encompassment in, 102–5, 109, 183
   grammar of orientalization in, 102, 106–7, 109–10, 180–81, 183
   Guerre de Fou in, 108–10
   role of a *huab tais* in, 105, 108

segmentary grammar in, 102, 105–6, 109–10, 180–81, 183, 185, 186
trinominal classification in, 104, 184–85
Latin America, 43
Leporello, 31
liminality, 87, 164, 166. See also rites of passage
lineage. See Nuer
linguistics, 28, 36, 46, 122, 128, 130, 132,136, 149, 198. See also language (ethno) linguistic group, 119, 126, 183–84
London, 26, 31, 158. See also England

Madrid, 28. See also Spain
Mali, 121
Marxism, 15, 28, 41
marriage exchange systems, 37, 48n. 2.
metalanguage, 39
metaphysics, 9
métissage, xi. See also ambiguity
Milton Keynes, 158–59. See also London, England
modernity, 7, 36, 60, 70, 72–73, 85, 183, 185, 187
morality/moralism, x–xi, 3–16, 41, 45, 47, 151, 192, 195, 198
mulattas, 80
multiculturalism, 92–93, 124, 201. See also immigrants
music, 33–34
Muslims, 30–31, 40, 112–15, 120–22, 125, 158, 160–62, 201. See also Islam
myth, 38, 56, 108, 181–82

nationalism, ix, 9, 12, 31, 40, 63, 70, 71–73, 93, 102, 119, 123, 145, 195
Hindu nationalism, 26, 160. See also *Hindutva*
nation-state, 23, 28, 63–64, 73, 86, 95, 101, 104, 123, 174, 176, 179, 180, 183–87, 196
Natural Sciences, 41
National-Socialists/Nazis, 42–45, 63, 73–76, 92, 134, 143. See also anti- Semitism, Germany
Neo-Marxism, 15
Neo-Structuralism, 14
Nepal, 53–61
grammar of encompassment in, 58–60
grammar of orientalization in, 58–61
the ritual of *Ghantakarna* in, 56–60
segmentary grammar in, 53, 58–61
Netherlands, 39
Newar. See Nepal
Nomads, 37, 121

non-grammar, 110. See also anti-grammar
Norddeutscher Bund, 64
norms/normative, xi, 6, 41, 60, 139, 193, 197–200. See also morality
Northern Ireland, 28
Notre Voie. See Côte d'Ivoire
NSDAP. See National-Socialists
Nuer, 38, 175. See also Sudan

Old Testament, 30, 55, 174
ontology, 8–9, 11–13, 15, 176
orientalism, x, 14, 19–20, 48, 55, 74, 82, 110
grammar of orientalization, 20–21, 25, 27–36, 38–41, 46–49, 168, 173, 176–77, 187–88, 190n. 1., 194, 198–203. See also Brazil, Côte d'Ivoire, Denmark, Germany, *Hindutva*, Laos, Nepal
and *métissage*, xi
traced diachronically, 65–73
Ostpolitik, 27

Paris, 66. See also France
parole, 18, 42, 44–45, 157–69
'People of Faith', 30
phenomenology, 6–9. See also Heidegger
poiesis, 116. See also Côte d'Ivoire, genocide
Poland, 36–37
politics, 18, 21–22, 23, 27–28, 35, 40, 42, 47, 58, 63–77, 173. See also citizenship, immigrants, nation-state, power, race, rights
popular culture, 31, 116
pornography, 32
positivism, 71
postcolonial, xiv, 13, 24, 117, 120, 123, 129, 135, 201
theory, 6, 9–11, 121
postmodernism, 6–8
power, 22–24, 28, 46, 64, 81, 92, 119, 121, 127, 130, 158–159, 162, 166, 173, 177, 199. See also equality, inequality
centres, 24, 48, 184
hegemonic power, 101, 123, 187
and hierarchy, 178, 192
of propaganda, 76
relations, 6, 65, 167, 169, 174, 177
structures, 23, 58, 87
pragmatics, x, xiv, 16, 110
primitivism, 33, 201
proselytism, 30
Protestants, 29, 65, 74, 91
Prussia, 64–65, 69
psychoanalysis, 7, 9–11, 13, 41, 54, 196
Punjab, 26, 163. See also India

race/racism, 9, 40, 42, 44, 74, 79–82, 88, 96, 97n. 1., 112, 115, 122, 125, 145, 150, 161, 164. *See also* anti-Semitism, difference, immigrants
Rashtriya Swayamsevak Sangh (RSS). *See* Hindutva
Ravenna, 69
religion, 18, 27, 29–31, 35, 40, 42, 47, 116, 163, 167, 186. *See also* Brazil, Buddhism, Catholics, Christianity, Hinduism, Islam, Jainism, Judaism, Protestants, Sikhs
rights, 44, 79, 81, 85–86, 90, 94–95, 127, 196, 200
rites of passage, 36, 149, 151. *See also* liminality
ritual possession, 87
Rmeet. *See* Laos
Roma, 37. *See also* Gypsies
Roman Catholic Church, 66. *See* Catholics
Romans, 66–67
Rwanda, 42, 46, 115

Sancho Panza, 31
scapegoating, 53–61, 195
Scotland, 28
segmentation, x, 21, 46–47, 86, 176. *See also* Sudan
segmentary grammar, 21–24, 27–35, 38, 46–49, 173, 175–76, 187–89, 194, 198–203. *See also* Brazil, Côte d'Ivoire, Denmark, Germany, Laos, Nepal
segmentary identity, 24
traced diachronically, 64
semiotics, 38, 159, 168
Serbia, 45
sexuality, xiv, 59, 192, 199–200
'scientific revolutions', 41
shamanism, 179
Sherpas, 54, 56
'signification', 38
Sikhs, xii, 26, 31, 38, 163, 167–69, 175
social cohesion, 53–61
Social Science, 7, 12, 36, 41–42, 45, 47, 71, 194, 203
Southall. *See* London
Spain, 5, 28–29, 38, 64
stigmatization, 54–55, 59
subjectivities, x, 6–7, 9–11, 13–14
Sudan, 21–24, 28
Sufism. *See* Islam
syncretism, 81, 166

taxonomy, 35. *See also* classification
Thailand, 101, 178, 180
Tibet, 54, 56
Torah, 30. *See also* Old Testament
transdisciplinarity. 12, 15. *See also* interdisciplinarity
Turkey, 177
Tutsi, 42
Tyrol, 29, 72

United Nations, 24, 113–14, 117, 134
U.S.A., 30, 34, 105, 122. *See also* Vietnam War

Vietnam War, 101, 105, 148, 150, 195
violence, 42–49, 55, 76, 113–15, 136, 142, 144, 177, 187, 192. *See also* anti-grammar, genocide
as communication, 66
exceptional, 109–10, 195, 197
rebounding, 59, 149–52
system-immanent, 197

Walloons. *See* Belgium
Wandervogel, 71
Wales, 29
witchcraft, 41, 54, 58
World Hindu Council (VHP), 158
'World Music'. *See* music
World Trade Center, 30

xenophobia, 21, 54, 97n. 1., 134, 150. *See also* race/racism

Yugoslavia, 45. *See also* Bosnia, Croatia, Serbia

Name Index

Abercrombie, N., 167, 170
Adorno, T.W., 43, 49
Agamben, G., 115, 138
Aijmaer, G., 190n. 5., 190
Albert, Albert, 65
Alvares, S., 81–84, 97
Alleton, I., 105, 109, 111
Almond, G., 160, 170
Alpha Blondy, 120, 135, 137n. 10., 138
Amselle, J-L., 138n. 14., 138
Andersen, W., 158, 170
Anderson, M., 56, 57, 61
Appadurai, A., 115–17, 135, 138
Appiah, K., 49, 201, 203
Apter, A., 116–17, 138
Aquinas, T., 25
Ardener, E., 91, 97n. 3., 97
Ardener, S., 97n. 3.
Arendt, H., 8
Arndt, E., 68
Aristotle, 25
Arnaut, K., xiii, 73, 112–41, 165, 188, 193, 195–96, 205
Asad, T., 29, 49, 197, 203
Ashcroft, B., 10, 16

Baba Kaké, I., 129, 132, 138
Bahr, H., 70
Bakary, K., 134, 138
Ballard, R., 169n. 7., 170
Bana, M., 31, 49
Banton, M., 77
Barthes, R., 38–40, 47, 49
Barth, F., 3
Bartók, B., 34
Bateson, G., 88, 91, 97
Bakhtin, M., 118, 138
Baumann, G., ix–xiv, 1, 18–50, 55, 86, 95–98, 102, 108, 110, 115, 117, 125, 136, 142–43, 145, 169n. 5., 170, 173–75, 178, 184, 187–88, 189n. 1, 192–204, 205
Bauman, Z., 169n. 4., 169
Bayart, J.-F., 121, 137n. 2., 139
Bazin, J., 138n. 14., 139
Bazin, L., 117, 122, 139

Bédié, H., 124–28, 131, 135–36, 138n. 15., 139
Bein, A., 143
Ben-Ari, E., 146–47, 149–50, 152n. 8., 153
Benedict, R., 14, 16
Benveniste, E., 35–38, 49, 136
Berg, A., 32
Bertaux, 70, 77
Bhabha, H., 9, 16
Bhatt, C., 158–59, 170
Billings, D., 137n. 2., 139
Bismarck, 69, 71, 76n. 4.
Blé Goudé, C., 114–15, 134
Bloch, M., 58, 61, 149, 152n. 17., 153, 165, 170
Blücher, F., 70
Boddy, J., 87, 97
Boone, C., 121, 123, 137n. 4., 139
Bourdieu, P., 3
Bourke, J., 146–47, 151, 153
Brandt, W., 27
Brontë, A., 32
Brontë, C., 32
Brontë, E., 32
Bülow, Prince, 72
Bülow, P.v., 66–69, 77
Bubis, I., 76
Buschmann, M., 146, 153
Bush jr., G., 144, 202
Bush sr., G., 144
Butler, J., 13, 16
Byron, R., 6, 16

Calderón, P., 32
Capurro, R., 6, 16
Carrier, J., 77
Caldera, R., 81
Cervantes, M.d., 31–32
Champagne, R., 157, 170
Chapman, M., 97n. 3.
Chauveau, J.-P., 123, 139, 140
Chomsky, N., ix
Cialdini, R., 198, 203
Craib, I., 157, 170
Chrétien, J.-P., 115, 139

Clausewitz, C.v., 45
Cohen, A., 3
Cole, J., 77
Comarof, J., 139
Comte, A., 71

Da Cunha, G., 85, 95, 97
Dagnino, E, 97
Dahn, F., 69, 77
Da Matta, 83–84, 97
Damle, S., 158, 170
Dang Nghiem Van, 182, 190
Debussy, C., 34, 201
Delafosse, M., 121, 139
Deoras, B., 163, 170
Derive, M.-J., 120, 137n. 4., 139
Derrida, J., ix, 6, 10, 15–16
Descola, P., 157, 168, 170
Diarra, S., 123, 139
Dilthey, W., 71
Douglas, M., 35, 49, 157, 169n 4., 170
Dozon, J.-P., 123–24, 128, 137n. 7., 139
Dumont, L., x, 19, 25, 47–49, 60–61, 64, 77, 83, 110, 173–75, 178, 184, 187, 189n. 1., 190, 193
Dvorak, A., 34

Ebrokié, C., 134, 139
Eden, T., 10, 16
Eijsvogel, J., 152n. 15., 153
Elias, N., 70, 77
Eriksen, T., 159, 169n. 4., 170
Ermey, L., 148–49
Ernst, M., 201
Escobar, A., 97
Ettinger, E., 8, 16
Eulenburg, P.z., 68, 77
Evans, G., 184–85, 190
Evans, R., 74, 77
Evans-Pritchard, E.E., x, 19, 21–24, 41, 47, 49, 86, 110, 176, 190, 194

Fabian, J., 14, 16, 20, 49
Ferlus, M., 182, 190
Firchow, P., 65, 77
Fillitz, T., 1
Flaubert, G., 21, 48
Forgacs, D., 43, 49n. 3., 49
Foucault, M., 173n. 2.
Fowler, R., 153
Fox, R., 16, 32, 202–3
Frankel, D., 152n. 14.
Frawley, D., 160, 170
Frazer, J., 53
Freud, S., ix, 12, 14, 54

Frevert, U., 65, 77
Freyre, G., 80, 97
Freytag, G.., 68, 71, 774
Frykenberg, R., 160, 170

Gadafy, M., 144
Galey, J.-C., 25, 50
Ganghofer, L., 72
Gbagbo, L., 112–13, 119, 124–26, 134, 139
Gellner, D., 58, 62
Gelman, S., 161, 170
Gennep, A.v., 36, 50, 149, 152n. 16.
Gershwin, G., 34
Ghandi, I., 26
Gide, A., 21, 48
Gierke, O.v., 66
Gillespie, M., 169, 170
Gilroy, P., 80, 97
Gingrich, A., ix–xiv, 1, 3–18, 32, 46, 50, 192–205
Gluckman, M., 88, 97
Godelier, M., 14, 17
Goebbels, J., 43, 134
Goldman, M., 79, 98
Goldschmidt, L., 90, 98
Golwalkar, M., 160–61, 163–64, 170
Gottschalk, P., 166, 170
Gramsci, A., 116, 137n. 2.
Griffiths, G., 11, 16
Grossberg, L., 5, 17
Gubernatis, A.d., 72
Guéï, R., 112, 124, 126, 131
Gunn, G., 110–11

Hackford, G., 148
Hall, S., 159, 166, 169, 170
Hanchard, M., 81, 97
Handelman, D., 159, 171
Hansen, T., 158–59, 163, 165–66, 171
Hastrup, K., 97n. 3.
Hegel, G.W.F., 9, 14
Heidegger, M., 6–13, 14–15, 17, 50, 197
Heimbach, E., 105, 111
Henfry, C., 84, 97
Herzfeld, M., 63, 68, 72, 76n. 6., 77
Hill, J., 119, 139
Hill, S., 170
Hinnenkamp, V., 137n. 6., 140
Hinton, P., 182, 190
Hitler, A., 41, 43–44, 46, 73–76, 76n. 7., 77
Horkheimer, M., 43, 49
Houphouët-Boigny, F., 113, 123–24, 126, 136
Hume, D., 40, 47, 50
Hussein, S., 144
Husserl, E., 14

Ibn al-Mujawir, 200, 203
Ingle, D., 151, 152nnn. 7, 8, 15., 153
Izikowitz, K., 179, 190

Jackson, M., 115, 117, 140
Jaffrelot, C., 159, 171
Jakobson, R., ix
Jamous, R., 197, 203
Jeggle, U., 151n. 1., 153
Jeismann, M., 65, 77
Jenkins, R., 159, 171
Judersleben, J., 146

Kammerer, C., 181, 190
Karlson, H., 146, 153
Karner, C., xiii, 157–72, 193, 195, 205
Kastoryano, R., 98
Kaysone, P., 105
Khader, N., 94, 97
Ki-Zerbo, J., 120, 140
Klemperer, V., 43–44, 49n. 3., 50, 74–76, 78, 143, 153, 195–96, 199, 203
Knudsen, A., 90, 97
Koch, H., 91–92, 97
Kodaly, Z., 34
Koenigsberg, R., 143, 153
Koné, D., 128–33, 134, 140
Koselleck, R., 77n. 8., 78
Kossikov, I., 102, 111
Koulibaly, M., 113, 140
Kourouma, A., 120, 135, 138n. 10., 140
Kramer, F., 87, 97
Kubrick, S., 148
Kuhn, T., 35, 41, 50
Kunin, S., 157, 160, 168, 171
Kuper, A., 22, 50
Kvist, J., 97

Labrie, A., 144, 153
Lacan, J., 7, 9–15, 17, 144, 197
Lagarde, P.d., 143
Lakoff, G., 161, 169n. 3., 171
Langbehn, J., 65, 71, 76n. 1., 78
Launay, R., 121, 140
Leach, E., 35–36, 50, 159, 171, 178, 182, 191
Leaman, G., 8, 17
LeBlanc, M., 121, 140
Lévi-Strauss, C., 35–37, 49n. 2., 50, 145, 153, 157, 159, 168, 171
Levy, C., 148, 153
Levy, R., 59, 62
Lewis, B., 121, 138n. 11., 140
Lewis, T., 59, 62
Lindell, K., 182, 191
Löfgren, O., 200, 203

Lohfink, N., 54–55, 61n. 2., 62
Lohourignon, M., 125, 140
Loucou, J.-N., 140
Luhrmann, T., 35, 41, 50
Luther, M., 71

Malinowski, B., 30
Malla, K., 61n. 9., 62
Mamdani, M., 121–23, 140
Mann, T., 32, 71
Manor, J., 159, 171
Margolis, J., 7, 17
Marguerat, Y., 121, 140
Marlitt, E., 69, 78
Marre, D., 1, 48n. 1.
Marvin, C., 151, 152nnn. 7, 8, 15., 153
Marx, K., 14
Mbembe, A., 116–17, 136, 140
McClintock, A., 78
McDonald, I., 158, 171
Mead, M., 10, 14
Medin, D., 163, 171
Memel-Fotê, H., 123, 140
Mesthrie, R., 137n. 6., 140
Miller, W., 148, 153
Miran, M., 121, 140
Moerman, M., 178, 191
Mohanty, C.T., 13, 17
Moltke, H.v., 68
Moore jr., B., 144, 153
Monier-Williams, M., 57, 62
Mosse, G., 72, 74, 77n. 8., 78
Mottin, J., 108–11
Mozart, W.A., 29–31, 50
Mróz, L., 35–38, 50
Mühlich, M., xiii, 53–62, 194–95, 199, 206
Müller, A.F., xiii, 63–78, 115, 136, 143, 187, 193, 194–95, 206
Müller, K.v., 65, 78
Mukta, P., 159, 171

Nash, M., 1, 48n. 1., 50
Nebesky-Wojkowitz, R.d., 54, 62
Nebout, A., 121, 138n. 13., 141
Neiburg, F., 79, 98
Neruda, F., 127, 129, 141
Ngaosyvathan, M., 108, 111
Niangoran-Bouah, G., 124, 141
Nida-Rümelin, J., 17
Nielsen, F., 80, 90, 98
Nietzsche, F., 76n. 3., 78

Osborn, A., 97n. 1.
Ouattara, A., 114, 116, 124, 126–28, 131, 135

Pandey, G., 160, 162, 171
Partman, G., 137n. 8., 141
Paul, R., 54, 62
Person, Y., 120, 135, 137n. 9., 138n. 11., 141
Pholsena, V., 184, 191
Pierce, P., 61n. 1.
Pinto, P., 3, 17
Pitrè, G., 72
Pius II, Pope, 66
Place, T., 147, 153
Platenkamp, J., 109, 111, 184, 185, 191
Plato, 25
Pol Pot, 41
Popper, K., 18, 35, 40–42, 47, 50
Postert, C., xiii, 73, 101–11, 165, 177, 184, 193, 195, 206

Quigley, D., 25, 50, 60n. 1., 62

Racine, J., 32
Raj, D., 162, 171
Rajagopal, A., 158–59, 169n. 4., 171
Rajah, A., 185, 191
Rampton, B., 118, 141
Ramos, A., 82, 98
Rao, T., 160, 170
Raulet, G., 71, 78
Rauschning, V., 74, 78
Ravel, M., 34
Rawson, C., 151n. 2., 153
Reagan, R., 144
Reinhardt, V., 66, 78
Rembrandt, 71
Ricoeur, P., 6, 17
Rockmore, T., 7, 17
Røgilds, F., 93, 98
Rosa-Ribeiro, F., 82, 88, 98
Rosch, E., 163, 171

Said, E., x, 14, 17, 19–20, 48, 50, 55, 62, 110, 194, 200, 203
Salamon, K., 90, 98
Saler, B., 159, 171
Samori, 120, 129, 131, 135
Saussure, F.d., 159, 168
Savarkar, V., 162-3, 171
Savina, F., 105, 108–9, 111
Scheper-Hughes, N., 197, 203
Scheuer, B., 114, 134
Schieder, T., 76n. 7., 78
Schiffauer, W., 92, 98
Schumacher, J., 152n. 14.
Schwartz, J., 80, 91–92, 98
Scott, R., 152n. 14.
Segato, R., 81, 98

Seshadri, H., 162, 165, 172
Shakespeare, W., 32–33
Sheriff, R., 84, 98
Sikand, Y., 166, 172
Silverman, S., 1
Simana, S., 182, 184, 191
Simon, P., 34
Singh, V., 163
Sjørslev, I., xiii, 1, 79–98, 193, 194–95, 201, 206
Skidmore, T., 80, 98
Smith, B., 147
Smith, S., 97n. 1.
Sokrates, 25
Soumahoro, B., 114–15
Spitzemberg, Baronesse, 75
Spivak, G., 7, 9–15, 17, 197
Sprenger, G., xiv, 73, 110, 173–91, 192–95, 199, 201, 207
Stalin, J., 41, 46
Stern, F., 70, 78
Sternberger, D., 43, 50
Stolcke, V., 93–95, 98
Stouffer, S., 147, 153
Storz, G., 50
Stuart-Fox, M., 181, 191
Strathern, M., 13, 17
Stravinski, I., 34, 201
Sudarshan, K., 162
Suesskind, W., 50
Swahn, J.-Ö., 191

Tambiah, S., 115, 117, 141
Tamot, K., 61nnn. 1, 4, 9.
Tapp, N., 101, 105, 109, 111
Taussig, M., 87–88, 98
Tayanin, D., 190n. 3., 191
Taylor, C., 6, 17, 50, 201, 203
Theoderic, King, 69, 76n. 6.
Theweleit, K., 152n. 11., 153
Thiesse, A.-M., 72, 78
Tiffin, H., 10, 16
Tillman jr., G., 152n. 14.
Toren, C., 7, 17
Touré, S., 124, 129, 141
Trawny, P., 8, 17
Triaud, J.-L., 122, 141
Tshechow, A., 32
Tudor, A., 168, 172
Turner, B., 170
Turner, V., 35, 50, 87, 98, 169n. 4., 172

Vajracarya, D., 61n. 9., 62
Vajpayee, A., 162
Veer, P.v.d., 21, 50, 160, 166, 172

Verdi, G., 21, 32
Verrips, J., xiii, 115, 136, 142–54, 187, 196–97, 199, 207
Vertovec, S., 98
Vézies, J.-F., 56, 62
Victoria, Queen, 65
Virchow, R., 68

Wamsley, G., 146–47, 154
Wattenmaker, W., 163, 171
Weber, M., 66–67, 78
Werner, M., 66, 78
White, D., 144, 154
White, H., 198, 203
Wiegerling, K., 6, 17
Wilden, A., 157, 172
Wilhelm I., 64, 68
Wilhelm II., 65, 69, 70
Williams, R., 77n. 8., 78, 115
Winslow, D., 146, 148, 150–51, 152nnnn. 8, 9, 14., 16, 154
Wolf, E., 43, 50, 75, 77–78, 196, 203
Wolin, R., 7, 17

Young, J., 8, 17

Zadi Zaourou, B., 141
Žižek, S., 144, 152nn. 4, 5., 154

Rektor Georg Winckler

in aufmerksamer Unterstützung

für Ihr Wirken!

10.11.05

André Gingrich